VIETNAM

THE SECOND REVOLUTION

Nicholas Nugent

In Print

In Print Publishing is registered with the Publishers Licensing Society in the UK and the Copyright Clearance Center in the USA.

British Library Cataloguing in Publication Data: a catalogue record for this book is available for the British Library.

ISBN 1 873047 66 5

Cover design by Russell Townsend
Typeset by Brighton Typesetting
Printed by Bell and Bain

First published in 1996 by
In Print Publishing Ltd, 9 Beaufort Terrace, Brighton BN2 2SU, UK.
Tel: +44 (1273) 682836. Fax: +44 (1273) 620958.

Contents

Nicholas Nugent works in London for the BBC World Service, where he helps deploy an extensive network of foreign correspondents who report on radio and television. He has himself reported from many parts of Asia, including Vietnam. He was one of the first journalists to report from Cambodia after the Khmer Rouge had been ousted from power by the Vietnamese army, and also reported from the frontline during the Iran-Iraq war. The author's links with Asia go back 28 years and include stints spent as a teacher in India and working for the United Nations in Indonesia.

A graduate in law from the University of Cambridge, Nicholas Nugent was a major contributor to *Born in Fire* (University of Ohio, Athens, 1988), a history of the Indonesian independence struggle, and is author of a biography of the late Indian prime minister, *Rajiv Gandhi: Son of a Dynasty* (BBC Books, London, 1990).

Preface

Vietnam as a country deserves to be as well known as Vietnam the war, especially the Hollywood version. Vietnam today is in any case vastly different from the war-torn country of more than 20 years ago, having in the meantime undergone one of the most extraordinary changes of economic policy direction of any nation. Its adjustment to what can only be seen as the post-communist era merits comparison with the very different way that Eastern European nations have made their adjustments.

It is 50 years since the virtually unknown figure of Ho Chi Minh drew on the words of the US president, Thomas Jefferson, to declare Vietnam's independence and more than 20 years since the end of what is called in Vietnam the 'American war' actually brought independence to the reunified country. Yet Vietnam has enjoyed the fruits of its independence for only a handful of years. With its current phenomenal rate of growth it seems to be trying to make up for lost time and to 'leapfrog' technology in its enthusiastic rush to join the ranks of the 'Asian dragons'.

Vietnam is the 13th most populous nation in the world with 72 million people inhabiting a land rather larger than Italy. This gives it some claim to importance for present-day rather than historical reasons. Its resources – hydrocarbon, mineral, agricultural and human – make it one of the richest countries in South East Asia. The Association of South East Asian Nations (ASEAN), the economic community which Vietnam joined in 1995, embraces more citizens than the European Union.

Many people in Vietnam, the UK, the USA and elsewhere have helped in providing me with facts, thoughts or contacts and several have reviewed draft chapters. I am particularly grateful to those in Vietnam, some of whose stories I have told. Most preferred not to be named. Instead I extend my appreciation collectively to all who were kind enough to help in whatever way. My main written

v

sources, the many books that have been consulted, are acknowledged in the text or in footnotes, while the *Far Eastern Economic Review* deserves a special mention for its ever strong coverage of Vietnam and South East Asia.

I have tried to keep terminology neutral but this is not easy. Does 30 April 1975 mark the 'fall' of Saigon or its 'liberation'? Did Vietnam win the 'American war' or did the victory belong to North Vietnam? These questions have no neutral answers. The very name of the southern capital – Saigon or Ho Chi Minh City – implies a political judgement, though strictly speaking the latter term describes a larger entity than the former, which remains in common use to describe the 'inner' city. I have alternated between Saigon and Ho Chi Minh City according to context.

With the notable exception of Ho Chi Minh, Vietnamese are known by their last name rather than the family name which comes first. Thus Vo Nguyen Giap is known as General Giap, or simply as Giap. Vietnamese settled abroad often reverse their order of names to comply with Western practice.

In her great book on the Vietnam war and its origins, *Fire in the Lake*, the American writer Frances Fitzgerald wrote: 'To the Vietnamese of the twentieth century "peace" means not a compromise between various interest groups and organisations, but the restoration of a single, uniform way of life. The Vietnamese were not interested in pluralism, they were interested in unanimity.'[1] This book explores how, more than 20 years after the coming of peace, Vietnam is still striving to achieve that unanimity.

Nicholas Nugent
Wimbledon
October 1995

[1] Frances Fitzgerald, *Fire in the Lake*, Little Brown and Co, Boston, 1972, p 17.

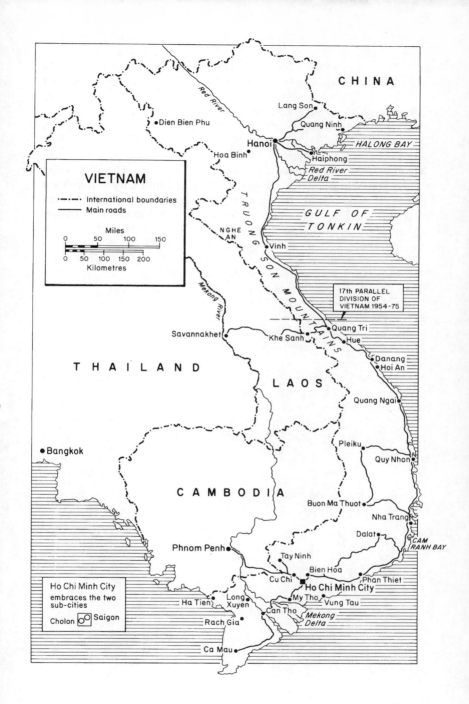

1

Three Decades of Conflict

Few countries have had such a miserable 20th century as Vietnam. For the first half century the country was dominated by the French, not the most benevolent of colonial rulers. The next quarter-century was spent at war – first against the French and then the Americans – or against each other according to the perspective of many southerners. The country's very name became synonymous with war for a whole generation. Only for the final quarter-century has Vietnam been united as one country, free of foreign domination and outwardly at peace. But for the first half of that quarter-century, unity and freedom were qualified by an intense struggle for survival: a war against poverty had superseded the previous military conflict. This is the story of how Vietnam overcame that poverty by overthrowing much for which it had previously fought.

It was France's determination to recover power in its colony after the Second World War defeat of Japan (which occupied Vietnam from 1942 to 1945) that drew Vietnam into war. The Vietnamese did not regard the capitulation of Japan in 1945 as the victory that the West celebrates as Victory over Japan (VJ) day, or as the end of the war; it was merely a stage in the ongoing independence struggle. Yet the Japanese defeat did provide the opportunity for the communist and nationalist leader, Ho Chi Minh, to declare the country independent as the 'Democratic Republic of Vietnam'. The struggle to win true independence was to take another 30 years.

What the West knows as 'the first Indochina war' started as the French tried to re-establish their rule. As far as Ho Chi Minh was concerned, it was no different from the wars for independence being fought by Indonesian nationalists against the Dutch colonial administration and by Indians against British rule in India, where civil disobedience was the main weapon. The French were intent on recovering a lucrative colony to help them rebuild metropolitan France after the devastation of the European war. As we shall see,

1

the USA was increasingly drawn in on the French side to further its completely separate objective of containing communism.

The 'French war' (as the Vietnamese call it) was largely a war of attrition fought between Viet Minh guerrillas, who dominated the countryside, and the French army, who controlled the cities. France exercised its rule through Bao Dai, who prior to his 1945 abdication had been their 'puppet' emperor. Bao Dai was the last of the Nguyen dynasty whose first ruler, Emperor Gia Long (1802-19), is credited with having unified Vietnam under one ruler. A subsequent Nguyen ruler, Tu Duc, had lost power to the French, though the emperors retained their thrones and some nominal authority. All real power and authority were with the French who ruled Vietnam and the adjoining states of Laos and Cambodia from Paris.

Ho Chi Minh can hardly have anticipated how long the war would last nor how many Vietnamese would die when he told the French in November 1945: 'The Vietnamese people do not want bloodshed...but we are determined to sacrifice even millions of combatants...to safeguard Vietnam's independence and free her children from slavery.'[1] By 1947, India and Pakistan had won their independence from Britain and two years later the Dutch had conceded independence to the Indonesians, whose four year struggle was initially as bloody as that of the Vietnamese. In contrast to the determination of the French, the British and the Dutch had ultimately withdrawn from India and Indonesia respectively, accepting the inevitability of home rule rather than risking military defeat. However, in neither India nor Indonesia was the independence struggle led by a declared communist supported with arms by external communist forces. It was these factors which led the USA to bankroll France's war effort and subsequently to replace French with American troops.

The first Indochina war lasted nine years, ending decisively at an engagement in the north-west of the country 170 miles west of Hanoi. In an attempt to prevent the Viet Minh from carrying the war into Laos, and also hoping to block a supply route from China, the French dropped 15,000 paratroopers into the Dien Bien Phu valley in November 1953 only to find themselves surrounded by 50,000 Viet Minh guerrillas in this remote and strategically disadvantageous spot. The 11 miles long by 5 miles wide valley was one of the last regions of Indochina to have been subdued by the French. The

---

[1] Quoted in Bernard Fall, *Ho Chi Minh on Revolution*, Pall Mall Press, London, 1967, p 159.

French had been hoping for a strategic victory which would end the war, but they had seriously underestimated both the numbers of guerrillas and the extent of their armaments, which included heavy guns. The Viet Minh had made a similar strategic calculation and were prepared to sustain heavy losses to gain victory. They were spurred by the fact that France, Britain, the USSR, the People's Republic of China and the USA were to meet in Geneva in May to try to reach a settlement in Indochina. They wanted to resolve this 'loose end' left over from the Second World War. The Viet Minh were determined to maximize the territory under their control before the Geneva meeting.

The Viet Minh led by Vo Nguyen Giap attacked on 12 March 1954 killing 500 French troops in the first few hours of the battle. As casualties at the French underground hospital mounted, so the territory under French control diminished. The Viet Minh penetrated ever further by digging trenches. After a 55 day siege and with their food and ammunition exhausted, the French surrendered to the Viet Minh on 7 May, the day before the big powers met in Geneva. General Giap called it taking the French 'by the throat'. The French lost 3,000 men, the Viet Minh probably more than twice that number. Some sources suggest the USA had a contingency plan to intervene on the French side at this stage which was never put into effect.[2] Operation Vulture, as it was dubbed, may even have included a plan to drop atomic bombs on Viet Minh positions, though it is unlikely that Congress, which had authorized budgetary support for the French, would have sanctioned such action.

As a humiliation of a European power by the non-Europeans it was attempting to subdue, Dien Bien Phu ranks alongside the defeat of the Romans at Carthage, of the Italians by the Abyssinians at Axum and of the British in the Afghan wars. It was the first ever such defeat of the French and of a better-equipped and trained army by a rag-tag guerrilla force. General Giap, the former teacher who led it, says Ho Chi Minh used to joke that he had won the battle without losing a single plane or tank – because they didn't have any to lose![3] Giap made use of a supply technique that was later employed against American forces: rice, weapons and even armour-plated heavy guns known as 'steel elephants' were transported great distances through the jungle by peasants on foot and on bicycles.

Dien Bien Phu was not the end of war, only the end of war

---

[2] Notably the late President Nixon writing in his *Memoirs*.
[3] Told in Justin Wintle, *Romancing Vietnam*, Viking, London, 1991, p 406.

against the French. The Geneva Conference partitioned Vietnam
along the 17th parallel, effectively granting independence to the
northern half, where Ho Chi Minh's government consolidated its
power as the French withdrew their army and their administrators.
The second Indochina war (or the 'American war') was a contest
for the south of the country. The USA backed the southern regime
under Ngo Dinh Diem, who replaced Bao Dai when the latter chose
to go into exile in France. Once again there was confusion over
objectives. Nominally the USA was fighting for South Vietnam's
independence, whilst the North was fighting for the country's
reunification, which had implicitly been promised in the Geneva
accords. In reality the USA was fighting to prevent the 'fall' of the
southern half of the country to communism, which had successively
taken over China, North Korea and then North Vietnam. With the
protagonists having such different objectives it is hardly surprising
that Vietnam was to remain at war for another 21 years.

Ngo Dinh Diem was hand-picked by the USA for the job. Born
into a noble Catholic family from central Vietnam, Diem was
educated in Hué and Paris and spent a period as interior minister
under Bao Dai before entering a seminary in New Jersey to train as
a priest. There he met such influential American Catholics as
Cardinal Spellman of New York and Senator John Kennedy. They
seem to have been impressed by his nationalism, although his
Catholicism stood him in good stead also when, after the Geneva
accords, Washington needed a new leader in Saigon. The summons
actually came from Bao Dai, who first made Diem his prime
minister. Diem spent his first few years consolidating his power by
suppressing a prominent criminal organization and the private
armies operated by two religious sects, the Hoa Hao and Cao Dai.
He managed to alienate the majority Buddhists by his blatant
favouritism towards Catholics. Nearly a million Catholics had taken
advantage of a period of grace before the 17th parallel was sealed to
flee from the North to the South, thus providing Diem with an
enhanced constituency. In 1963, Buddhist monks from Hué set
themselves on fire in the streets of Saigon to draw world attention to
Diem's repression of Buddhists. Diem's weakness was his
authoritarianism; he was an autocratic mandarin of the old school to
whom it would not have occurred to share power or to test the will
of the people he led.

As it happened, this suited his sponsors in Washington for they
had no intention of holding the nationwide elections that the Geneva
accords had said should be held within two years. Instead Diem

declared the South the 'Republic of Vietnam', establishing a semblance of permanence for what should have been only a temporary state. The USA financed Diem's government and sent its own army to support him – at first as 'advisers' then, after 1965, as combat troops. To challenge Diem's rule, Hanoi set up the National Liberation Front (NLF) to represent southern communists. It was under this umbrella organization that the communist war in the South was fought. The USA always believed the NLF was acting under orders from Hanoi – and that Ho Chi Minh himself was getting his orders from Moscow or Beijing or both (although a State Department document, whose existence was revealed in the *Pentagon Papers*,[4] could find no hard evidence that Ho Chi Minh actually took his orders from Moscow). Hanoi argued that the war in the South was not ideologically inspired but was a spontaneous uprising against the cruelty and despotism of Ngo Dinh Diem.

The USA never actually declared war on the north. Its involvement was gradual – first (from 1950) as paymasters of the French war effort, then as 'advisers' to the Diem regime and ultimately as combatant. The Gulf of Tonkin resolution passed by both Houses of Congress on 7 August 1964 paved the way for US forces to be sent to Vietnam by authorizing the US president to take 'all necessary action to repel attacks against US forces and to prevent further aggression in South East Asia'. Only two senators voted against it, such was the sense of outrage in both Houses at two allegedly unprovoked attacks by North Vietnamese forces on US destroyers off the coast of North Vietnam. Subsequently it has become clear that there was only one attack and that, far from being unprovoked, the vessel attacked had been engaged in intelligence gathering well inside the North's territorial waters. This revelation led to suggestions that the claimed second attack was a pretext to get Congress to give its blanket approval for US military action against North Vietnam.

Within the USA, the resolution was considered to have more to do with Lyndon Johnson's imminent presidential 'battle' against the Republican candidate, Barry Goldwater, who had accused the incumbent president of being 'soft on communism'.

---

[4] What became known as *The Pentagon Papers* were commissioned by Secretary of Defence Robert McNamara in June 1967, compiled over many years by 36 anonymous historians eventually to fill 47 volumes. They were leaked to the *New York Times* in 1971 and remain one of the most comprehensive records of US involvement up to that time (*The Pentagon Papers*, Routledge & Kegan Paul, London, 1971, p 592).

The resolution retrospectively approved the air strikes President Johnson had already ordered against four North Vietnamese patrol boat bases as well as oil storage tanks at the port of Vinh on 5 August. It is considered to have authorized the extensive bombing programme against the North that began in March the following year. Operation Rolling Thunder, as it was called, was to last for three and a half years. Millions of tons of bombs were dropped – twice as much as had been dropped on Germany during the whole of the Second World War. North Vietnam said two-thirds of its 5,788 villages were hit and thousands of non-combatants killed. Railway tracks, bridges, factories and storage depots were all destroyed in an operation which set back the North's economic growth by at least 10 years. As an attempt to stop the North supporting the communist insurgency in the South, by breaking its resolve and depriving it of supplies, it clearly failed. It did, though, bring the USA ever deeper into what by now was undoubtedly the 'American war'.

The Gulf of Tonkin resolution is cited as the legal basis for the sending of full combat forces to Vietnam. They came ashore at Danang in March 1965, supposedly to defend the huge airbase there from which aircraft engaged in Operation Rolling Thunder were taking off. Nearly 20,000 US military personnel were already in Vietnam as part of (from 1950) the US Military Assistant Advisory Group (USMAAG) and from 1962 became the US Military Assistance Command (USMAC) whose role was to advise and train the South Vietnamese army. As the strikes against Vinh and other targets demonstrated, US personnel had already engaged in combat before Congress gave such actions its sanction. The landings at Danang marked the build up of a US combat force which was eventually, four years later, to exceed half a million. By the end of 1965, there were 184,000 US troops in Vietnam. They escalated the war as the North responded to the arrival of US troops by apparently infiltrating more guerrilla fighters into the South. Later, smaller forces from several other countries – Australia, New Zealand, South Korea, Thailand and the Philippines – arrived to fight alongside the Americans in response to a call by President Johnson for other nations to help the USA 'save' South Vietnam.

A clash in 1963 between the South Vietnamese army and communist guerrillas at the Mekong delta village of Ap Bac, in which a small guerrilla unit inflicted heavy losses of men and equipment, including five helicopters, had paved the way for the deployment of US forces. Three US advisers were among those killed. US observers, dismayed at the way the South Vietnamese army fought, concluded that the communists could only be defeated by the direct involvement of US forces,[5] although it could equally well illustrate that 'grasshoppers can defeat elephants' – to use the terminology applied by Ho Chi Minh to portray the discrepancy between forces.

As Operation Rolling Thunder demonstrated, the USA was set on using technologically superior weaponry to defeat the enemy. In the South, artillery and air power were used against the 'VC' or 'Viet Cong', the derogatory American abbreviation for the phrase 'Vietnamese communists'. These southern successors to the Viet Minh, who had so successfully fought the French, were thought to number well over 100,000, with many more non-combatant sympathizers. The US objective was to find and 'eliminate' them in so-called 'search and destroy' operations. Their problem all along was how to recognize the enemy, since to the Americans one Vietnamese peasant looked much like another and a farmer by day could become a guerrilla fighter at night. Their task was made more difficult by the fact that, as the Americans admitted, the guerrillas enjoyed a high level of support. There was plenty of evidence that they were nourished and protected by at least some of the population.

Although the Americans were there to assist the South Vietnamese government (all talk of reunification having been forgotten), the war increasingly became one between the USA and Vietnamese communists – rather than the civil war that southerners regarded it as. The success of US military operations was measured by 'body counts', often with little care given to establishing whether the bodies were genuinely those of communist guerrillas or of civilians. The euphemism 'collateral damage' signified that civilians, or non-combatants, had also been killed. The My Lai massacre is the most notorious example of the way in which the objectives seemed to sideline the morality. Such incidents gave the US army a bad reputation among the Vietnamese and in the world at large, strengthened by comments like that attributed to one US commander in Ben Tre province: 'We had to destroy the village in order to save it.' One senior US air force officer openly advocated bombing North Vietnam 'back into the stone age'. On the ground, the communist side was no less brutal, but it was the words and actions of the USA military that were more open to national and international scrutiny.

[5] This was the conclusion of John Paul Vann, whose story is told in Neil Sheehan's biographical history of the war, *A Bright Shining Lie*, Jonathan Cape, London, 1989.

From an early stage the Americans knew they must win 'the hearts and minds' of the Vietnamese people if they were to counter both communist propaganda and a natural antipathy towards the foreign 'invader' born of years of French rule. It was much less clear how it was to achieve this since its 'search and destroy' tactics tended to antagonize the very people the Americans hoped to 'save' from communism. A technique borrowed from Malaysia, where the British had fought communist guerrillas in the 1950s, was to create so-called 'strategic hamlets' – herding village people into secure housing units surrounded by barbed wire with the object of protecting them from communist guerrillas who were thus denied the means of obtaining food. Another project was Operation Phoenix – in effect a programme by CIA agents to identify and eliminate suspected 'Viet Cong'. In Vietnam the phoenix, or *phung hoang*, is a mythical royal bird which, it is said, can see everywhere. The implication of the Phoenix programme was that communists could be 'seen' wherever they were hiding. The programme suffered from the same weakness that afflicted the whole US operation in Vietnam: the difficulty of deciding which peasants were communists and which were not. Communists were only clearly communists if they were carrying a weapon.

Control of territory was another unclear concept. Quite often the South Vietnamese army controlled territory by day, but at night communist guerrillas took over. The remarkable tunnels running over several miles at Cu Chi to the west of Saigon – now a tourist attraction – give some indication of how the guerrillas lived and were able to remain undetected through the years of war. The communists also had a base, which included a field hospital, inside the hollowed-out Marble Mountains to the south of Danang, close to the US airbase and a stone's throw from China Beach where American troops had first landed and where they went for their 'R and R', rest and relaxation. Furthermore, South Vietnam's hostile terrain, the thick tropical jungle, was more of an obstacle to unfamiliar GIs than to Vietnamese.[6] The communists therefore

[6] However, the novel *The Sorrow of War*, written by Bao Ninh, who fought as a soldier in the North Vietnamese 27th Youth Brigade, vividly demonstrates that the jungle was 'lethal' too for the communist fighters. The novel's hero suffers from nightmares about the time he spent in 'the jungle of screaming souls' (Bao Ninh, *The Sorrow of War*, Secker and Warburg, London, 1993). Another writer, Nguyen Huy Thiep, powerfully contributes to an understanding on the impact of the war on the Vietnamese in his story *The General Retires* about a general who is alienated by the moral emptiness of the society to which he retires (Nguyen Huy Thiep, *The General Retires*, Oxford University Press, Kuala Lumpur, 1992).

directed their operations from the jungle and built their main supply route, the infamous Ho Chi Minh trail, through jungle-clad terrain.

By 1967 world opinion was swinging away from supporting the Americans. Even in the USA itself, attitudes towards the war were beginning to sour – as a result largely of the military draft and the high level of casualties being sustained by 'our boys'. The first 'television war' was nightly being viewed in American sitting rooms, causing Americans to doubt repeated official claims that the USA and its allies were winning the war. The dropping of chemicals such as napalm with little regard for its impact on human victims or on the land laid the USA open to charges of ruthlessness. Secretary of State Robert McNamara was himself having doubts about the prosecution of the war and its effect on public opinion. In May he wrote to President Johnson: 'There may be a limit beyond which many Americans and much of the world will not permit the USA to go. The picture of the world's greatest superpower killing or seriously injuring 1000 non-combatants a week while trying to pound a tiny backward nation into submission on an issue whose merits are hotly disputed is not a pretty one.'[7] The *Pentagon Papers*, which McNamara had commissioned, subsequently revealed widespread doubts within the administration about both the merits and the winability of the war.

The following year, 1968, provided clear proof that US forces and their South Vietnamese allies were not as close to defeating 'the VC' as was being claimed. On the occasion of the Vietnamese New Year festival, or *Têt*, communist guerrillas penetrated more than 100 Southern towns and cities. In the imperial city of Hué, the guerrillas held the ancient citadel for more than three weeks, flying their flag from its flagpole. In Saigon they even penetrated the compound of the US embassy. Though the communist side suffered very heavy losses, they inflicted a severe psychological shock on the Americans by demonstrating the limits of US and Saigon government control. Some analysts believe the attacks had a greater impact on US public opinion than anything previously and were responsible for the anti-war demonstrations on campuses that year. The setback of the *Têt* offensive was instrumental in President Johnson's decision in March 1968 not to stand for re-election, as well as on the opening of peace talks in Paris.

It was eventually US public opinion that brought about a US troop withdrawal. Richard Nixon was elected as president in 1968

[7] Quoted in *The Pentagon Papers, op cit*, p 592

by promising to end the war, or at least US involvement in it. He intended to do this through a programme of 'Vietnamization' whereby US forces were to be withdrawn and the South Vietnamese army was to be left to fight on alone. However, Nixon first escalated the war by taking it into Cambodia and by the 1972 Christmas bombing of Hanoi and Haiphong, attempting to force the North Vietnamese into making concessions at the Paris peace talks. Ironically too, the hand of friendship Nixon extended towards China in 1971 had removed the main US reason for the war. 'If the communist Chinese were now friends of the American people, why are we still trying to "save" the South Vietnamese from their communist brethren?' questioned Americans. President Nixon's visit to Beijing in February 1972 was just as traumatic for the North Vietnamese, who sensed that their ally and major arms supplier, whom they had never entirely trusted, was about to betray them to their enemy.

Peace accords were eventually signed on 27 January 1973, much to the indignation of the South Vietnamese government which believed, with some justification, that it was being deserted by the USA. It refused to countenance sharing power in Saigon with the communist Provisional Revolutionary Government (PRG). The accords provided for a cease-fire and for the withdrawal from Vietnam of all US forces. The troop withdrawal was completed within two months and was reinforced by Congress imposing its own bar on any further US military activity in Indochina. In late 1973, North Vietnamese negotiator Le Duc Tho and US Secretary of State Henry Kissinger were jointly awarded the Nobel Peace Prize for signing the peace, although the former refused to accept his share, saying that peace had not yet come to Vietnam. The peace accords did not bring peace. The war continued between the Vietnamese combatants with heavy fighting in Quang Tri province, just south of the DMZ, and in the Mekong delta. Both sides claimed the other had attacked first.

In late 1974, 18 months after all US forces had left, the North Vietnamese mounted a massive assault on the South, which resulted in the capture of successive South Vietnamese towns – Hué, Danang, Pleiku, Buon Ma Thuot and so on. They surprised themselves at how rapidly they progressed. Their speed of progress, especially after President Thieu made a tactical withdrawal of South Vietnamese forces from the Central Highlands, set up panic in the South. Columns of refugees started heading south for Saigon along Highway One while well-connected Vietnamese took flights out of the country. President Thieu was one of those who left. Eventually the North Vietnamese army, also travelling on Highway One but with tanks, captured Saigon itself on 30 April 1975. The campaign commander, General Van Tien Dung, said later he had expected the final campaign to last two years, but it took only three months. It was a strategic victory for the North Vietnamese army rather than the spontaneous uprising of the people of the South against their government that communist propaganda had predicted. Even so, one of Saigon's best known streets, *Rue Catinat*, was renamed *Duong Dông Khoi* – General Uprising Street!

Even this conclusive end to the 'American war' (or the second Indochina war) did not bring lasting peace to Vietnam. Three and a half years later, it responded to provocations across its south-eastern border by sending troops into Cambodia, ousting the ruthless Pol Pot government from power in Phnom Penh. That action, which may have been justified in both humanitarian and self-defence terms, led to a subsequent border war between China and Vietnam as China 'punished' Vietnam for its action. Much of the rest of the world, led by the USA, punished Vietnam too by imposing an economic embargo.

The Vietnam War is one of the most analysed conflicts in history. The main focus of attention has been to the question: 'How could a technologically superior fighting force be defeated by a poorly equipped and largely irregular army?' Communist Vietnamese believe they won the war because their cause was just and because for them it was quite literally a matter of survival. 'Unlike the Americans, we could not go home when our year-long tour of duty was over', said one, 'We had nowhere else to go.' Another Vietnamese analyst says it was a war between technology and determination and the latter triumphed. Northern Vietnamese say they never doubted that they would eventually win and the country would be reunified, although there must have been times when they doubted whether they would live to taste that victory. Southerners are less sanguine, many still feeling that they lost the war. At least 3 million Vietnamese died, the vast majority of them non-combatants. Many others were disabled, or have not been able to lead normal lives. The impact of the war on family life too was enormous – absent or disabled fathers, widowed mothers, and, for many years after the war's end, a significant shortage of adult men in relation to women.

The psychological effects on the Vietnamese, northerners and southerners, of the long years fighting are not nearly as well documented as are those on the Americans although they are beginning to become apparent as Vietnamese feel freer than they did previously to write about their war experiences. The physical impact is more evident: ecological devastation where napalm and other chemicals were used, together with the destruction of towns and cities. Many feel the death and destruction were too high a price to be paid for reunification and bitterness remains between north and south. Liberation commemorations still fail to recognize the right of southerners to be as proud of their contribution to their war as of northerners: instead such commemorations only remind Southerners that they were the losers. Veterans of the South Vietnamese army receive no pensions and the South's 223,748 dead soldiers are not commemorated. 'Reunification came in 1975, but we have yet to achieve national reconciliation', claims one embittered southerner, 'They, the communists, are not even graceful towards us in victory.'

Twenty years on, Vietnamese in both the north and south of the country still have a strong sense that they were the victims of a conflict that only partly concerned them. US forces had left Vietnam before the final defeat of its ally, the South Vietnamese government, but South Vietnamese blame the USA for the defeat, saying it deserted them in their hour of greatest need.

Perhaps the best analyses from the American side of why superior manpower and fire-power did not defeat an army of peasants come from two of the men most intimately involved in American policy making. Henry Kissinger recognized that the USA's most basic error was that 'we fought a military war; our opponents fought a political war; we sought physical attrition; our opponents aimed for psychological exhaustion.' This might have gone down in history as an instance of being wise after the event, except that Henry Kissinger wrote it *before* he assumed office in the administration of Richard Nixon. With remarkable prescience his article, in the January 1969 edition of the journal *Foreign Affairs*, went on seemingly to predict the reason for the US defeat: 'We lost sight of one of the cardinal maxims of guerrilla war; the guerrilla wins if he does not lose; the conventional army loses if it does not win.'[8] This was written before President Nixon's escalation of the

[8] Quoted in William Shawcross, *Sideshow: Kissinger, Nixon and the Destruction of Cambodia*, Fontana Paperbacks, London, 1980, p 87.

war and its disastrous extension into Cambodia, for which Nixon and Kissinger were chiefly blamed.

The other prosecutor of the American war who could be credited with anticipating its outcome was President Kennedy, who in 1961 was responsible for sending the first large contingent of US military advisers to Vietnam. Seven years earlier, while still a senator, Kennedy had also appeared to be wise before his time when he wrote: 'I am frankly of the belief that no amount of American military assistance in Indochina can conquer an enemy which is everywhere and at the same time nowhere, an enemy of the people which has the sympathy and covert support of the people.'[9]

---

[9] Quoted in David Horowitz, *From Yalta to Vietnam*, Pelican, London, 1967, p 159.

2

Big Brothers

Vietnamese see their history as a long struggle against one colonial master or another. As the writer Bao Ninh expresses it: 'Most foreigners coming to Vietnam brought along either a sword or a pistol.' Up until 939 AD the country was dominated by China. Today many of Vietnam's heroes and heroines commemorated in street names – figures like Tran Hung Dao, Le Loi and the two Trung sisters (*Hai Ba Trung*) – are venerated because of their resistance to the Chinese. Although Vietnam subsequently enjoyed independence from China, it was never free of threat from its powerful northern neighbour, which has had difficulty accepting Vietnam as a separate nation state. It sees itself as a 'big brother' and has expected and even demanded that Vietnam show it due respect.

Vietnam's European colonizers, the French, considered they had a civilizing mission towards the inhabitants of Vietnam. Although the French did not colonize Vietnam until the mid-19th century, European missionaries had started arriving as early as the 17th century. It was an early French missionary, Alexandre de Rhodes, who gave Vietnam a version of the Roman alphabet in which to write the Vietnamese language, which had previously been rendered in *chu nom*, a Chinese-like script. The Vietnamese have reasons to be grateful to him: he distanced them further from Chinese influence by making their language distinct from Chinese. But de Rhodes was part of the 'foreign domination' that Vietnam was fighting against, so his name was taken off street names in the north after 1954 as part of the process of exorcising the memory of the French. It was removed from the south after 1975. Now that Vietnam is pursuing Western-oriented economic policies, it is grateful to have a romanised script which makes doing foreign business much easier. There is a movement to rehabilitate de Rhodes and restore a statue of him that used to stand in Saigon, to acknowledge the country's debt to this Frenchman.

During the mid-19th century struggle by European powers for global influence, the French cited the persecution of Roman Catholics in Vietnam as justification for seizing power there. They did this without actually deposing the Nguyen dynasty emperors, who had ruled from the imperial seat of Hué since 1802. The French technique was gradually to consolidate their power. In 1859 they took Saigon, subsequently adding the adjoining provinces of what they called Cochin China, which became the first of three French protectorates. France had become the new 'big brother'. The French drive north came 20 years later and was largely commercially motivated. They wanted to control the country's natural resources and to trade with southern China via the Red River.

Vietnam's emperor at the time, Tu Duc, called on the Chinese for help in resisting French hegemony, the first time ever a Vietnamese leader had called on the Chinese for help! Chinese moves into northern Vietnam only strengthened the French determination to bring Vietnam fully under its control and gave them a pretext to move into areas to the north of the Red River delta which the Chinese had garrisoned. Under a treaty with Emperor Hiep Hoa signed in 1883, France added the two further protectorates of Tonkin in the north and Annam in the centre, thus completing its conquest of Vietnam. French rule of Vietnam was to continue until its defeat at Dien Bien Phu in 1954. The anti-French struggle, which got under way almost as soon as they had consolidated their hold on the country, bred a new set of Vietnamese nationalists of whom Ho Chi Minh became the best known. His opponents, however, saw him as nothing more than an opportunistic communist.

During the Second World War, Japan occupied Vietnam but allowed the Vichy French to retain administrative control – at least until the last few months of the war when Japan took full control. Japan's weakening of the France's hold on Vietnam gave Ho Chi Minh the chance to organize a resistance movement, which he did through the underground Indochina Communist Party. In 1941 the Party's central committee met at Pac Bo on Vietnam's border with China to set up the League for the Independence of Vietnam, which came to be known as the Viet Minh. Its objective was to challenge both Japanese and French rule and thereby win Vietnam full independence from all foreign powers.

The most crucial period in modern Vietnamese history followed the ending of the Second World War with Japan's capitulation on 10 August 1945. Ho Chi Minh moved fast to proclaim Vietnamese independence in Hanoi's Ba Dinh Square on 2 September, the very day Japan was formally signing its surrender document on a ship in Tokyo Bay. Ho Chi Minh had hoped the French would not attempt to re-impose their authority, since they had been ousted from power in Vietnam by the Japanese in March that year. The victorious allies, Britain, the USA and the USSR, had already decided that the Chinese should supervise the disarming of the Japanese in the north of Vietnam while the British fulfilled a similar role in the south.

When it became clear that the French were intent on re-establishing their rule, Ho made his famous remark characterizing the French as a lesser evil than the Chinese: 'It is better to sniff French shit for a while than eat China's all our lives.'[1] The Vietnamese, who have a 700 mile frontier with China, have often had cause to remember a lesson learnt at this time: that their country does not have the resources to fight several enemies at once, so a degree of compromise is inevitable when faced with threats from more than one direction. Unlike Emperor Tu Duc, who in 1876 had sought Chinese help in resisting the French, Ho Chi Minh at first opted for at least an understanding with the French in order to resist the Chinese, who were pillaging Tonkin with 'an appetite and a lack of discipline which threatened to bring anarchy and ruin to northern Indochina.'[2]

However the relationship deteriorated into open warfare as it became increasingly clear that the French would not voluntarily relinquish control of their most profitable overseas territory. In their determination to oust the French, the Viet Minh were ready to take arms from any source and the communist Chinese, who were on the verge of taking power in China, became the most enthusiastic supporters of what they regarded as a communist rather than a nationalist revolution in Vietnam. The Viet Minh were both inspired and armed by Mao Zedong's communist army. From this time onwards there has been a pro-Chinese faction in the Vietnamese Communist Party. Other Party members who are more sympathetic to Moscow considered the Viet Minh's dependence on China to be a regrettable mistake. With hindsight, it is clear that this dependence on China was a crucial factor in bringing the USA into the Vietnam war.

After their decisive defeat at Dien Bien Phu in 1954, the colonial

---

[1] From Paul Mus, *Vietnam, Sociologie d'une Guerre*, p 85, quoted in Jean Lacouture, *Ho Chi Minh*, Pelican, London, 1969, p 104.

[2] Jean Lacouture, *ibid*, p 101.

power retreated from Vietnam. It took the French even longer to get over this humiliation than for the Americans to come to terms with their subsequent defeat. When President Mitterand visited Vietnam in February 1993 he apologized for the attempt 40 years earlier to reimpose colonial rule. Mitterand had been a junior minister in the government of the time and this belated visit by a French leader marked an important stage in overcoming the bitterness that lingered on both sides since Dien Bien Phu. A further stage in the process of normalizing relations with the former colonial power takes place in 1997 when Vietnam hosts the seventh summit of *La Francophonie,* the international 'club' which links France with other French-speaking nations.

During nearly a century of colonial rule of Vietnam, the French had never been regarded as benefactors. Yet that is how China and the USSR were seen during the subsequent wars against the French and then the Americans. First China and then the USSR also gave the young communist republic moral and material support out of shared ideology and a sense of international solidarity. Both had been slow to recognise Ho Chi Minh's Democratic Republic of Vietnam, which they eventually did in January 1950 after Mao Zedong had taken power in Beijing. Both communist powers were subsequently drawn into giving increasing quantities of military and other aid as the government of South Vietnam received more and more support from the USA.

Given Vietnamese rulers' traditional wariness of becoming too dependent on China, it was ironic that Vietnam was being forced by US support for the South into a strategic alliance with a neighbour it did not trust, but it had little choice. This dependence on China echoed the situation in the mid-19th century when Vietnam had sought help from the Chinese to resist an invasion from more distant parts: the Americans had now replaced the French. Accepting support from the USSR was less of a problem because it was further away and thus not perceived as being in any way a threat to Vietnam. In any case, by accepting help from both the USSR and China, Ho Chi Minh's fledgling republic managed to play them off against each other thus avoiding becoming over-dependent on either.

It was something that happened outside Vietnam and over which Vietnam had no influence that changed this situation: the ideological split between Moscow and Beijing that emerged during the 1960s. At first this was not a particular problem while both supported the communist war effort in Vietnam. Later it became harder for Vietnam to balance the support it received from these two big rivals. To confuse matters further, China and the USA were now on speaking terms, even friends, leaving the USSR out in the cold. Before the Sino-Soviet ideological split occurred, the close relationship Vietnam enjoyed with both was seen as being based on ideology, which transcended all other considerations. After Moscow and Beijing fell out, accusing each other of not being 'true communists', it was less easy for Hanoi to balance its relations with these two benefactors. For historical, ideological and practical reasons, Hanoi selected the USSR as its new 'big brother'. It had never felt threatened by the USSR, it regarded Moscow as the headquarters of international communism and Moscow was underwriting the war effort to the tune of around a US$1 billion a year. In 1978 Vietnam became a full member of the Eastern European trading bloc, the Council for Mutual Economic Assistance (COMECON), and signed a treaty of friendship with the USSR.

Conversely, relations with China took a rapid downturn. After Vietnam invaded Cambodia in late 1978, to replace Pol Pot's Khmer Rouge with a government more to its liking, China responded (in February 1979) by engaging Vietnam on its northern border for a short but bloody and damaging war. Vietnam was reminded of what it had managed to forget during the war years: the proximity and hostility of its closest neighbour. The Chinese invasion provided an excuse for a wave of anti-Chinese nationalism directed at the ethnic Chinese community within Vietnam itself. Thousands of Chinese were forced to leave the country by threats against themselves or their property. When China then retaliated by ending its economic support, Vietnam became even more dependent on the USSR and its other East European allies.

A concrete demonstration of this dependence was the way the USSR took over from China the task of building the Thang Long bridge over the Red River, which nowadays carries the road connecting Hanoi's Noi Bai airport to the city as well as the railway connecting Hanoi to the Chinese border. Further south in the Red River valley, Moscow had constructed the largest hydro-electric plant in South East Asia, which remains the country's major source of power and is now connected to a grid serving the entire country. By the early 1980s, with China and Vietnam estranged, Vietnam was effectively being kept afloat by the USSR.

During this period it was possible to characterize the USSR as Vietnam's only true friend.[3] It was a friendship based on ideology and support. Nowadays, Vietnamese in both the north and the south are anxious to point out that *Lien Xo* – the Vietnamese name for both the USSR and its citizens – were never popular with the Vietnamese people. They say Russian culture lacked the appeal of that of the French or Americans and that the Russian language is 'unpleasant'.

Then it was the USSR's turn to let down its South East Asian ally, if not deliberately so. This 'let down' had several stages. By the late 1980s Moscow was signalling that it would not (or could not) continue to support Vietnam as it had done previously with special trading rights, subsidized fuel and by helping to build the country's infrastructure, like the Hoa Binh hydro-electric plant. In 1989 Moscow reached a rapprochement with Beijing, which once again put Hanoi into a difficult spot. Earlier that year the USSR had withdrawn its forces from Afghanistan, with obvious implications for its support of the parallel deployment of Vietnamese forces in Cambodia. Finally in 1991 there was the demise of the USSR itself, accompanied by the banning of the Communist Party. This was a major blow for communist-ruled and Soviet-funded Vietnam, mitigated to some extent by the fact that it had already embarked on the most radical revision of its economic policy, to which we shall return in Chapter Five.

Vietnam has its own version of the Cinderella story which tells of an orphan, Tam, living with a cruel step-mother who reserves all her favours for her natural daughter, Cam. One day Cam steals all Tam's catch of rice-field shrimps, presenting them to her mother as her own. Her mother rewards Cam by giving her a crimson dress. Meanwhile, Buddha appears to Tam and comforts her by giving her a small fish, but the spiteful Cam kills the fish. A big festival dawns on the occasion of *Têt* and the King is due to be there. Cam and her mother go. Tam wants to as well, but her step-mother tries to prevent her going by setting her the seemingly impossible task of

[3] See, for example, the reminder by former foreign minister Nguyen Co Thach that the USSR is the only one of the five permanent members of the United Nations Security Council that Vietnam has not fought against, quoted in Michael Williams, *Vietnam at the Crossroads*, Pinter/RIIA, London 1992, p 1.

separating husked from unhusked rice. Buddha sends a flock of sparrows which do the job swiftly. On her way to the festival, adorned in new clothes provided by Buddha, Tam loses a silken shoe, which the young King finds. It is so beautiful he vows to marry its owner. Tam and the King marry but her step-mother and sister subsequently engineer her death, putting Cam in Tam's place in the King's palace. The story runs through several more episodes before Tam is eventually reincarnated.

A contemporary version was being told in Hanoi in the early 1990s, without an ending, happy or otherwise. Russia and China used to be married: Vietnam was their offspring. Now the Russian father was dead and the Chinese mother was looking for a new spouse. She wooed the rich American, but he was less keen on the Chinese than he had been when the Russian was still on the scene. The American was not interested in the Chinese any more. But the child had views too. Vietnam was keen to be adopted by the American. With its father dead, it desperately wanted a counter-balance to its unloved, bullying mother. But the American could not forget how beastly the growing child had been to it earlier and could not easily bring itself to adopt the grown offspring.

In this 1990s version, the character who most closely resembles the fairy tale version is Vietnam itself as Cinderella, or Tam. The Vietnamese have a strong sense of themselves as a victim, the ill-treated progeny, and an equally strong feeling that they deserve a degree of help which only a fairy godmother, or Buddha, or a rich step-father like the USA can provide. While the original version reflects the Confucian value that hard work deserves to be rewarded, the contemporary version could be said to demonstrate that the process of reincarnation or rebirth, through which Vietnam is currently passing, can come about as a result of an individual's own efforts.

Vietnam normalized relations with China in November 1991 following the Sino-Soviet rapprochement of 1989 and the Vietnamese withdrawal from Cambodia later the same year. The subsequent demise of the USSR only served to confirm the wisdom of the shift in its foreign policy away from near total dependence on Moscow towards a policy described succinctly in a government publication: 'Vietnam wants to be friends with all countries of the world.'[4] General Giap, the *éminence grise* of the Vietnamese political establishment and a firm supporter of the new policies, characterizes the 'new' foreign policy as being 'friends with everyone but still being Vietnamese'. This 'open' foreign policy is the second track of the reform programme of which *doi moi*, or economic renovation, is the first track. Vietnam is trying to move away from a dependence on military might as the cornerstone of its international relations and is instead aiming to advance its interests through a combination of diplomacy and economic strength.

Though normalized, relations between Vietnam and China are correct rather then warm. It is no more true today that the two countries are 'as close as lips and teeth', as China used to claim in the mid-1970s, than it was then. Some analysts believe that Vietnam would not have normalized its relations with China at that juncture if Washington had itself restored full relations with Hanoi once its troops were pulled back from Cambodia, as it had indicated it would. China and Vietnam are today economic rivals and that has focused attention on their remaining unresolved dispute over the two groups of islands in the South China Sea known internationally as the Spratlys and the Paracels. Both countries have awarded exploration concessions to foreign oil companies in areas of the sea claimed by the other. (Interestingly, it is American companies that are most exposed to the wrath of the rival claimant, with Crestone Energy Corporation exploring for China an area adjacent to one being worked for Vietnam by Mobil Oil.)

In 1988 China sank two Vietnamese patrol vessels in the Spratly islands killing 70 sailors while reasserting its claim to the islands. The incident reinforced suspicions in Vietnam about its northern neighbour's intentions. The two countries subsequently agreed to settle matters of demarcation peacefully, but several years on the maritime dispute remains unresolved. In 1995 China turned its attention towards islands in the Spratly group occupied by the Philippines, demonstrating that it has no intention of giving up its claims on the entire group. China is concerned at its imminent need to import oil to fuel its economic revolution, which makes it disinclined to give up a claim to waters believed to be rich in oil. The precise extent of what China calls its 'historical claim' in the

[4] *Vietnam: The Blazing Flame of Reforms*, Statistical Publishing House, Hanoi, 1993 p 119. The policy may not in fact have been that new since Ho Chi Minh is reported to have said in an interview in September 1947 that his vision was 'to make friends with all democratic nations and make enemies with none' (quoted in the *Far Eastern Economic Review*, 29 June 1995, p 33).

South China Sea is undefined and its naval presence may have more to do with enhancing its bargaining power towards the shared development of resources in the area, which Beijing has advocated.

In late 1994 there was a serious and little publicized incident in Ho Chi Minh City when an unidentified person threw a grenade at a member of a visiting Chinese trade delegation as it returned to the city's Floating Hotel. Several of the visitors were injured, two of them seriously, necessitating urgent repatriation to China. The incident overshadowed the subsequent visit to Vietnam by Communist Party General Secretary Jiang Zemin and heightened a war of words between Hanoi and Beijing over the disputed waters. The fact that the Ho Chi Minh City incident had such repercussions, and that it was hushed up, underlines just how delicate relations are between Hanoi and Beijing.

Vietnamese leaders resent any suggestion that the country's economic reforms are mimicking those China introduced earlier. Nevertheless, they cite the Chinese model to argue that ending the Communist Party's monopoly on power is not a prerequisite to becoming a world economic power, as they believe China is on the way to becoming. There is no doubt, though, that China's thriving economy is helping to drive Vietnam's. Chinese goods are flowing across their common frontier to satisfy Vietnamese demands. A vivid example of the impact of such trade comes from beer. The preponderance of Chinese beer in Vietnam spurred Vietnamese entrepreneurs, led by state companies, to enter into joint ventures with foreign partners. The resulting alliances, with Carlsberg of Denmark and Tiger of Singapore among others, have produced good local beers, like Halida in Hanoi and Huda in Hué, stemming the flow of Chinese beer. Similar efforts are underway to stem the flow of Chinese biscuits. The desire to check the flow of Chinese goods, or simply to better them, has provided an important spur to the recent development of Vietnam's manufacturing industry.

Vietnam's problem is that China-made goods are invariably either cheaper, like the electric fans which China is accused of dumping in Vietnam, or technically superior, like the sewing machines and bicycles which are said to last three times as long as those made in Vietnam. Whilst few people favour drinking Chinese beer even though it is cheaper than Vietnamese beer, most people prefer to own a more expensive China-made bicycle. For China, Vietnam is an important and profitable market for the products of its manufacturing industry, which may be a reason why it prefers to resolve the offshore demarcation disputes peacefully, rather than going to war thus risking Vietnam closing its border to Chinese goods. Trade across the Vietnam–China border offers a powerful demonstration of market forces in action, as each country's newly liberated entrepreneurs, led by the state corporations, try to satisfy the demands of consumers on the other side! Nor is the flow all one way. During 1995, a shortage of rice in China was overcome by importing large quantities from Vietnam, among other sources.

Relations with China have a direct corollary in tolerance towards the ethnic Chinese, or *Hoa*, community within Vietnam. When relations between the two countries are good the *Hoa* thrive, when they are tense the *Hoa* feel threatened. Before 1975 the *Hoa* population was 2 million strong, but as many as half a million left as a direct or indirect result of the anti-Chinese campaign of the late 1970s. At first they left unobtrusively – travelling by land to China or flying out to join relatives in Taiwan or Hong Kong. When communist officials, in an orgy of nationalist xenophobia, started searching the homes of *Hoa* citizens of Vietnam for illegal gold or hoarded currency in 1978, many others took to the sea in the first mass exodus of what came to be known as 'boat people'. If it was not actually encouraged, this exodus of Chinese Vietnamese was welcomed by the authorities, the more so since it was accompanied by the sharp downturn in relations with China itself. The persecution left the communist government of newly-united Vietnam with a badly tarnished human rights image that was to darken further when ethnic Vietnamese followed the example of the ethnic Chinese and fled the country in small boats. Early refugees from communist Vietnam were readily offered resettlement in the USA, Australia and elsewhere, so a significant proportion of overseas Vietnamese resettled in those countries is of ethnic Chinese origin.

Chinese Vietnamese were among the first to see the opportunities presented by the new economic policies and to capitalize on them – helped by their knowledge of the country and language. A significant number have now resettled in the country from which they earlier fled. Most of those returning come to Cholon, the Chinese quarter of Ho Chi Minh City, which is still the main Chinese 'camp' in Vietnam. (Curiously the central street in Cholon is named after Tran Hung Dao who is celebrated for defeating the Chinese!) Cholon literally means 'big market' and that is just what

Cholon is. Founded in the 18th century by Chinese returning after another forced exodus following the 1778 Tay Son rebellion, Cholon has for two centuries been the main commercial centre of Vietnam as well as Saigon's commercial quarter. It used to be the centre of the rice export trade. Even during the austere early 1980s Cholon retained its reputation as the centre of the gold trade and place where the free-market exchange rate between Vietnam's currency, the dong, and the US dollar was set.

Business may be Cholon's main *raison d'être* but it is not its only one. Writers from Norman Lewis (in *A Dragon Apparent*) to Graham Greene (*The Quiet American*) and Marguerite Duras (*The Lover*)[5] have portrayed Cholon's reputation for hedonism and licentiousness, its nightlife, gambling and opium smoking, not to mention its links to the rebellious undercurrent of the moment. It was through a dancing girl in a Cholon nightclub that Norman Lewis established contact with a Viet Minh leader in 1950. Cholon is today returning to life in all the respects that have given it this notoriety and have earned it the respect and admiration of those who do not live there but perhaps visit occasionally. That admiration is evident today. Non-Cholonese seem to be saying: 'If Cholon can restore its business life and sense of fun then communist rule cannot have penetrated very deeply. It seems that no power in distant Hanoi can stop Cholon functioning as it always has done'.

Cholon's return to the bustle of the early 1970s is the main evidence that the *Hoa* are returning. Around a third of the estimated 1.8 million *Hoa* in Vietnam today live in Cholon, which is renowned for the way the Vietnamese and *Hoa* communities live happily side by side. It is not easy to find out numbers, but a Cholon-based banker confirms they are coming back and bringing big money with them. The shops of Cholon are well stocked with Vietnam-made and imported goods. The electrical market is piled high with boxes of Japanese and Korean televisions and hi-fi equipment. It is once again true that you can find anything in Cholon – at a price! The banker, who works for the private, Chinese-owned Viet-Hoa Bank (which was allowed to open in 1992 as part of the new encouragement of private banking), says the

---

[5] Norman Lewis's *A Dragon Apparent* (Jonathan Cape, London 1951), one of the finest travel books of the era, is set against the background of the first Indochina war; Graham Greene's novel *The Quiet American*, also set in French times, tells the story of early American involvement in Vietnam through fiction (Graham Greene, *The Quiet American*, Heinemann, London, 1979); while Marguerite Duras's romance is a study of relations between the French and Chinese Vietnamese in colonial times (Marguerite Duras, *The Lover*, Flamingo, London, 1986).

bank's main business is financing the import trade. It is funding the import of factory equipment, all types of vehicles and photographic 'mini-labs', one of the most popular and profitable small-scale enterprises now being installed in towns the length and breadth of the country and rivalling the photocopier as a street business.

One of the first Chinese Vietnamese to come back was Lo Ky Nguon. In 1985 he returned from Cambodia to where he had fled from Cholon in the late 1970s as political pressure on the *Hoa* intensified. From a modest office behind a shop selling plastic household goods, Nguon has built up a large construction, hotel and banking empire which includes the Viet-Hoa Bank and the popular Caesar Hotel, restaurant and nightclub. His trump card was to take over the financing of a new market after its Singaporean backers pulled out. Nguon himself found alternative funding for the market from Taiwanese sources and took over the project. Cholon's An Don market is now one of the largest in Vietnam and the first with escalators! Cholon is thriving on investment from ethnic Chinese sources – from Taiwan, Hong Kong or wherever Cholon's former inhabitants fled in the late 1970s. Many have made fortunes abroad, but they are not slow to see the potential back in Vietnam. These émigré Chinese Vietnamese do not need to return to live in Vietnam because they still have contacts there through whom they can channel funds from Taiwan or Hong Kong. Chinese Vietnamese now living abroad have put much more money into the city than the more numerous overseas Vietnamese, or *Viet kieu*.

Philip Chow was another early returnee to the city of his birth and upbringing. His family had migrated to Hong Kong where they developed a sizeable business empire embracing retail trading and restaurants. Arriving back in 1987, Chow's particular mission was to persuade the authorities, in the wake of their new economic policies, to allow him to reopen Cholon's once popular racetrack at Phu Tho. Receiving their approval after demonstrating how much they stood to gain from taxes on betting stakes, he achieved his target within two years. The race track became so profitable that the city authorities decided they could do without Chow. While Chow moved on to other business activities, Phu Tho earns the city authorities a sizeable income from its twice weekly race meetings, which have attracted the sponsorship of the French cognac manufacturer, Martell!

Investment in Cholon comes not only from Chinese Vietnamese, but from other ethnic Chinese too. Cholon's hotels and nightclubs are full of Taiwanese businessmen, who are renowned for their love of the pleasures that accompany business. It is questionable whether the business opportunities or the nightclub hostesses present the greater attraction. For several years Taiwan has headed the list of nations investing in Vietnam. Its business community has seized the opportunities presented both by Vietnam's liberal foreign investment code and the fact that Japan felt bound by the US embargo and thus held back on its own investment. By the time the embargo was lifted and Japanese businessmen started arriving in large numbers, Taiwanese businessmen had invested in well over 100 joint venture projects, making them the most powerful foreign commercial interest in Vietnam. Taiwan is certainly the dominant economic power in Cholon. A senior member of the People's Committee for District 5, which encompasses Cholon, reacted with horror to the suggestion that Taiwanese investors were taking the area over: 'We're not going to let Cholon become a Taiwan satellite', she said. 'We want to keep the district Chinese Vietnamese. Every project has to be approved by the state.'[6]

As well as clearing the way for the normalization of its relations with China, Vietnam's troop withdrawal from Cambodia in 1989 removed the obstacle standing in the way of friendly relations with the member countries of the Association of South East Asian Nations (ASEAN). Vietnam joined this economic and security grouping, consisting of Thailand, Malaysia, Singapore, Indonesia, the Philippines and Brunei, in July 1995. Some analysts believe Vietnam's realization that its future lay as a member of the South East Asian community rather than of the ailing Soviet bloc was just as significant as its adoption of new economic policies.[7] While for historical reasons Vietnamese leaders are unable to admit to any admiration for China, their admiration for the way countries like Singapore, Malaysia, Thailand and Indonesia have become economically strong characterizes the 'new' thinking in Vietnam today. Collectively, the phenomenal growth of these countries in the 1980s and 1990s seems to provide proof for Vietnam's contention that economic development needs firm political control. Both politically and economically the ASEAN nations are Vietnam's latest 'big brothers'.

[6] Quoted in an article by Julia Wilkinson in *Discovery*, the Cathay Pacific in-flight magazine, July 1993, p 67.
[7] See Michael Williams, *Vietnam at the Crossroads*, p 73 for example.

ASEAN was founded in 1967 to provide a bulwark *against* the communist nations of the region like North Vietnam. Its member nations were especially critical of Vietnam's 1978 invasion of Cambodia and enthusiastically supported the international ostracization of Vietnam that resulted. That Vietnam has now joined an organization which it used to believe had hostile intentions towards it is one of the more obvious ironies of contemporary South East Asia. Other ASEAN members have not changed their policies, although these days they put less stress on the anti-communist sentiments that originally brought member nations together. They now feel that both individual and regional security will be enhanced if all South East Asian nations join. With China appearing to assert its so-called 'historical claim' over large parts of the South China Sea, ASEAN nations are united in their shared suspicion of China's regional intentions and concerned at its unwillingness to outline precise details of its claim. They take some comfort from the fact that China's eagerness for investment means it would be unlikely to go to war as that would certainly deter foreign investors.

Most ASEAN members also share Vietnam's belief that political stability is the most important prerequisite for economic development and that this best comes from tightly regulated political activity – what Indonesia used to call 'guided democracy'. The emphasis on the primacy of development interests over civil and political rights has sometimes been referred to as the 'Asian view of human rights'. Only one ASEAN member, the Philippines, has challenged this belief in the primacy of economic development as part of a process of re-examining its own priorities set in train when 'people's power' overthrew former President Marcos in 1986. President Fidel Ramos told a conference of Asian politicians and intellectuals in late 1994 that his country had reversed its previous strategy and was now seeking economic recovery under a democratic system.[8] He disputed the notion that 'democracy does not mix well with economic development' and said the depiction of a conflict between the West, where rights and freedom are emphasized, and the East, where cooperation, community and discipline are stressed, was too simplistic. Other ASEAN member governments point to the fact that economic growth in the Philippines has fallen way behind that of the rest of ASEAN including Vietnam. They say this proves the contrary argument.

[8] The speech, on 4 November 1994, was widely reported – by AFP amongst others.

Just how complete Vietnam's transformation is from COMECON to ASEAN member is illustrated by the former foreign minister, Nguyen Co Thach. He says: 'Russia got things upside down by doing political reform first. Economic reform must come first and it should be strengthened by political reform.'[9] Thus at one stroke he distances his country from its former chief ally and benefactor and makes clear who its best friends are these days. By his next comment he underlines that point: 'Our foreign policy must serve the change in our economic policies. Around the world economic policy is driving foreign policy.'

Vietnam sees ASEAN as a guarantor of its security too, even if that aspect of membership is not clearly spelled out. The USSR has ceased to exist and Russia has made clear it does not want to take over the role of economic and strategic guarantor. The USA has retreated from the region. China will always be Vietnam's neighbour and is perceived as a threat however peaceable relations might seem. Vietnamese distrust of China cannot be over-estimated and is the main reason Vietnam wanted to join ASEAN so that these 'big brothers' could become the latest counter-balance against China - a role Ho Chi Minh had wanted the USA to adopt in 1945. For similar reasons, Vietnam is in no hurry to evict the Russian fleet from Cam Ran Bay in southern Vietnam. The real transformation of attitudes in Hanoi is that security is now perceived to come not from membership of one organization or another but from economic strength and self-sufficiency resulting from the sort of policies that it now pursues.

It is economic policies which drive ASEAN forward. All other ASEAN members, including tiny Brunei, are already economically active in Vietnam. Indonesia was the first foreign country to open a bank there and Thailand and Malaysia have followed in the banking path. Malaysian businessmen are much in evidence in Vietnam, trading, manufacturing and looking for investment opportunities. Thailand, which has bigger historical obstacles to overcome – its troops fought in Vietnam alongside the Americans – now self-interestedly pursues an economic and foreign policy it describes as 'turning battlefields into markets' which has resulted in huge Thai investments in Vietnam, Cambodia and Laos. Intense competition in the region has led a Thai diplomat to remark: 'Now the market itself has become the battlefield.' Manpower from the Philippines is helping Vietnam's economic revolution: many Filipinos occupy

[9] In conversation with the author in November 1994.

managerial and other positions – running restaurants for example. They are filling vacancies created by the exodus as boat people of skilled and trained Vietnamese.

Vietnam's special 'big brother' within ASEAN is undoubtedly Singapore. Singapore had few scruples about trading with 'the enemy' in the 1970s and 1980s; its foreign policy was dictated by economic self-interest long before such a course became fashionable. In late 1991, Prime Minister Vo Van Kiet asked Singapore's former prime minister, Lee Kuan Yew, to assume the role of economic adviser to the Vietnamese government, which indicated just how far Vietnam's foreign policy had changed. Unconsciously casting Vietnam once more in the Cinderella role, a Singaporean investor explained the appeal at that time: 'To the Singaporean businessman Vietnam is like a beautiful but young girl. He proposes now even though she is too young as yet to marry, because if he waits till she's old enough someone else may have secured her hand in marriage.'

This allegory well illustrates the romance of Vietnam–Singapore relations – for the Singaporean business community in Ho Chi Minh City see their country as a suitor rather than a 'big brother'. They think their years of economic friendship are now paying off. Another Singaporean in Vietnam says what really counts is the 'shared Confucian culture' which makes Vietnam easy for a Singaporean to understand. Singaporean companies are well represented in the list of foreign investors, while the extent of trade is indicated by the fact that roughly one in every three ships in Saigon harbour at any time is from Singapore. Most of Vietnam's two major exports, its oil and its rice, are shipped through Singapore.

Vietnam's leaders are happy with their new 'big brothers' within ASEAN. They are economically strong, they share Vietnam's new thinking, which puts economic strength first, and through their investment they are helping make Vietnam strong, or so Hanoi hopes. Vietnam's leaders are full of praise for ASEAN leaders like Lee Kuan Yew of Singapore, Dr Mahathir of Malaysia and President Suharto of Indonesia and are taking up golf, the sport of diplomacy on the ASEAN circuit! But they have not given up hope that an even bigger and stronger brother, the USA, will get over its remaining inhibitions and help rescue Vietnam from its poverty and backwardness.

3

American Generals

There were few links between Vietnam and the USA prior to the Second World War. The first recorded visit to Vietnam by Americans was when the clipper ship *Franklin* docked at Saigon in 1820. At an official level, an envoy of President Jackson visited Vietnam in 1832, while Emperor Tu Duc, who had sought Chinese help against the French, also sent an envoy to Washington. There is no record as to what reply he brought back, if any. There was little historical reason to attract Ho Chi Minh to the USA. Nonetheless, as a young man working his passage as a kitchen hand on a French steamship, Ho Chi Minh is thought to have called at the ports of San Francisco and Boston before settling for as long as a year in New York. He worked there as an itinerant labourer around 1915. In New York, Ho developed an excellent command of English – and a taste for Jack Daniels' Tennessee whiskey! He was less admiring of another product of Tennessee: the racist Ku Klux Klan which he described in an article published in France in 1924 as 'a group of snobs and idlers, without political or social purposes'. He wrote that 'cunning elements' made use of the KKK 'to serve their political ambitions'.

With his interest in relations between races, Ho became an admirer of Abraham Lincoln whose writings appealed to him. According to one of Ho's biographers, he regarded Lincoln as 'the complete anti-racialist' and champion of the cause of 'the emancipation of oppressed peoples'.[1] The twin evils, as Ho saw it, of colonization and racism became his preoccupations and he quoted often from Lincoln in articles he wrote on these subjects. The American president at that time, Woodrow Wilson, inspired Ho by his fourteen-point doctrine of self-determination, which seemed to endorse everything Ho was seeking for his own people. Later, after Ho had settled in France, it became the basis for an eight-point

[1] Jean Lacouture, *Ho Chi Minh, op cit,* pp 225-226.

programme in which he demanded greater freedom for the Vietnamese people and representation in the French parliament, but stopped short of demanding complete independence from France. Ho tried but was prevented from delivering his appeal personally to President Wilson when the latter arrived in France for the Versailles peace conference of 1919.

Ho retained his admiration for US political traditions despite his subsequent exposure to the works of many great European and Chinese statesmen and intellectuals, including Marx and Lenin. To him the USA was the first colony to win its independence through revolution, an example he hoped Vietnam would one day follow. Later he was to borrow from the American declaration of independence in proclaiming Vietnam's independence in Hanoi's Ba Dinh Square on 2 September 1945. His declaration began: 'All men are created equal. They are endowed by their Creator with certain inalienable rights. Among these are life, liberty and the pursuit of happiness.' In adopting those words of Thomas Jefferson, Ho Chi Minh was demonstrating that three American presidents – Lincoln and Wilson being the others – had inspired him. Franklin Roosevelt, with his well known opposition to colonial rule, was to make a fourth.

Ho clearly expected US recognition for his declaration of Vietnam's independence and appealed for it in his proclamation. He also appealed directly to President Truman. The *Pentagon Papers*, the secret official US history of the war leaked to the *New York Times*, found that Ho sent a total of eight messages to Washington but could find no evidence that any of them received a reply. Ho believed Americans would appreciate that what the Vietnamese aspired to was what they had themselves fought for in their revolution, namely independence and freedom from foreign domination. He was particularly anxious to gain US support at that crucial time because the USA had no claims on Vietnam. He could not trust any of the other victorious wartime allies who were supervising the surrender of the Japanese. The Chinese had strong interests of their own, which they hoped to advance by giving power in Vietnam to their own nominees. The Russians, Ho felt, would be too exhausted by their war effort to back Vietnam in a struggle against the French. He reasoned that the British would be unlikely to support independence for Vietnam for fear of giving encouragement to the people of its own colonies. The Americans would most likely be supportive, Ho calculated. He may have been inspired by Mao Zedong and Zhou Enlai, leaders of the Chinese communists who were at that time trying to seize power in China. Early in 1945 they had proposed a meeting at the White House with President Roosevelt – or perhaps they had made the same calculation as Ho.

Truman's predecessor, President Roosevelt, had made clear his opposition to the restoration of French rule after the defeat of the Japanese. Roosevelt believed colonialism was a major cause of the Second World War and particularly of the Japanese attack on Pearl Harbour, which brought the USA into the war. He wanted the fledgling United Nations to take over the administration of former colonies as they were liberated. But Roosevelt died five months before Ho declared Vietnam's independence. His successor, Harry Truman, was fired by a different preoccupation in Asia, namely the containment of communism.

Ho's hope for American support was based not only on his reading of history. It derived from his personal experience of the later war years, 1944-45, when the fore-runner of the CIA, the Office of Strategic Services (OSS), had supported Ho and his Viet Minh guerrillas with small-arms and money in their operations against Japanese occupation forces. In return, the Viet Minh had given the Americans access to an intelligence network which stretched the length and breadth of Vietnam, behind Japanese lines. The fascinating and extraordinarily ironic story of how Ho courted the Americans in the hope that they would help Vietnam secure its independence from France and how the Americans in turn cultivated Ho, hungry for the intelligence he could provide, is told by one of the OSS officers involved, Archimedes Patti, in his book *Why Vietnam?*[2]

It would be nice to think the Americans suspected they were backing Vietnam's future leader, but Major Patti suggests otherwise, saying Ho at that stage was 'a very little fish in a big pond' and that 'it is much to be doubted if any American discerned the importance of his future role in Vietnam.' But they did consider he had an important role in the anti-Japanese war, in which Viet Minh interests were identical to those of the USA. A month before the Japanese capitulation, an OSS team parachuted into northern Vietnam to train 200 guerrilla fighters under Vo Nguyen Giap in the use of the latest American weapons and guerrilla tactics. Reflecting on the irony many years later, Patti wrote: 'Some of us may have suspected that

[2] Archimedes Patti, *Why Vietnam? Prelude to America's Albatross*, University of California Press, Berkeley, 1980, from which the following quotations are taken.

in the future the weapons and training might be used against the French, but no one dreamed they would ever by used against the Americans.'

According to Patti, who came to know Ho Chi Minh well, the US department of war information considered recruiting Ho to broadcast propaganda from San Francisco back to Vietnam. During the time they worked closely together, Patti tells how Ho made good use of the facilities of the American Office of War Information in several cities of southern China 'to improve his English and knowledge of American history, customs and current world events.' Ho also appealed through Patti for American technical help to re-establish Vietnam's industry, as well as American trade, investment and training and he looked forward to the day when 'France was not the only place to study... when students could also study in the USA.' In late 1944, the Viet Minh helped smuggle an American pilot through French and Japanese lines back to China when his plane came down with engine trouble over northern Vietnam after a bombing raid on Japanese-occupied Saigon – an early example of Vietnamese communists helping an American missing in action! *En route* to China, the pilot was taken to meet Ho, which was a learning experience for them both.[3]

President Truman was too preoccupied with determining post-war borders in Europe, and with developing a new and less friendly relationship with the USA's wartime ally Josef Stalin, to give much thought to the developing struggle between Vietnamese nationalists and the French in Indochina. Possibly he had already concluded that the restoration of French rule in Vietnam was an essential bulwark to the spread of communism in Asia. If that was not his view in 1945, it certainly was by 1950. Mao Zedong's communists had taken power in China and the communist leader in Korea, Kim Il Sung, who controlled the north, was attempting to reunite the two halves of the country militarily.

By this time also, Indonesia and India had won their independence from the Dutch and British respectively, which made the Viêt Minh even more determined to settle for nothing less from the French. The USA, which had not initially helped the French re-establish their rule in Indochina, was by now funding the French war effort against the Viet Minh, seeing it as being in US interests. The Americans had not wanted the French back in Vietnam, but

---

[3] This episode has found its place in fiction too, in Anthony Grey's epic novel *Saigon*. The true story is told in Patti's book.

wanted communists much less. What they may not have appreciated at the time was that, in rejecting the Viet Minh's appeals for support, the USA drove it into a much greater dependency on the communist powers, both the USSR and China, than Ho Chi Minh wanted. The cold war was on in earnest and, although it was not obvious at the time, Vietnam was on the way to becoming one of its main battlefields.

By the time the first Indochina war came to an abrupt end with the French surrender at Dien Bien Phu, the USA was paying about 80% of France's war costs. Ho realized that the French colonialists were by now acting on the orders and with the assistance of 'their masters, the American interventionists'.[4] So it is hardly appropriate to draw a clear demarcation between the first and second Indochina wars since the USA was already deeply involved in the first, and not only financially. An American airman was killed flying US supplies to the French in Dien Bien Phu. What was decisive about Dien Bien Phu was that it broke the French will to continue the fight to retain their colony, making it inevitable that any future resistance to communist rule in Vietnam was going to come from the USA directly.

The defeat of the French did nothing to diminish US resolve to keep communism at bay. By the time the major powers met to consider Indochina at Geneva in July 1954, the USSR had exploded its first atomic bomb, which was many times more powerful than that dropped on Hiroshima. It was on the eve of the Geneva conference that President Eisenhower first articulated the 'domino theory' to justify his country's support for the government of South Vietnam: if Vietnam was allowed to 'fall' to communism then the rest of South East Asia – Thailand, Burma, Malaya – and quite possibly Australia and New Zealand would be at risk too. It demonstrated a preoccupation with containing communism that had guided US foreign policy since 1945, coupled with the pathological fear of communism in the USA that followed Mao Zedong's takeover in China in 1949 and was encouraged by Senator Joseph McCarthy's anti-communist witch hunts.

While the Geneva conference was underway the British Prime Minister, Winston Churchill, remembered for the way he had initially opposed the granting of independence to India, made his oft-quoted remark that 'to jaw-jaw is always better than to war-war'. He was speaking at the White House and, whilst not specifically referring to Vietnam but rather to East–West relations in

[4] Quoted in Lacouture, *op cit*, p 234.

general, the remark was interpreted as showing that Britain favoured a more conciliatory approach over Vietnam than Washington was prepared to make. The US objective at Geneva was to avoid a sell-out to the victorious communist side. However, the chief architect of the temporary division of the country along the 17th parallel, which was agreed at Geneva, was the Chinese Prime Minister, Zhou Enlai.[5] The Americans took little part in the negotiations and did not fully endorse its decisions. Instead they threw their full support behind the government in the south, now led by Ngo Dinh Diem, as the best way of preventing a communist takeover of all Vietnam.

With Diem and the Americans primarily concerned to build a bulwark against communism, it was no surprise that the elections which participants at the Geneva conference agreed should take place by 1956, to be followed by reunification of the country, were never held. Even President Eisenhower believed they would have been won by the communists. Instead the USA gave more and more support to a regime in the south that had no intention of giving up power or contesting elections and whose commitment to democracy was not strong. Successive South Vietnamese governments were dependent on finance from Washington to underwrite their war effort as well as their economy, which thrived on US imports. Just how dependent it was is illustrated by the former prime minister and vice president, Nguyen Cao Ky, who tells in his autobiography how American GIs distributed packets of Uncle Ben's rice to villagers. Ky himself had crates of Tabasco sauce shipped to him from Louisiana. That a rice and pepper-growing country should need to import such condiments beggars belief![6] Ky casually admits in his book that there was widespread corruption within the Saigon regime. By the beginning of 1965 the Saigon government was disintegrating and there were suspicions that it was about to do a deal with the government in the north.

The USA was determined to thwart this and sent ground forces to Vietnam for the first time. They came ashore at the very spot where French forces had landed 107 years earlier, but it is unlikely that they saw the similarity of the two 'invasions'. The Americans did not see themselves as colonizers, believing only that their mission

[5] This is clear from the account of the conference in Stanley Karnow, *Vietnam: A History*, Penguin, London, 1991.
[6] Nguyen Cao Ky, *Twenty Years and Twenty Days*, Stein and Day, New York, 1976. As Saigon fell, Ky fled to California where he opened a liquor store. In the mid-1990s he moved to Hong Kong to do business with Vietnam.

was to protect the people of South Vietnam from communism. The French, it will be recalled, had arrived with a similar mission to protect Christian missionaries and had subsequently established a protectorate. Only later did they administer Vietnam as a colony. There was no doubt though that many patriotic Vietnamese, including some who were staunchly anti-communist, looked upon the landings as the arrival of any army of occupation. The extent to which the Saigon government depended on the USA as well as the size of the American force – half a million by the end of 1967 – reinforced this impression. The comparison of the relationship between the Saigon government and the USA with that between Vietnam's 'puppet' emperors and their French rulers is not inappropriate. The leadership in Hanoi always referred to the government in Saigon as 'the US puppet regime'.

Well over 3 million Americans served in Vietnam; 58,183 lost their lives. The names of the dead are recorded on the Vietnam Veterans' Memorial, a polished black stone in Washington DC which stands as a painful reminder of the nation's first and only military defeat. Just as painful are the 1,621 names of US servicemen registered as missing in Vietnam, because their bodies have never been recovered. In the mid-1990s the US administration has been spending around $100 million annually trying to locate and recover their bodies from the jungles of Vietnam. Around one tenth of those Americans who returned from the war had been wounded whilst as many as half a million suffered from what has been labelled 'post-traumatic stress disorder'. The herbicide Agent Orange has allegedly affected not only veterans but their offspring as well. There have been many and various estimates of the financial cost to the American people of the war, depending on exactly what is tallied. One puts the cost over the eight years when US troops were 'officially' deployed, from March 1965 to March 1973, at $120 billion.[7]

The war had a profound and lasting effect on American psyche, which was compounded by the eventual defeat. 'It is bad enough to lose so many men', runs the argument, 'but we have nothing to show for it. The communists still won the war.' No amount of euphemistic talk about 'peace with honour' (in President Nixon's

---

[7] Stanley Karnow, *Vietnam: A History, op cit*, p 31.

phrase) or its depiction as 'a limited war' can paper over the fact that the war demonstrated US impotence, symbolized by the ignominious evacuation of US diplomats and South Vietnamese soldiers from the roof of the American embassy in Saigon, an episode re-enacted in the musical *Miss Saigon*.

Nowadays US attitudes towards the war are no less mixed than they were at the time. Military men tend to endorse their commanders' view that the US military was trying to fight a war 'with one hand tied behind its back', or that the American people let the army down by not giving the war their wholehearted support. While those who feel they lost something in Vietnam –their youth, their innocence or a year of their lives – often exhibit an overwhelming feeling of bitterness, some politicians involved in prosecuting the war admit it was ill-conceived or that defeat was inevitable. Two former secretaries of defence, Robert McNamara and Clark Clifford, have both conceded that it was a mistaken war. McNamara, who more than any other American is seen as the war's chief architect, maintained years of silence before speaking of 'the ignorance, the flawed thinking and lack of courage' of those members of the Kennedy and Johnson administrations who 'acted according to what we thought were the principles and traditions' of the USA. 'We were wrong, terribly wrong,' said McNamara in an interview to launch his memoirs of the war. He said the USA had totally underestimated Ho Chi Minh: 'We saw him first as a communist and only second as a Vietnamese nationalist.'[8]

McNamara's army chief of staff, General Maxwell Taylor, who subsequently became US ambassador in Saigon, shares his former boss's view that the USA did not properly understand what it was doing in Vietnam: 'We didn't know ourselves...we didn't know our South Vietnamese allies. We never understood them....And we knew even less about North Vietnam.' Former Secretary of State Henry Kissinger summed up what the war had done to the American psyche. 'Vietnam', he said, 'has created doubts about American judgement, about American credibility, about American power – not only at home but throughout the world. It has poisoned our domestic debate. So we paid an exorbitant price for the decisions that were made in good faith and for good purpose.'[9]

[8] Robert McNamara, *In Retrospect: The Tragedy and Lessons of Vietnam*, Times Books, New York, 1995. Quotations are from press interviews given on 9 April 1995.
[9] Quotations are from the opening chapter ('The War Nobody Won') of Karnow, *op cit.*

What Henry Kissinger referred to is dubbed 'the Vietnam syndrome'. In later years, when the USA contemplated armed intervention abroad – in Central America, the Caribbean, Somalia or the Gulf – those who opposed it warned of 'another Vietnam'. In this context, 'Vietnam' had come to mean 'a quagmire' – and not just in relation to the USA as in the description of Afghanistan as 'the Soviet Union's Vietnam', in other words a situation that was more difficult to get out of than to get into in the first place. The 'Vietnam syndrome' can equally be cited as the main reason the USA did not intervene militarily in Iran during the hostage crisis, and only belatedly in Bosnia despite its sympathy for the Muslim side there. It also lay behind its cautious search for United Nations endorsement before embarking on the war to liberate Kuwait. Significantly President Bush reacted to the subsequent defeat of Iraq by saying: 'By God, we've kicked the Vietnam syndrome once and for all.'

A jokey report in the magazine *Paris Match* during the war years suggested that Vietnam and the USA should swap generals. America, it said, might find its war effort improved with the services of General Vo Nguyen Giap, the victor of Dien Bien Phu, and General Van Tien Dung, who led the forces that eventually captured Saigon. Vietnam would certainly benefit from the attentions of General Foods, General Motors and General Electric! Following its economic reforms, it is ironic that there is nothing the Vietnamese want more than the attentions of US corporations. US companies were initially prevented from taking part by the trade and investment embargo, after Vietnam's change of economic policy encouraged foreign investors. Washington had imposed the embargo on North Vietnam in May 1964 and extended it to the entire country after the communist victory in 1975. President Clinton came under intense pressure from US companies to lift it. They felt they were losing the opportunity to take part in the revolution that was transforming Vietnam. The Boeing Corporation argued that it risked losing orders for the 80 passenger jets that Vietnam Airlines said they would purchase by the year 2005. An equally vociferous lobby representing the families of Americans listed as 'missing in action' in Vietnam opposed the lifting of the embargo.

The embargo was eventually lifted in February 1994, the same month that Washington extended most favoured nation privileges to

China despite earlier demands that Beijing should first attend to human rights shortcomings. Both moves showed the power of commercial lobbying, and were preceded by an announcement that human rights and commercial concerns would henceforth be 'de-linked', which greatly pleased American businesses. Vietnam had in any case cooperated with the USA in elaborate searches for the bodies of those Americans unaccounted for in Vietnam. The Vietnamese seemed willing to facilitate Americans in all their pursuits, making visas available to almost anyone – government officials and members of the armed forces, business people, aid workers and missionary representatives, journalists, academics, veterans and tourists. Among the last category, a large number of young back-packers flocked in even before the embargo was lifted. Some were sons and daughters of veterans who had fought there, others just curious to see the backward country that had so humiliated their own.

Non-governmental aid and development agencies from the USA were also active in Vietnam before the embargo was lifted. Many were set up by Vietnam veterans' associations which wanted to put something back into the country. One such is the Veteran Vietnam Restoration Project which provided funds for a health clinic in Vung Tau as early as 1989. Another is the Denver-based Friendship Bridge which ships medical supplies to Vietnam and is now helping to provide pure drinking water in conjunction with the Water for People organization. Many US veterans have revisited Vietnam on behalf of such charities. Friendship Bridge has also sent Vietnamese health workers for training in the USA. The veterans behind Friendship Bridge try to avoid the suggestion that they are acting out of feelings of guilt, saying they prefer to see it as 'feelings of reconnection motivated by compassion towards a country that history has not treated well.' 'There is still an awful lot we have to learn from Vietnam', says Joseph McMahon, Jr, one of the organization's moving spirits and himself a Vietnam veteran. Another veteran now a US senator, John McCain of Arizona, spent five years as a prisoner in North Vietnam after his naval aircraft was shot down, yet he has been a staunch advocate of normalization. Some veterans feel as strongly about what the long US economic embargo has done to the country as they do about the war itself.

Whether from feelings of guilt, compassion or simply commercial pragmatism, the US government started its own reconnection with Vietnam by trying to help such non-governmental organizations (NGOs). The State Department has quietly directed funds to NGOs operating in Vietnam and organisations such as World Vision, Save the Children Fund (USA), World Learning and World Education have all been spending government money in Vietnam, some of it on programmes aimed at re-integrating those 'boat people' returning from South East Asian camps after being rejected for resettlement elsewhere.

The main US interest in Vietnam today is undoubtedly commercial. One US businessman set himself up in Hanoi as a trade and investment consultant when he realized how far ahead the Japanese were in researching the market. 'If the Japanese were interested in the world's twelfth largest market, then the US should be as well', he reasons. He aims to introduce US investors or traders to potential partners in Vietnam. Many Americans hoping to trade with or invest in Vietnam see it as a potentially profitable market with good prospects, or else they are attracted by the cheapness of its labour. A Vietnam-America Chamber of Commerce has been formed to promote investment and trade links.

As with aid workers, there are US businessmen too who have emotional or altruistic reasons for 'coming back'. One such is Dick Pirozzolo, who owns a public relations company and returned to Vietnam for the VietnAmerica trade shows in 1994. 'I was in Vietnam in 1971 as a public information officer, so I learned my trade there in the air-force. I continued to have an interest in Vietnam and came here as soon as the opportunity presented itself. I've been here three time within six months, to help get these shows going, trying to enter the Vietnamese market.' He was a whole-hearted supporter of normalising US trade and diplomatic relations with Vietnam: 'Veterans of World War II have had the chance to make amends with Germany and Japan and resume normal relations. It's a way of putting closure on an event that was not particularly happy in many people's memories. The veterans of this war by and large want to put that same closure on their involvement in Vietnam. They want to make amends.' Pirozzolo sees nothing ironic in US companies trying to interest Vietnamese customers in, amongst other things, rice cookers, several different brands of beer and wines, toothpaste and soap. 'Vietnamese have always been interested in American products because they go for the best and we can offer the best', he says. The rush to buy US goods at the trade shows bore out his assessment.

Another veteran now back as a businessman is William Willert, whose company, Willert Home Products, is one of the largest manufacturers of disinfectants in the USA. His $1 toilet deodorizers were selling well at the Ho Chi Minh City trade show, but his motives too were not entirely commercial. 'I want to start a factory here to make products which I currently make in Korea or Thailand. I want to transfer production here to employ Vietnamese people.' Pressed as to why Vietnam, Willert insists it is not the low wages which have been a major factor in attracting other investors, but because he is a Vietnam veteran: 'I was here in 1968 in the US navy. I think it is time the Americans did something to help the country out. We should be doing more. Hopefully I can set up a factory to employ Vietnamese. That's the best thing America can do to help the Vietnamese economy.' Willert believes normalization should have happened ten years earlier and is very critical of successive governments for failing to bring it about. 'If you polled all the veterans of the Vietnam war I believe they would overwhelmingly vote for normalization. It's a small group of veterans that don't want to because they have hard feelings. The Vietnamese didn't attack us, we attacked their country and we lost the war, so why are we mad at them? We're mad because we lost!'

Before the embargo was lifted the Vietnamese government asked a similar rhetorical question: 'How much longer must we be punished for winning the war?' They recognized that there are many people in the USA who strongly opposed normalization and have long since dropped their demand for the millions of dollars worth of war reparations that they say President Nixon promised them. They belatedly realized that a presidential promise was not worth much without public or congressional support. The difficulty for the US government was the unwillingness of some organizations to abandon their unsustainable claim that there are live Americans still being detained in Vietnam. (It has been suggested that this myth was first created by the US administration in 1969 to serve its own purposes and was used as a bargaining counter at the subsequent Paris peace talks.[10]) Vietnamese cooperation in the search for the remains of Americans unaccounted for in Vietnam became a US precondition for the lifting of the economic embargo and any strengthening of diplomatic relations. Hanoi went out of its way to assist the search.

In July 1995, 20 years after the end of hostilities, Washington restored full diplomatic relations with Hanoi. This coincided with Vietnam's incorporation as the seventh member of ASEAN, a move

[10] This is the main allegation of H. Bruce Franklin, *MIA – Mythmaking in America,* Lawrence Hill Books, New York, 1992.

which helped gain Vietnam the necessary international standing for the USA to overcome years of hostility and extend the hand of friendship. Some veterans groups protested at the normalization, most accepted its inevitability while others rejoiced, declaring the move to have been 'long overdue'. It had in fact been a much quicker start to the healing process than with Cuba, for Vietnam had shown signs of having abandoned communism as a creed which made it seem less of a threat to the USA. The US business community was relieved at the removal of another obstacle in the way of trading with and investing in Vietnam. One US businessman in Vietnam drew a deliberate comparison with the war-time claims of military commanders saying: 'I've been trying to do business here with one hand tied behind my back.' Another had previously claimed: 'More Americans are being hurt by the lack of normalized ties than are being helped by the status quo.'[11]

Vietnam wanted relations with the USA as a counter-balance to China. Just as in 1945 Ho Chi Minh was balancing foreign influences in an effort to secure Vietnam's independence, so in the 1990s a similar balancing game is going on. This time it is more about balancing economic might than diplomatic might. Vietnamese leaders reason that US investment in Vietnam would provide a counter-balance to the domination of the economy by 'Chinese' money coming from China, Hong Kong, Taiwan and Singapore; Danish, Singaporean and French investment, for example, has been welcomed into the brewing industry as a means of keeping China-made beer at bay. Encouraging all comers, but especially the USA because of its economic strength, is part of a new strategy to use economic power rather than military might to strengthen the nation's security. It is a lesson learned from the ASEAN countries.

Since the embargo was lifted Americans have been coming back to Vietnam, although US investors are not arriving as rapidly as the Vietnamese had hoped they would. Some of 'the generals' have arrived – Kraft General Foods are importing processed foodstuffs and General Electric are hoping to play a part in power generation projects. Chrysler and Ford are on their way too. Mobil Oil is resuming where it left off in 1975, annoyed no doubt that the embargo denied it the opportunity to develop the promising Bach Ho oil field that it discovered and that other countries' oil companies have secured some of the more promising offshore

[11] This and the previous quotation are taken from the *Far Eastern Economic Review*, 4 May 1995, p 25.

exploration areas. Nevertheless, it is clearly sufficiently encouraged by the results from Vietnam's oil fields still to want to take part. Caterpillar, with an eye on the huge amount of construction already underway and the upgrading of Highway One (funded by loans from the World Bank and Asian Development Bank) are hoping that its presence in South Vietnam before 1975 will stand the company in good stead. The brand name is well known and the company's representative in Vietnam estimates that as many as 700 Caterpillar bulldozers and earth-movers left behind by the US military are still in use, many with the army.

Individual Americans are coming sight-seeing and, whether or not they previously served in Vietnam, are eager to see the former US embassy building in Saigon. Some with a sense of history are keen to see the one-time US consulate in Hanoi, which now houses an office of the Vietnam Fatherland Front, a communist organization. Veterans are keen to retrace their own war. As one put it: 'I'm fed up with seeing Oliver Stone's war. *My* war was very different and lasted for the year I was here, no more and no less. It was a deeply personal experience for me. In coming back to Vietnam I am re-living that painful period, possibly even exorcising it. I shall never forget it and the impact it had on me.'

Another had promised himself that when he retired he would return to Khe Sanh, in the extreme north-western corner of the former South Vietnam. He was one of several hundred American soldiers besieged there for 77 days by more than 20,000 North Vietnamese troops in 1968. Around 250 American lives were lost there. Though communist casualties were much greater, Khe Sanh was compared on US television to the French defeat at Dien Bien Phu. When US forces withdrew from Khe Sanh a few months later, they comprehensively destroyed the base, ensuring it could not be used by the other side. Today there is virtually nothing, apart from a memorial stone, to mark the scene of one of the worst American setbacks of the war. That does not stop veterans from making what is something of a pilgrimage for them. (Khe Sanh achieved some sort of immortality in the Bruce Springsteen song, *Born in the USA.*) On the way to Khe Sanh veterans pause to look at a stretch of the fabled Ho Chi Minh trail, the network of paths along which men and supplies were transported southwards to fuel the communist war machine.

Returning Americans are struck by a number of ironies. Coming out of Hanoi's Noi Bai airport, they are confronted by a large and isolated billboard advertising American Express which stands in a paddy field still scarred by bomb craters. The Government Guest House in Hanoi was one of the first establishments in Vietnam to accept the American Express card after the embargo was lifted. They may be surprised to find how widely accepted US dollar bills are. Since 1975 the 'greenback' has been a parallel currency. More than $1 billion of US currency is circulating in Vietnam. For Vietnam it is the currency of stability, as the Hong Kong dollar is in southern China and the Deutsche Mark is in Eastern Europe. The US dollar is used by Vietnamese for large cash purchases such as buying vehicles, while foreign visitors are often required to pay their hotel and transport expenses in dollars. Buying a train ticket from a provincial town, foreigners may be surprised to be given change for a $100 dollar bill in relatively clean US currency. In an effort to give greater stability to the national currency, the dong, the government decreed in October 1994 that bills must henceforth be presented in dong, but the dollar has continued to be as acceptable a currency. Even *cyclo* (rickshaw) drivers accept dollars and can be seen in banks changing them into dong, a dollar at a time!

People in Vietnam today are proud if a little bemused by their unofficial link with the USA, home to around 1 million Vietnamese, the largest community outside Vietnam. Large numbers of families, especially in southern Vietnam, have relatives there. The largest numbers of Vietnamese Americans live in 'the golden state' of California (or 'Cali' as the Vietnamese call it), especially in San Jose and in Orange County near Los Angeles with its Little Saigon business area. The *San Jose Mercury News* was the first US newspaper to open a bureau in Vietnam after the embargo was lifted. Vietnam would like to open a trade office in San Jose because of the large community of Vietnamese Americans there, but San Francisco's Mayor Jordan, a leading advocate of normalization, wanted it to be in his city. He has already twinned San Francisco with Ho Chi Minh City and plans to introduce direct flights between the two. (Previously, Ho Chi Minh City was twinned with the second city of the USSR, Leningrad.) Vietnamese rice, beer and gems are already exported to the USA. Veterans can once again enjoy Saigon-made '333' beer as they did while serving in 'Nam.

Seattle, another US city with a large population of Vietnamese and strong trading interests with East Asia, was the first to send a trade mission to Vietnam. Two of Seattle's best-known companies, Boeing and Microsoft, have opened offices in Hanoi. In Microsoft's case it is more a question of checking software piracy than a judgment that Vietnam will be anything other than a relatively small market. Computer companies were amongst the first US companies to arrive in Vietnam – ready and willing to service the large amount of hardware that had been smuggled in before the embargo was lifted. American Standard, who make sanitary ware, are planning to open a manufacturing plant in Vietnam which, the company says, could save the country the $10 million it spends each year importing (mainly from Thailand) toilets, basins and baths!

Twenty years on, the Americans are back in Vietnam and this time their objectives are peaceful. The war going on now is a commercial war, a battle for business and profits. Nor is the USA fighting a Vietnamese enemy. It is one US company taking on another, or perhaps competing against East Asian companies. Asia, Europe and America are all fighting for a share of this new emerging market, or competing to be allowed to develop its mineral and other resources. Vietnam is engaged in its own battle to catch up with its richer neighbours – and this time it is welcoming foreigners of all sorts with open arms to help it do battle and win its war against underdevelopment.

4

The Ho Chi Minh Legacy

The transition of Washington's Indochina policy from opposing colonialism to opposing communism was spurred by a belief that Ho Chi Minh was an agent of Moscow and Beijing. Though the State Department in 1948 could find no firm evidence that he actually took his orders from Moscow, it was firmly believed in Washington that he did. After Mao Zedong came to power in China, it was similarly assumed in Washington that the Viet Minh were acting at Beijing's bidding in carrying communism into South East Asia. This belief was the basis for Washington's demonization of Ho Chi Minh.

Washington's hatred of Ho spurred on its war effort. It also led to provocations. For example, the communist government of Calcutta renamed the street on which the US consulate stood 'Ho Chi Minh Street' so that Americans had to use the hated name in their address! Later American students chanted 'Ho, Ho, Ho-Chi-Minh' on college campuses to symbolize their opposition to the war and provoking the deployment of the National Guard, which on several occasions opened fire. The same Ho Chi Minh who had inspired the Vietnamese peasantry now had a following among young American intellectuals.

Ho Chi Minh was not a pawn of either Moscow or Beijing. Washington's view of him, and thus its commitment to the defence of 'free' South Vietnam, was based on a misreading. Although US OSS officials in southern China advised Washington that the aim of Ho and his Viet Minh was to prevent the French from regaining power in Vietnam, President Truman's administration saw him only as a factor in the spread of communism. By 1950, Ho was being judged by the actions of the USSR, which was trying to subvert the governments of Greece and Turkey, of Mao Zedong's army, which had taken power in China and of Kim Il Sung, who was trying to seize control of Seoul. Events in China, Korea and Europe rather than in Vietnam led

46

Washington to support France and ultimately to its own costly involvement in Vietnam.

Ho was, though, avowedly a communist. He had helped to found both the French and the Indochinese communist parties and was a member of two others, those of the USSR and China. He spoke and wrote in communist journals using the language of a communist ideologue. Yet Ho's image as a communist was never as clear-cut as those of other communist revolutionaries because (as his writings show) the American and French revolutions had as great an impact on him as did the Russian revolution. He may also have been inspired by the success of the Chinese revolution, but one of his biographers, Jean Lacouture, points out that Ho seems to predate Maoism with the emphasis he placed on the importance of the peasantry in opposing colonialism. During his time in Paris and London, Ho had read French and English writers, including Zola, Hugo, Dickens and Shakespeare.

It has become fashionable to debate whether Ho was first and foremost a nationalist or a communist. This seems to miss the point since it is clear from Ho's writings that he saw communism as the means to free Vietnam from colonial rule. One view is that he became a communist whilst in Paris because only the far left supported calls for independence for the French colonies.[1]

Subsequently, Ho was particularly inspired by the writings of Lenin. In an article published on his 70th birthday, Ho wrote: 'Initially it was patriotism, not communism, that led me to have confidence in Lenin and the Third International. By studying Marxism-Leninism...I gradually realized that only socialism and communism could liberate oppressed nations and the working people throughout the world from slavery.'[2] Creating a socialist society was his ultimate goal, but his immediate aim was to gain Vietnam's independence.

Ho's fellow revolutionary, General Giap, has said it was nationalism that made him a Marxist and that is equally true of Ho Chi Minh. Ho believed socialism, which he referred to as 'final victory', would be implemented following the attainment of independence and reunification which, after the division of Vietnam, became his loudest clarion call. As early as 1945, Ho told Archimedes Patti, the OSS officer working with him, that members of the Indochinese Communist Party were 'nationalist first and

[1] See Neil Sheehan, *Two Cities: Hanoi and Saigon*, Cape, London, p 59.
[2] Quoted in Jean Lacouture, *Ho Chi Minh, op cit*, p 32.

party members second' although that assertion has to be judged in the context that Ho was urgently seeking US support at that time. A testament Ho wrote shortly before his death in 1969, which dwells on a time when 'compatriots in the North and the South will be reunited under the same roof', goes on to express his pride at seeing the growth of the international communist movement, suggesting he did not by this stage in his life see a clear distinction between his nationalist and communist ambitions for Vietnam.

The irony of the US belief in his close relationship with other ruling communist parties is that Ho Chi Minh actually felt badly let down by them. As early as 1924, he berated French and British communists for not taking the issue of colonialism seriously. After the Second World War, he complained that French communists, who were by then partners in the socialist government in Paris, were not supporting Vietnamese independence. He accused them of being more nationalistic than ideological. Ho resented the fact that the USSR took more than four years to recognize his Democratic Republic of Vietnam, doing so only after Mao Zedong's communists had come to power in China. Ho could not easily forgive China's communist government and Prime Minister Zhou Enlai in particular for supporting the division of Vietnam at Geneva, causing Prime Minister Pham Van Dong to remark 'he has double-crossed us.'

To Ho these actions – or inactions – confirmed that national self-interest runs deeper than ideology and justified his decision in 1945 to turn to the USA for support. He believed the Americans had no territorial ambitions in Vietnam. However, he failed to realize that they were to have ideological ambitions – to keep Vietnam, or as much of its as possible, out of the hands of communists. The recognition of Ho's government by China and the USSR had, in Washington's eyes, merely confirmed North Vietnam's place in the communist pantheon – although there was no realization of the role the USA had played in driving it there. Another irony of the US belief that North Vietnam was China's agent was that by the mid-1950s Washington and Beijing clearly shared an interest in keeping Vietnam divided. China felt more secure with a disunited Vietnam while the USA saw the division as a means of keeping communism out of the south of the country. It was not until the China–Vietnam border war of 1979, long after US troops had been withdrawn and the country reunified under communist rule, that the USA came to appreciate just how little love there was between Beijing and Hanoi.

Ho's victory over the French at Dien Bien Phu had gained him a following throughout Vietnam. Expert advice was that he would win the nationwide elections provided for in the Geneva accord. President Eisenhower accepted that fact and the then Senator John Kennedy told the Senate in April 1954: 'Despite any wishful thinking to the contrary, it should be apparent that the popularity and prevalence of Ho Chi Minh and his following throughout Indochina would cause either partition or a coalition government to result in eventual domination by the communists.'[3] The USA was determined to prevent this happening, so they connived with Ngo Dinh Diem to ensure that the elections never took place. From Geneva onwards the USA was engaged in a conspiracy to prevent the reunification of Vietnam. The war increasingly became a conflict between the most powerful nation on earth and a small communist nation, rather than the civil war that south Vietnamese prefer to depict it as.

Archimedes Patti, who described French colonialism as 'one of the worst possible examples of peonage, disregard for human rights and French cupidity', had little doubt that the Viet Minh would succeed in their military objective of defeating foreign powers in Vietnam. He wrote, admittedly with the benefit of hindsight, that they enjoyed 'that all-important ingredient, popular support from the Vietnamese people – an ingredient which we totally ignored in the sixties and seventies, much to our sorrow.' After the widespread famine of 1944-45 Patti began to realize that the revolutionary movement in Vietnam was closely linked with the instinct for survival: 'If national independence could assure a Vietnamese of survival, he saw the Viet Minh as the answer. It mattered not to him whether the medium was democratic, socialistic or communistic. The question was to be free from want, to enjoy the fruits of one's labour and to exist unmolested.'[4]

The *Pentagon Papers* provide some evidence that the USA did come to reassess the wisdom of its policy towards Vietnam and to reassess Ho Chi Minh himself. There are hints of recognition that, far from being in Moscow's pocket, he could have been something of an Asian Tito, distancing himself from Moscow and presiding over a broadly neutral, albeit communist, government. But the reassessment came too late (the *Papers* were compiled from 1967 onwards and leaked in 1971) except in so far as it was a factor in President Nixon's decision to start talks with the North Vietnamese.

---

[3] Quoted in David Horowitz, *From Yalta to Vietnam, op cit*, 1969, p 148.
[4] Archimedes Patti, *Why Vietnam?, op cit*, pp 125-132.

It was one of President Kennedy's Vietnam advisers, General Maxwell Taylor, who publicly conceded later that the USA may have judged Ho wrongly. Listing US failings in the war he concluded: 'Who was Ho Chi Minh? Nobody really knew. So until we know the enemy and know our allies and know ourselves, we'd better keep out of this kind of dirty business. It's very dangerous.'[5] The ignorance was reciprocated. Ho Chi Minh told a Polish diplomat in 1963: 'Neither you nor I know the Americans well', although he went on to predict that 'one day they will begin to analyse our ideas seriously' and conclude that it is 'possible and even worthwhile to live in peace with us.'[6]

Ho Chi Minh – which means Ho, the enlightened one – was one of at least a dozen pseudonyms assumed during his lifetime by the man born Nguyen Tat Thanh in 1890.[7] It was the name by which he was known in 1945 when, aged 55, he assumed the role of president of the Democratic Republic of Vietnam. If the Americans realized belatedly that they did not really know him, the vast majority of Vietnamese were little wiser. His habit of using pseudonyms or frequently changing his name has preserved an obscurity and created a mystique. Even today, the 30 years he spent away from Vietnam between 1911 and 1941 are shrouded in mystery. He never kept a diary and no biographer has been able to answer all the lingering questions from his roving years. Did the French ship on which he was working call at San Francisco? In New York did Ho stay in Harlem or Brooklyn? Was he really assistant to the celebrated French chef Escoffier whilst working at the Carlton Hotel in London? Did he visit Moscow in the early 1920s in time to meet Lenin, or only arrive there two days after Lenin's death in January 1924? Which ranking members of the Chinese Communist Party did the then obscure Nguyen Ai Quoc meet during his years in China? And, most intriguing of all, did he ever marry? There are no clear answers to these questions. When the French writer, Bernard Fall, met Ho in 1962 and tried to elicit answers to some of these questions, especially the last, Ho defended his secrecy thus: 'An old man likes to have a little air of mystery about himself. I like to hold

[5] Quoted in Karnow, *op cit*, p 23.
[6] Quoted in Neil Sheehan, *Two Cities: Hanoi and Saigon, op cit*, pp 58.
[7] These are the most widely accepted name and year of birth, although there are others.

on to my little mysteries. I'm sure you will understand that!'[8] The mystery has enhanced the mystique.

During the war, at least from Dien Bien Phu onwards, Ho Chi Minh's name became synonymous with invincibility – a symbol of the enemy who could not be seen. Thus the Americans coined the term 'Ho Chi Minh trail' for the route used to bring men, arms and supplies south. According to some accounts it was actually Ho Chi Minh who ordered the construction of this remarkable network of paths, tracks and river crossings stretching around 12,000 miles in all. The trail followed a route from Nghe An province south of Hanoi, into the Truong Son mountain range, darting across the jungle-clad border into Laos and Cambodia before re-entering South Vietnam at Tay Ninh province into what the Americans called the 'iron triangle', the thickly jungled communist 'sanctuary' to the north of Saigon. (Somewhere in this area was the legendary COSVN, the National Liberation Front's Central Office for South Vietnam which was believed to coordinate the communist guerrilla war, which the Americans never located.)

Down the Ho Chi Minh trail (known to the communist side rather less prosaically as the Truong Son trail) thousands of tonnes of supplies were transported between 1959 and 1975. Initially loads were carried on foot by porters wearing the equally highly functional 'Ho Chi Minh sandals' carved from old vehicle tyres. It took several months to complete the journey. Later, drawing on the experience of Dien Bien Phu, the route was adapted for the use of bicycles which could carry as much as 440 pounds of rice at a time. Echoing the 'steel elephants' of Dien Bien Phu, the bicycles used to carry ammunition were dubbed 'steel horses'.[9] Later still, the trail was traversed by as many as 5,000 Soviet and Chinese six-tonne trucks for the same purpose of supplying guerrillas in the south. Latterly the trail encompassed underground hospitals and billets and was the means by which units and tanks of the North Vietnamese Army were infiltrated into the south to take part in the final campaign to capture Saigon.

The Ho Chi Minh trail symbolized the seemingly impossible odds faced by the communist side against the massive military might of their enemy. At the same time, it demonstrated the nearly

[8] See Bernard Fall, *Ho Chi Minh on Revolution*, Pall Mall Press, London, 1967, p 354.
[9] This also echoed the legendary Vietnamese hero, Phu Dong, who more than 4,000 years ago is said to have had a gigantic iron horse made for him to go to battle against invaders from the north.

impossible task faced by the US armed forces trying to detect an enemy hidden from view by Vietnam's natural vegetation. Part of the difficulty of targeting the trail was that so much of it lay outside Vietnam where political considerations initially prevented US forces operating, although on one notorious occasion in 1971 South Vietnamese forces thrust into Laos, but failed to find their objective. Later both Laos and Cambodia were subjected to US bombing, but even within Vietnamese terrain US aircraft had little chance of making more than occasional random hits on the trail despite using elaborate electronic surveillance from a base in eastern Thailand. In 1968, a massive US aerial bombing wave known as Operation Delaware targeted a sector of the trail in the A-Shau valley, not far from the US airbase at Khe Sanh, apparently without much success. Here, in a location chosen because of the frequency of cloud cover, the communists were known to have a large ammunition stockpile which one North Vietnamese general described as the North's Cam Ranh Bay, referring to one of the main US supply bases. Thousands of pounds of bombs were dropped close to the trail but it continued in use, obstructions being quickly removed and the roadway repaired. In the process, the mountainous region through which it passed suffered severe defoliation.

Dubbing this formidable feat of military engineering with the name of their enemy may not have been intended as a compliment, but it helped strengthen Ho Chi Minh's image of invincibility. The communists fighters, who were just as capable of playing on their late leader's image, called their final 1975 springtime assault on Saigon the 'Ho Chi Minh Campaign', vowing to capture the southern capital before Ho's birth anniversary on 19 May. Though Ho had been dead four and a half years, it seemed fitting that the campaign be named after the figure who had inspired the war by his commitment to the twin goals of winning independence and reunifying Vietnam. According to an account by campaign leader General Van Tien Dung,[10] the forces advancing on Saigon were inspired by the knowledge that defeating the Americans would 'make Uncle Ho happy'. On capturing Saigon, a decree was issued from Hanoi renaming it Ho Chi Minh City.

[10] In his account of the campaign, *Our Great Spring Victory*, Monthly Review Press, New York and London, 1977.

In Vietnam, *Bac* (Uncle) Ho is widely revered as the father of the nation. One of his most oft-quoted sayings is that 'nothing is more precious than freedom and independence'. Most Vietnamese give *Bac* Ho the credit for having won that freedom and independence and for bringing about the reunification of the nation, although these objectives were not accomplished until after his death. However, there remain those in the south who do not regard reunification as a blessing, as we shall see in Chapter Seven. The Communist Party still accords god-like authority to the sayings and teachings of its founder. The post of party chairman has not been filled since Ho died. Twenty five years after his death, Party propaganda continues to insist that 'Uncle Ho was so great that even his enemies loved him'. In the political arena, advocates of one particular point of view try to strengthen their case by arguing that it would have had Uncle Ho's support. In society at large, the appropriateness of what Ho Chi Minh stood for is these days a matter for debate: his economic principles, his attitude towards religions and even the wisdom of the war itself.

For example, there has been much acclaim for the novel *Noi Buon Chien Tranh* – in English *The Sorrow of War*[11] – by former soldier Bao Ninh. The novel tells of the author's war, including his role in the Ho Chi Minh Campaign. There is plenty too about the less glamorous war that preceded the final success. The book's real poignancy lies in the impact of the war on the author, thinly disguised as the novel's hero. Having gone to fight the Americans out of a sense of idealism and, despite taking part in its most glorious moment, the capture of Saigon, he returns home a broken man having lost his father, his girlfriend, his youth and his idealism. Although the author is reluctant to interpret his work saying 'each reader must interpret what I have written in his own way', it is difficult to read the book other than as a powerful indictment of war in general and his war in particular, a stark reminder of its horror and the fact that large numbers of Vietnamese from both sides, most of them non-combatants, lost their lives. 'Was it all worth it?' is the rhetorical question hanging over the graphic and powerful story, leaving the reader with little doubt that the author believes not. The fact that the book has been acclaimed and rewarded with the Vietnam Writers' Association prize demonstrates either that the climate for writing, and thus of free speech, has improved considerably, or else that many in authority share the author's

[11] Bao Ninh, *The Sorrow of War*, Secker and Warburg, London, 1993.

questioning of the war. The Writers' Association is a Communist Party-backed organization, so the prize has official approval.

The Sorrow of War is not the only novel pointing up a deep sense of disillusionment amongst Vietnamese intellectuals though it is the most acclaimed. Another, which illustrates the economic misery of peasants who were heavily taxed during the immediate post-war years, is credited with helping to change the Communist Party and bring about decollectivization.[12] If true, this suggests that writers, who have always been venerated in Vietnam, have lately become figures of some influence. This has coincided with the Party losing respect as a result of its failure to improve the people's living standards. As part of the thinking which ushered in the new economic policy and started to open the country up, the Party officially encouraged writers and journalists to depart from Marxist orthodoxy and assume the role of social critics. This led to a wave of literary works criticising the excesses and corruption of the Party and bureaucracy, often in thinly disguised satire. Writers departed from the 'wishful thinking' approach, which was little more than propaganda, and instead told the truth by portraying things as they saw them.

One writer who responded to the encouragement was Duong Thu Huong,[13] herself a member of the Party and one-time fighter with the Youth Brigade, who wrote frankly and openly of what she has called 'the dehumanization of her country'. As she joined public calls for political pluralism and economic reform, her books, which were already best-sellers, were banned by the same Party which had earlier encouraged more openness. In 1991, Duong Thu Huong was expelled from the Party and charged with having ties with reactionary foreign organizations and smuggling documents – the manuscripts of her books – out of the country. She was imprisoned for seven months. As a review in the Bangkok newspaper, *The Nation*, put it: 'She had put into print what the people of Vietnam know: that the way things are is different from the way they are supposed to be.' In her most famous novel, *Nhung Thien Duong Mu*, or *Paradise of the Blind*,[14] she writes about the cruel effects of the communist land reforms of the 1950s, inspired by those of China. The story is told by a young and privileged woman of the 1980s

---

[12] *That Night, What a Night* by Phung Ba Loc (1985) – not available in English.
[13] Duong Thu Huong's books include *Beyond Illusions* (1987), *Fragments of Lost Life* (1989) and *Paradise of the Blind* (1988) – the last published in English in 1993 by William Morrow, New York.
[14] *Ibid.*

whose disillusionment with her country's economic system is evident. Duong Thu Huong's most recent novel, *Tien Thuyet Vode*, or *An Untitled Novel* (1990), gives an account of the life of a soldier on the Ho Chi Minh trail comparing it to that of an animal. Vietnamese take particular offence at people being likened to animals.

As Bao Ninh breaks one taboo by questioning the value of the reunification war, Duong Thu Huong implicitly breaks another by questioning the nature of heroism. Both are challenging the official propaganda about the 'gloriousness' of the war. As former fighters, both Bao Ninh and Duong Thu Huong make particularly powerful writers and social critics. The fact that both also have Communist Party connections (Bao Ninh's father and daughter are members) makes their writing especially poignant in a society that is, with some difficulty, questioning its own ideological foundations. Their novels provide evidence for the fact that, as with US veterans, the psychological scars of war are taking longer to heal than the physical ones. Some Vietnamese writers proclaim they are free to write what they like, but others have been imprisoned for doing so. The 500 members of the Vietnam Writers' Association receive a subsidy from the Minister of Culture, which must surely be a disincentive to criticizing the country's rulers.

The official encouragement of 'free' writing created problems for the authorities as their failures were exposed. Nguyen Huy Thiep, a good example of the group known as renovation writers, used his short stories to expose the government's failure to satisfy consumer expectations and what the critic who translated his stories into English has called 'the poverty and injustice of the dark age'.[15] Although it is difficult to find firm proof, this consumer frustration has surely played a key role in the change of economic policies of the late 1980s. Thiep, a former history teacher, has also contributed to the challenge of the nature of heroism by casting heroes of Vietnamese history in an unheroic light. For example, he portrayed the 18th century hero, Nguyen Hué, as having a lascivious passion for beautiful girls. This caused one Writers' Association official to suggest disapprovingly: 'If we denigrate Nguyen Huê today, tomorrow we will denigrate Uncle Ho.'[16] Clearly in the eyes of the

[15] See the introduction by Greg Lockhart to the English edition of Nguyen Huy Thiep, *The General Retires and Other Stories*, OUP, Singapore, 1992, for a discussion of renovation writers and Thiep in particular.
[16] Quoted in Greg Lockhart's introduction to *The General Retires and Other Stories*, *ibid*, p 8.

Party leadership literary freedom had gone far enough. The decline of communism in Eastern Europe provided an excuse for the Party to clampdown again and official guidance was given to writers and journalists on how this event was to be portrayed. Nonetheless, this literary 'Hanoi spring' has had at least two important consequences. The writers have been agents of change, a role widely understood in Vietnam where, since the foundation in the 11th century of the Temple of Literature in Hanoi, the power of writers has been recognized if not always welcomed. Second, the renovation writers have enhanced awareness outside Vietnam of its difficulties by revealing life behind the state propaganda. This has mainly been through translation, but the works of these writers are also widely available and read in Vietnamese by overseas communities in California and elsewhere. In Vietnam, the officially encouraged flowering of Vietnamese writing in the late 1980s is not seen as being positive. Officials are inclined to dismiss it with a comment about 'the limits of creativity'.

The clampdown on literary freedom has not stopped a lively debate about all aspects of life in Vietnam. Both traditionalists and reformers seek to associate Ho Chi Minh with their position, though more usually his name is invoked to lend support to current reformist thinking. For example, many people are at pains to argue that he would have approved of the turnaround in economic policy, known as *doi moi*, set in motion by the Communist Party in 1986. Either out of respect or self-interest, there is a strong desire to solicit his approval for something that is widely perceived as being for the good of the country. 'Of course he would have approved' runs the argument, 'because he was a patriot and *doi moi* is making Vietnam strong.' This argument inevitably casts some doubts on the patriotism of those that followed Ho and ruled Vietnam pre-*doi moi*. They are implicitly being blamed for running the country into the ground, for any rational assessment that *doi moi* is a success needs to accept that the economic policy that preceded it was a failure, even a disaster. 'It helped keep us poor', says one critic of the leadership of Le Duan, who followed Ho Chi Minh at the helm of the Communist Party.

The Vietnamese are not yet ready to blame Uncle Ho for any of their country's misfortunes, which leads to some strained rationalizations. It is suggested, for example, that *doi moi* itself is based on Uncle Ho's teaching, which is a little difficult to conceptualize. 'Had he lived beyond the end of the war', runs the argument, 'he would have wanted to make Vietnam economically great so *doi moi*, which is doing so, is perfectly compatible with his teachings.' Former foreign minister Nguyen Co Thach goes further in saying that Ho Chi Minh was so intelligent that had he outlived the war he would have implemented *doi moi* long before his successors actually did. The Party's mistake, according to Thach, was to have deviated from his path in the immediate post-war years. Another line of reasoning invokes Uncle Ho's name to condemn the excesses of *doi moi* saying 'he would never have tolerated all this corruption'. Do Muoi, the Party leader who helped usher in the reforms, appeared to credit the revitalization of the economy they brought about on 'the correct application of Ho Chi Minh's thoughts' although he urged Vietnamese to apply them further in order to resolve 'complicated issues' in the economic renovation process. He may have been thinking of the corruption and abuse of power that has accompanied *doi moi* when he added that to understand Ho's thoughts on solving theoretical and practical problems 'has become more urgent than ever'.[17]

In all this *post hoc* rationalization, one hears little about the disastrous land reforms in North Vietnam of the 1950s, for which Ho Chi Minh apologized but over which he presided. Uncle Ho's reputation remains high and his people have good reasons to be grateful to him – but his economic philosophy is not one of his strong points. Communist Party members say the country has yet to achieve the socialism for which Ho struggled. Others are more pragmatic in saying that socialism failed Vietnam and has now been rejected. It would probably not occur to them to blame Ho for this failure.

Ho Chi Minh is often credited with having a broad-minded attitude towards religion. The main evidence for this comes from his choice of government members in 1945, which included Catholics alongside communists and socialists. Even his declaration of independence makes reference in its American-inspired opening sentence to 'the Creator', raising the enigma that Ho Chi Minh may have looked beyond Marx and Lenin to a more spiritual inspiration. Ho may have recognized the importance of religion in Vietnam, where Confucianism, Taoism, Buddhism and Catholicism have all had a profound impact on people's lives. Living for a period in Thailand in the 1920s, Ho adopted Buddhist robes, but this was a means of setting up communist cells rather than a commitment to the path of the Buddha!

---

[17] Do Muoi was speaking in Hanoi on 19 May 1995 to mark the 105th anniversary of Ho Chi Minh's birth.

As with economic policy, there is a body of opinion in Vietnam today that applauds the return to what are alleged to be Uncle Ho's spiritual values and away from the persecution of the post-reunification years. The publicized visits by Party secretary general, Do Muoi, to a pagoda and a church during the 1993 *Têt* (new year) celebrations were intended to demonstrate this change. However, there are plenty of clergy from all Vietnam's main religions who believe government policy still has a long way to go and that meddling in the organization of their religions negates any supposedly more enlightened attitude towards religions. Asked whether there is a new more tolerant policy, a foreign ministry official quotes a Vietnamese proverb that 'a person down a well cannot see clearly around', the implication being that previously the leadership had their heads down a well! Asked to elaborate, the official confirmed that what had changed was that the leadership – Party and government – now have a greater awareness of the important part played by religion in the lives of the people.

Vietnam has a long tradition of religious persecution, it is not something particular to communist rulers. The French justified their colonization of the country as a response to the persecution of Catholics by Nguyen dynasty emperors in the 1830s and 1840s. More recently President Ngo Dinh Diem of South Vietnam, a staunch Catholic, was accused of persecuting Buddhists. This led to the celebrated incidents of self-immolation by Buddhist monks in 1963. He also suppressed the armies that had developed around two important religious sects, the Hoa Hao and Cao Dai. By contrast, there is no evidence to suggest Ho Chi Minh was vindictive towards adherents of any particular faith although discouragement of religious worship in the north may have been more subtle than in the south. After reunification, there was a clampdown on most religions and religious bodies were required to 'offer' their lands to the state. Catholics, regarded as stooges of the West, were treated with particular suspicion and many were sent for re-education. However, the Cao Daists, who claimed 2 million followers at that time, say things became much easier for them, reflecting the degree of repression previously.

Vietnam's constitution guarantees freedom of religious faith but government resolutions, some dating from 1977, reserve to the government the right to approve all candidates for the priesthood or monkhood in any faith with 'good performance in their civic duties' as one of the criteria. They also grant the state the right to nominate members to the bodies controlling each religion. There is a level of indirect control too in that certain communist organizations, such as the Fatherland Front, are entrusted with the task of prohibiting any activity 'deemed to be contrary to the goal of building socialism', a cause which has been used to imprison Buddhist and Catholic priests. A charge sometimes used against imprisoned priests is (in the words of the constitution) that they have 'misused religion to violate state laws and policies'.

Buddhist, Catholic and Cao Dai clergy all complain of government attempts to 'manage' their church affairs through the appointment of state-sponsored management committees. The biggest battle has been between the independent-minded Unified Buddhist Church of Vietnam (UBCV), established in 1951, and the Vietnam Buddhist Church (VBC), which the government set up in 1981 while banning the UBCV. After the patriarch of the UBCV died in 1992, the government tried to prevent the appointment as successor of Thich Huyen Quang, who had openly criticized government policy towards religion. There were street protests in the city of Hué and, in a move reminiscent of the 1963 protests, one monk from the Thien Mu pagoda set himself on fire. Although the government denies the self-immolation was politically motivated – it claims it was a family matter – many monks were arrested and imprisoned on public order offences and Thich Huyen Quang was exiled to his home province of Quang Ngai, where he is confined to a pagoda.

Catholics too are engaged in a tussle which centres on whether the Vatican or the government in Hanoi should have the right to appoint bishops. Worshippers in the south may have flourished under Diem's rule, but after 1975 foreign missionaries were expelled, seminaries (priestly training colleges) were closed and many priests sent for re-education. Since the economic reforms and the re-opening of the country to outside influences, there has been a much more relaxed attitude towards the Catholic church, which in 1988 was allowed to re-open six seminaries and to ordain new priests. For the first time since reunification bishops were allowed to visit Rome. In 1994 Pope John Paul II made the Archbishop of Hanoi a cardinal – the last Vietnamese cardinal had died in 1990. Catholics consider the best test of how greatly attitudes have changed is whether an exiled bishop living in Rome, Nguyen Van Tuan, is allowed to return to Vietnam and whether the Vatican is allowed to establish a diplomatic mission in Hanoi.

Cao Daists similarly complain of government attempts to run their church by appointing their management board. Cao Daism, a peculiarly Vietnamese religion, draws inspiration from

Confucianism, Taoism, Buddhism and Catholicism for both its creed and its ritual. The faith has an impressively strong following, especially in Tay Ninh province near the Cambodian border where its 'holy see' is situated and in the Mekong delta. Ironically one of its panoply of saints (who include Jesus Christ, William Shakespeare and Joan of Arc) is Lenin, who is said to have appeared in a vision to the religion's founder, Ngo Minh Chieu, in 1926. Cao Daists believe Lenin was sent to earth by god and so deserves their respect. They appear not to have a view on whether Lenin's political philosophy was a good or bad thing, or to see any irony in the fact that they continue to respect Lenin's place in history even though the country's communist leadership has defected from his teachings (though his statue still stands in Hanoi). Another Cao Dai saint is the French writer, Victor Hugo, so it is even more ironic to note the claim by the reforming communist leader, Nguyen Van Linh, that it was not Karl Marx's *Das Kapital* but Victor Hugo's *Les Misérables*, an epic novel about the dispossessed of Paris, which 'pointed him towards communism', causing him to strive not just for national independence but for social revolution as well. 'It touched the strings of my heart very directly – I could not be satisfied with a society where there is an enormous gap between rich and poor', Linh told American writer Neil Sheehan.[18] It was Nguyen Van Linh who launched the revolution that has, in effect, eschewed communism in favour of what can only be called capitalism.

Given the way in which the government persists in trying to control religion by appointments to its management bodies, which are in turn controlled by a Religious Affairs Committee, it is no wonder that followers of all faiths complain of an absence of freedom of religion. Reports compiled during 1984 by Europe-based human rights groups[19] listed Buddhist and Catholic priests and a Cao Dai follower among 200 political prisoners held at a re-education camp in Phu Yen province, southern Vietnam. The harsh camp regime forbade preaching, the reciting of prayers, reading or the learning of foreign languages. Manual labour was obligatory. According to the reports, imprisoned religious leaders were treated more harshly than imprisoned writers. In a remarkable clampdown in late 1994, the UBCV was accused by the Fatherland Front of wanting 'to destroy the religion as well as national solidarity' by

[18] Neil Sheehan, *Two Cities: Hanoi and Saigon, op cit*, p 75.
[19] The reports are by Amnesty International (*Buddhist Monks in Detention*), the Vietnam Committee on Human Rights and the International Buddhist Information Bureau, a division of the UBCV (Report from A-20 Re-education Camp).

organizing its own programme of relief for victims of severe flooding in the Mekong delta and several monks were detained. In August 1995 – the month after relations with the USA were normalized – six monks involved in the relief programme, all members of the UBCV, were sentenced to jail terms of up to five years. There were indications that the UBCV leader, Thich Huyen Quang, and other church leaders would also be brought before a court. The government's treatment of the UBCV demonstrates its view that religious freedom does not include the right to appoint its own leaders, or to organize its own relief effort. From branches abroad in France and California, the UBCV actively campaigns for the release of the imprisoned monks, while international human rights groups publicize the detention of priests and monks as a major blemish on the record of the supposedly reformist government.

Vietnamese reformers consider Hanoi's attempts to control the various churches to be a departure from the philosophy of Ho Chi Minh that has not yet been rectified. In other words, they believe Uncle Ho would not have approved of such repression. They accuse the government of being unnecessarily paranoid and compare Hanoi's clampdown on the Buddhists with Diem's during the 1960s, or with the Chinese government's paranoia about the impact from exile of the Dalai Lama. One explanation offered for official wariness of religion is that since Ho Chi Minh himself enjoys near god-like status it is this 'faith' that deserves and gets government support. Ho may not be worshipped but he is deeply revered. Even 25 years after his death, his portrait is displayed in government offices and shops. More surprisingly it can also be found in many homes, usually on the home altar where Vietnamese families display photographs of their deceased forebears, to whom they make offerings on holy days. A visitor to Vietnam soon becomes aware of the cult status enjoyed by Uncle Ho. Probably the true explanation for the distrust of vocal religious leaders is more simple. Having survived the difficult years, political leaders are paranoid about any potential threat to their hold on power. However, there are signs of enhanced tolerance by the authorities towards religious worship, notably that new churches and pagodas are being built or restored and that attendances at both are rising. Even in Hanoi, churches are often full these days.

The subject of human rights is a sensitive one in Vietnam as it tends to be used as a stick by organizations in the West to 'beat' Third World governments. That at any rate is how it is seen by the government in Hanoi which resents being lectured to by anyone, especially foreigners, about human rights. It echoes a familiar Third World theme when it says there is more to human rights than the absence of political prisoners and that judged in terms of relieving people from the threat of famine Vietnam is doing very well these days. In another familiar line, the Vietnamese government takes a stab back at the human rights situation in the developed West, pointing out that Third World countries look after their old people much better than do Western nations. It takes a more specifically Vietnamese line in expressing astonishment, if not downright indignation, that organizations in the country that perpetrated the My Lai massacre of innocent villagers should take upon themselves the right to criticize what they judge to be human rights shortcomings in Vietnam.

The government concedes that it does hold without trial what it terms 'security prisoners' which under the new criminal procedure code it has no right to do. Others who are regarded abroad as political prisoners have been sentenced for various offences. Among those held during 1994 at A20 Re-education Camp in Phu Yen province are poets and writers. The offence of one was to send short stories about life in Vietnam for publication outside the country, while a professor there was sentenced to 15 years' imprisonment for peacefully campaigning for political reform through a study group he set up called Freedom Forum.

The term re-education camp is a euphemism for a prison. Officially the 're-education' of servants and soldiers of the former South Vietnamese regime ended in 1992 after about 100,000 had 'benefited' from it. Only a small number were detained throughout the 18 years. 'The only re-education going on these days is of government and Party officials in the ways of market forces and other devices of capitalist economics', according to a long-time government critic. Officials would not take kindly to that comparison, or to the irony. Meanwhile those former soldiers and others who suffered long years of re-education now mainly live in new homes in exile in the USA, representing a loss of the very skills, from foreign languages to business expertise, most in demand in present-day Vietnam.

Attitudes towards the right of political parties other than the Communist Party to exist are changing, according to the government, but in reality the change is imperceptible. Approved independent candidates were allowed to contest the 1992 National Assembly elections, and some were elected. But there are no signs of the Communist Party ending its monopoly by permitting other political parties to be formed. Vietnam remains a one-party state. The Communist Party seems determined to retain political control at a time when wealth rather than weaponry is becoming the main determining factor of who actually wields power. Party officials rule out any more broadly-based democracy just as adamantly as they insist that Vietnam remains a communist country striving to achieve 'true' socialism – and that Ho Chi Minh's ideals are those of the present government. They point to the mess they believe Russia is in as a result of having introduced multi-party democracy and seem proud not to have fallen into that particular trap. Others argue that political reforms, like the right of individuals to own property and to travel without permission, are an inevitable consequence of economic reform and the associated opening up of the country to foreign investors and other foreign influences as varied as missionaries, Americans, advertising, western love songs, *karaoke* bars and satellite television – all of which have had an effect in changing people's attitudes and aspirations.

One aspect of political reform that is coming only very gradually is freedom of the press. More than once the National Assembly has debated whether to allow the publication of independent newspapers or journals, but each time they have voted against. So Vietnam's 7,000 or so journalists remain dependent for their livelihood on the government-owned or controlled press. (Even the burgeoning number of nominally foreign-owned magazines are part owned by government or Party organizations.) One Vietnamese observer of the trends in the press says it was freer in the early 1990s – 'when Gorbachev was in power in Moscow' –but has weakened since then. He says a 1994 purge of senior editors of Ho Chi Minh City newspapers demonstrated how cowed the press is and also how the Party is attempting to reassert its control generally. The time when the press was relatively strong coincided with the moment when the Party was at its weakest. It seems that the power of the Communist Party and the freedom of writers and journalists to criticize the government and Party are a sort of 'see-saw' act: when one is up the other is down!

'If Ho Chi Minh were alive today', runs a popular discussion theme, 'he would either have deplored the departure from communist orthodoxy, or he would be rejoicing at the fact that Vietnam is now showing signs of being well fed and prosperous, even at the price of a widening gulf between rich and poor.' 'He might deplore the persecution of some religious leaders, writers and democracy campaigners, but then he might accept this as the price to be paid to keep a benevolent Communist Party in power, intent as it is on achieving one day the nirvana or eldorado of socialism.' It is impossible to know, so those with interests to protect are content to imagine their policies would have had Uncle Ho's support. It is an extension of the debate about whether he was more of a nationalist than a communist. That the debates take place at all demonstrates the important influence Ho still exerts, especially in binding together a country that has since the Second World War been split for longer than it has been unified.

It is clear that the time is not yet ripe for the sort of reassessment of Ho that Stalin and Lenin have undergone in Russia. Ho remains on a pedestal – literally and figuratively. The mausoleum in Hanoi where his embalmed body lies is a place of pilgrimage. However, there have been attempts within the Party to humanize Ho by stressing his credentials as a nationalist and liberator and down-playing his attachment to Marxism, Leninism and even Stalinism. The Institute of Marxist Study is now the Institute of Marxist and Ho Chi Minh Studies, suggesting a clear distinction between the two. Readers of the Party newspaper, *Nhan Dan*, detect signs of disagreement within the Party over how far this rebuilding of Ho's image should go. At least official visitors to London are clear on their priorities. They first go to visit the Haymarket where a blue plaque reads 'Ho Chi Minh, 1890-1969, founder of modern Vietnam, worked in 1913 at the Carlton Hotel, which stood on this site.' A recent visitor had tears in his eyes as he read the inscription. A second request is to visit Karl Marx's grave in Highgate cemetery. Only then do they indulge themselves with an enjoyable night out at *Miss Saigon*, the musical that portrays the humiliating helicopter retreat from Saigon of the last Americans!

Ho is credited with reuniting the country and thus his reputation is not open to question. He is like Gandhi is for Indians: the father of independent nationhood. Gandhi's relevance for young Indians is diminishing by the year, as is that of Nehru, whose foreign and economic policies have, like Ho Chi Minh's, undergone U-turns to suit current circumstances. Ho Chi Minh's reputation has stood the test of time because he is more remembered for defeating foreign invaders and unifying the country than for his disastrous economic policies. By contrast, the reputations of some of his associates, notably of Le Duan, have not long survived their deaths.

Sensitivity about Ho's reputation extends to his personal life. Officially Ho was a bachelor 'because he was so committed to his cause that he did not have time to enjoy family life'. Yet rumours of romances followed him as he travelled abroad. He is said to have had a French girlfriend in Paris, another girlfriend while he stayed in London and a third in Russia. It has even been reported that in Moscow he married fellow Vietnamese revolutionary, Nguyen Thi Minh Khai, who was later killed by the French. At least two Chinese women, one of them a doctor, were linked romantically to Ho whilst he was in China. Much of the mystery about Ho's private life derives from the paucity of information about his 30 years abroad.

Privately senior party members concede that Ho was a womanizer, but officially the image that Ho cultivated for himself of being 'married to the revolution' has been preserved. Uncle Ho's virginity is part of the myth that gives him quasi-divine status. In the early 1990s, a Saigon newspaper reported that Ho had a Chinese wife during his period in China, the marriage having been arranged by the Chinese Communist Party. It said he had left her behind when he left China but sent her some poems. The report may have been planted by the faction within the Party pushing for Ho's official image to be humanized and made more relevant to contemporary Vietnam, the same drive that is trying to down-play his communist leanings. Though the report was never denied, the newspaper's editor subsequently lost her job, showing that the press is not free of Party or government control and that the myth of Uncle Ho's virginity is not yet open to challenge. Unlike Chairman Mao, whose status in China is said to have been enhanced by revelations of his sexual appetite, Uncle Ho will officially retain his celibate status for some time yet.

And why did Ho Chi Minh's fellow revolutionaries not observe the wish expressed in his will that he be cremated and his ashes sprinkled on three hills in the north, centre and south of the country? The official answer is that as the war was still going on when he died in 1969 'we did not want to deny those in the other part of the country the chance to see his face, so we preserved his body.' Perhaps it was felt that preserving the body helped unify the nation and reinforces the myth of Ho's invincibility. For the present, modern Vietnam's founding father continues to enjoy in death a high degree of respect, even reverence. However, Vietnam's rulers may one day be faced with a similar dilemma to that currently being faced by the rulers of Russia: what to do with the body of a former hero whose relevance to contemporary life has diminished.

5

Doi Moi: Vietnam's Perestroika

In December 1986, Vietnam's National Assembly agreed on a programme of economic reform as radical as any in the communist world. Vietnam's way was to adopt the free market economic system whilst retaining Communist Party rule by ushering in what is known as *doi moi*. Its impact has been so great and lifestyles so transformed that Vietnamese use an old proverb more often associated with the chaos of war to indicate the magnitude of change. They say that 'heaven has changed'. Even a casual glance at how an impoverished country seems poised for economic take-off seems to justify the expression. Although *doi moi* bears comparison with Russia's economic reform programme, or *perestroika*, there are also key differences. The most obvious is that *doi moi* has not been accompanied by political reform, although its impact has been to loosen considerably previously tight political controls. *Doi moi* has in fact brought in its wake a measure of political reform, but that was largely an unplanned consequence rather than a deliberate intention by the Communist Party to loosen its hold on power.

Although it is common in Vietnam to talk of 'before' and 'after' *doi moi*, the reforms actually happened over a number of years. The retreat from agricultural collectivization began as early as 1979 when a new contract system allowed for households to be allocated land by collectives. After the major reforms of December 1986, the disappearance of Vietnam's main trading partner and benefactor with the collapse of the USSR and dissolution of the Eastern European COMECON trading union led to a further round of reforms. At the same time Vietnam's foreign policy was being re-oriented from alignment with the communist bloc to full membership of the South East Asian community of nations. Economic reform was not accompanied by political reform but it did coincide with (or give rise to) this strategic realignment.

Vietnam's leaders speak of the introduction of *doi moi* as a positive and highly enlightened policy. In reality, they had little choice but to go down the free enterprise road. Vietnam in 1986 was bankrupt. Industrial and agricultural output were static or falling, whilst the population was increasing. The country was not able to produce enough rice to feed its own people: as late as 1987 there was famine in northern Vietnam. Nor could it export enough produce to pay for its imports of food, fuel and other necessities. It depended on a Soviet subsidy which President Gorbachev had indicated would come to an end. By the time it did end in 1991, Vietnam owed the former USSR around US$15 billion.

Vietnam's economic predicament was made worse by its diplomatic isolation, largely the result of international disapproval of its invasion of Cambodia. There was a particularly visible indicator of the harshness of life in Vietnam with the departure of 'boat people'. As one commentator has put it, the deteriorating economic situation 'called into question not only the Party's competence but also its legitimacy to rule.'[1] It was in this crisis atmosphere that first the Communist Party and then the National Assembly adopted *doi moi* as a means of averting further disaster. A central tenet of faith of the reformers is that the survival of Communist Party rule in Vietnam is inextricably linked to the success of *doi moi*.

Doi moi represented the ending of the command economy under which bureaucrats in Hanoi determined what should be produced and in what quantities. It has put such decisions in the hands of the producers who respond to market demand. This has had its greatest impact in rural areas where the farmer is free to grow what crops he chooses, which he will decide according to anticipated demand and the cost and availability of seeds. He now knows that the more he grows the more he can keep for himself or sell privately. He is no longer fulfilling a state objective but is working for himself – although tax in produce still has to be paid for the use of the land. Since 1988, the household rather than the collective has been recognized as the basic unit of agricultural production, with the concomitant rights of the family both to use the land and to sell its surplus production. Technically what has been restored is the right of individual farming families to use land, although since they can also buy, sell and bequeath that right it amounts to land ownership in all but name.

---

[1] Michael Williams, *Vietnam at the Crossroads, op cit,* London, 1992, p 50.

Doi moi represented a belated recognition by the Party that collectivization of the land and state ownership of enterprise had failed Vietnam. It was the rapid decline in agricultural and industrial output that gradually brought this home to the authorities. As early as 1979 a minor faction within the Party was advocating change. It included the head of the State Planning Commission, Vo Van Kiet, who was later to become prime minister. As Vietnam's economic situation worsened, the reformists in the Party gained ground. But it was not until after the death in 1986 of Ho's successor as party leader, Le Duan, that the reformists were able to advance their alternative philosophy to any significant degree.

Le Duan's successor as Secretary General, Nguyen Van Linh, is generally regarded as the chief architect of the reforms. A northerner who had spent the American war as a guerrilla in the south, Linh had been greatly influenced by the relative prosperity of the south which led him to the conclusion that orthodox socialism, as practised in the north, did not serve the interests of the working people. He came to believe it was 'a foolish dream that would bankrupt the country'. The man who said he had learnt his communism from Victor Hugo's *Les Misérables* rather than from Marx also admitted that fighting the Americans had taught him another lesson: 'that nothing worked unless it was firmly grounded in reality'.[2]

Becoming Party secretary for Ho Chi Minh City after the war ended, Linh had set about waging what he calls 'economic guerrilla warfare' against Hanoi by, in effect, resisting the collectivization of the land and encouraging private initiative. He believed firmly that there should be a role for those he called 'patriotic capitalists', business people who had not fled the country but were willing to play a role in the new, re-unified Vietnam. Linh encouraged party leaders from the north to visit Ho Chi Minh City so that he could demonstrate to them what could be achieved through private initiative, even within state factories. Linh was outspoken in expressing his view, notably in newspaper articles, that Marxist orthodoxy had failed Vietnam.

Linh had been helped in his campaign for reform by a Harvard-trained economist who had served the former southern regime and was not afraid to express his views. Dr Nguyen Xuan Oanh once worked for the World Bank in Washington, returning to Saigon in 1963 to join the Diem government as Central Bank Governor and

---

[2] As told to American writer Neil Sheehan, *Two Cities: Hanoi and Saigon, op cit*, p 78.

deputy prime minister. Despite his association with the defeated regime, Dr Oanh decided not to leave the country when Saigon fell. He spent nine months under house arrest but was released, he says, 'when the new rulers realized I was not dangerous and that I was strictly a technician.' He immediately started trying to prove otherwise 'by writing against the government', as he puts it. In a series of articles in a Saigon newspaper, Dr Oanh outlined his ideas on management, banking and finance, all areas he believed needed urgent attention. Nguyen Van Linh asked him to set up a think-tank to refine his ideas. Many of these ideas were eventually adopted by the Party under the label *doi moi*, literally meaning 'renovation'. Dr Oanh prefers the translation 'restructuring'.

'*Doi moi*', says Dr Oanh, 'is not just about changing the machinery of the economy, but about changing the thinking too.'[3] Changing the thinking was the biggest challenge, but implementing the reforms was, and continues to be, a gargantuan task too. Dr Oanh explains the four big changes he believes were fundamental to the success of *doi moi*:

'The first requirement was to reform the management of the economy by allowing private initiative and ownership of the means of production. We needed to revive the market system and to let the people themselves take part. Secondly, since the banking system is the engine of a country's growth, it had to be revamped. In a command economy the banking system is just a window into the ministry of finance, with no real power of its own. We had to end the system whereby the council of ministers made the decisions and executed them through the planning commission, a characteristic of socialist economies. Banks needed to be allowed to function as banks, although under State Bank supervision of course. Thirdly, we had to reform foreign trade by breaking the monopoly under which foreign trade in a socialist country belongs to the government or its foreign trade ministry. It should be given to whoever is capable of doing trade. Now there are around 400 organisations licensed to trade abroad and it's going rather well – up from US$500 million worth annually to around US$7 billion. Fourthly, we had to encourage foreign investment. We needed foreign capital to help develop the country.'

What *doi moi* has meant in reality is many more things than Dr Oanh's list of four suggestions. The role of the formerly all-powerful

---

[3] Speaking in an interview with the author in October 1994. Unless otherwise sourced, all quotations in this chapter come from interviews with the author.

State Planning Commission has shrunk very considerably so that it concerns itself now with broad strategy, not the implementation of that strategy. The government has ceased to set prices, with the very limited exceptions of those charged for electricity, petrol, cement and transport. Central government control over all aspects of life has diminished and as a result provincial and city governments have greater autonomy. The withdrawal of subsidies to state-owned enterprises has caused many to collapse and others to 'go private'.

The Vietnamese currency, the dong, which was devalued massively in the early years of *doi moi*, now has a unified exchange rate and since 1989 has been allowed to float to its free market level. As a result of this monetary reform, inflation has come down to manageable levels. Then there are some indirect consequences. The opening up of the country to encourage foreign investment has resulted in large numbers of foreign visitors. Restrictions on Vietnamese having contacts with them have been lifted and foreigners no longer need a permit to travel around the country.

The most obviously beneficial results of *doi moi* are that agricultural output has risen dramatically: rice production is up from 17 million tones annually in the mid-1980s to over 25 million tonnes in the mid-1990s. In 1989 Vietnam stopped importing rice and soon afterwards became a major rice exporter – the third largest behind Thailand and the USA with annual exports of at least 2 million tonnes. Vietnamese rice has been sold to Indonesia, the Philippines, Singapore, the Middle East and to France for supply to African countries suffering shortages. A significant share of the country's foreign exchange earnings come from rice.

The impact of *doi moi* on the land is most visible in the Mekong delta, Vietnam's rice-bowl, from where almost all the rice for export comes. Can Tho, the delta's main city, has a new air of prosperity about it; one of the busiest shops is selling motorized ploughs, threshing machines and other mechanized farming equipment. According to Dr Nguyen Tri Khiem of the agriculture department at Can Tho University, the city's wealth is a direct result of increased agricultural output, which is in turn a consequence of granting individuals the right of land ownership once more. 'Now', he says, 'farmers can now use their land as collateral to obtain credit from the banks to enhance their production – by buying fertiliser or machinery, for example.' Dr Khiem says other factors, like improved rice strains, the use of fertilisers and new technology, have helped but *doi moi* is the most important because it has provided the incentive needed to grow more. *Doi moi* has given a boost to another policy which has benefited farmers: diversification, an attempt to help farmers move away from total dependence on rice production in favour of more profitable enterprises for the household, including growing other crops, animal husbandry (especially of pigs, chickens and ducks) and home fishing. Now that farmers are free to sell their produce and to buy their needs from others it is less important to concentrate on growing only one crop.

To demonstrate that *doi moi* has enhanced the prosperity of farmers, government figures in late 1994 show that 40% of farming households now have television sets and 65% have radio-cassette players. Certainly a profusion of television aerials testify to the relative prosperity of farmers in the Mekong delta.

In the cities, *doi moi* has brought the return of private traders, many of whom seem to be making up for lost time! Shops and market stalls have proliferated. Saigon, where by 1995 there were estimated to be as many as half a million private retailers, is bustling with economic activity and Cholon even more so. Even in relatively backward Hanoi it seems as if almost everyone is trading in goods or skills. Having a full-time government job does not stop state employees supplementing their modest wages. From a society where trading was discouraged if not actually illegal, Vietnam has become a society where trading is a basic instinct. Television carries advertisements once more and billboards advertising Japanese and American goods, from soft drinks to computers, are widespread. Goods are competitively priced lest the seller be undercut by the next shop or stall.

The real change is not just that *doi moi* has allowed such private enterprise but that it has created a supply of goods to be sold. By providing the incentives necessary for the production of foodstuffs and consumer goods, the things people want to buy, the change of policy has ensured that shortages are a thing of the past. As one elderly resident of Hanoi put: 'Never again need we stay up late in order to queue for rice.' The commission system is well understood: *cyclo* or bus drivers claim commission from a hotel or restaurant for delivering clients there. One of the most basic forms of street trading is provided by the motorbike drivers who congregate on street corners and offer a taxi service – so called *xe ôm*, meaning 'hug transport': the passenger holds on to the driver as he weaves his way through the city traffic!

A key feature of *doi moi* has been the coming of foreign money. A year after the National Assembly approved the economic reform programme, it approved a foreign investment law which is one of the most attractive in Asia to investors. Companies pursuing government priorities qualify for tax-holidays and are allowed to repatriate their profits in full. Priority objectives include making goods for export, satisfying local demands which are currently met by importing and applying new technology. Priority sectors are making or processing foodstuffs or consumer goods, labour-intensive industries making use of Vietnam-produced raw materials or natural resources, services contributing to the improvement of Vietnam's infrastructure, including banking, high technology industries and industries which earn foreign currency, like tourism and shipping.

Potential investment has to be approved by the State Committee for Cooperation and Investment (SCCI) which undertakes to give quick decisions, a commitment it has not always met. Most investments to date are on a joint venture basis. Foreign firms have found it helpful that a Vietnamese partner can provide local knowledge, land and labour whilst the foreign partner provides most of the capital and technological and managerial expertise. By late 1994, seven years after the foreign investment law was passed, more than $10 billion worth of foreign investment had been approved. More than a quarter of the total was for hotels, transportation and other tourist projects while oil and gas exploration, in which around 25 foreign companies are engaged, has also attracted a sizeable amount of foreign money. However, disappointingly for the government, only around a third of approved investment had actually been applied – suggesting some firms had cold feet about proceeding after gaining approval.

There has been criticism that the government approved the foreign investment law before its domestic equivalent. The government says it recognized that foreign capital was needed if Vietnam was going to be 'rescued' from its desperate economic straits, but critics allege that its decision in effect handed over the job of developing Vietnam to foreigners. This, they say, is having a severe impact on national identity: 'By giving foreign firms virtual *carte blanche* to exploit the country's resources, including its tourist potential, the government has exposed the country unnecessarily to foreign influences, good and bad', argues one Vietnamese entrepreneur: 'They should have learnt from China which made the same mistake.'

As a relative late-comer, Vietnam has had to make itself particularly attractive to foreigners. Prime Minister Vo Van Kiet is in no doubt that Vietnam is competing for foreign money against

China and other ASEAN countries which, like Vietnam, need investment to develop and exploit their full potential. In late 1994, Kiet told the Vietnam Investment Review that Vietnam could not be satisfied with its progress to date in attracting foreign investment for one simple reason: 'While we move forward with economic reforms, our neighbouring countries are not sitting idle. We live in a fiercely competitive global market and face acute challenges because our economy lags behind.' Prime Minister Kiet is well steeped in the competitive nature of foreign investment, but other leaders give the impression they believe foreign companies owe it to Vietnam to invest. They stress the need for infrastructural investment – transport and electricity supply for example – which offer relatively little return for the foreign investor. Similarly there is a contradiction in the government's stress on producing goods for export, as one of the main attractions for firms contemplating investing in Vietnam is the size of its domestic market of 72 million people.

The government prefers to stress not the size of the market but the cheapness of the labour, which is indeed another factor attracting investors to Vietnam and away from other Asian nations where the cost of labour is considerably higher. Prospectuses offered to potential foreign investors emphasise Vietnam's cheap, literate and well-disciplined labour force, a rapidly expanding agricultural base, its natural resources and mineral wealth and its 2,000 mile coastline.[4] The government also believes the fact that provinces now have considerable autonomy is a plus point as it tries to demonstrate that central planning no longer exists. By stressing the importance of high-technology, the government hopes to attract the very latest according to the leap-frog principle: 'We never had the earlier, now outdated, technology so it is much easier for us to start with the latest technology.'

Yet leap-frogging can give rise to a 'technology gap'. As a foreign banker puts it: 'What's the point of having the latest technology if you do not have the means to make the best use of it?' Vietnam has an advanced foreign investment law and willing joint venture partners, but its banking structure is so rudimentary that the personal cheque has only recently been introduced – and is not always understood or honoured. Even wealthy Vietnamese (of whom there are now plenty) have to use cash to pay their bills and

---

[4] See, for example, Nguyen Xuan Oanh and Philip Donald Grub, *Vietnam: The New Investment Frontier in South East Asia*, Publishing House of Ho Chi Minh City, 1992, p 1.

without high-value notes Vietnamese cash is cumbersome. The credit card is only just now arriving in Vietnam. Similarly, sophisticated street card-operated pay-phones have arrived but private subscriber telephones are in desperately short supply. The same 'technology gap' is evident with regard to Vietnam's resources. While Vietnam is thought to be sitting on large reserves of its major export, oil, the country still has to import petrol, diesel and kerosene because it has no oil refinery. Since 1989 it has enjoyed large surpluses of rice, but has not always had the means to transport it to regions of shortage so inadequate is the transportation network.

Shortcomings like these serve to remind just how backward Vietnam is as it strives for the investment to help it catch up with its neighbours. In statistical terms, Vietnam remains one of the world's poorest nations, a position from which it cannot escape overnight just because it has now adopted new economic policies which have worked miracles on the country's rate of growth. Away from the fertile delta regions, rural Vietnam has little to show by way of benefit from *doi moi*. Vietnam is coming from a long way back yet it ambitiously hopes to end up among the winners, or at least to secure a place in the finals.

To help towards that target, Vietnam hopes to be able to depend on oil and gas reserves which have been variously estimated at up to 10 billion barrels, or twice those of Malaysia. The liberal foreign investment regime introduced in 1987 was mainly designed to attract investment into the oil industry. Production sharing contracts with foreign companies have been awarded on favourable terms in an attempt to woo them into this new area. But Vietnam's reserves remain unproven. More than 20 years after America's Mobil Oil made the first offshore discoveries, only two fields are producing significant quantities of oil; Bach Ho or White Tiger, the field discovered by Mobil and now operated by a Vietnamese-Russian consortium, started producing in June 1986. Dai Hung or Big Bear started producing in October 1994, operated by an Australia-led consortium. Both producing fields are in the southern Cuu Long basin. Exploration off central and northern Vietnam has proved less promising.

Vietnam's annual oil production is increasing through the development of existing fields rather than from new discoveries. Now that the operators of the Dai Hung field, which had been proclaimed as one of the largest anywhere, have reduced their estimates of recoverable oil deposits sharply, the government's production target of 30 million tonnes of oil annually by the year 2000 looks unlikely to be realized. (Just over 7 million tonnes were produced in 1993.) By the end of the century Vietnam expects to have one or more refineries in operation to process crude for its domestic requirements. In the longer term, exploitation of the full offshore economic zone claimed (roughly twice as large as the country's land area) depends on the resolution of disputes with China. Like China, Vietnam is contemplating the fact that increases in domestic demand will limit the amount of oil available for export. Both countries badly need oil to sustain their rapid drives towards industrialization and neither wants to be the first of the region's oil producers (which also include Indonesia and Malaysia) to become a net fuel importer.

The fact that the government in 1992 took back oil fields and exploration areas (including parts of Dai Hung) from the Vietnam–Russia joint-venture shows how Vietnam's foreign policy, or foreign dependence, has changed. It also demonstrates how it is hoping to use technology to pull its economy out of stagnation. Soviet technology had been unable to develop such deep fields: Western oil companies have succeeded where the Russians failed. However, the 12 oil or gas discoveries since 1989 have heightened optimism but not proven much, according to the Chief Executive of BP Vietnam, Michael Yeldham. BP was one of the first foreign companies to arrive following the industry's opening to foreign investors. Yeldham says it is still too early to talk of 'another Malaysia'. He says most recent discoveries have 'fallen short' in quality terms – too waxy oil for example – or quantity terms, given the enormous investment needed to bring oil ashore. 'So far we haven't found the predicted billion barrel oil fields, but we remain hopeful and have not yet seen reason to revise upwards or downwards our early estimates of 5 billion barrel reserves', says Yeldham. He and other oil prospectors in the region believe that natural gas, brought ashore for the first time during 1995, may prove to be a brighter prospect for Vietnam than oil. To realize its full potential requires either the development of a market within Vietnam, or else the building of a costly liquefaction plant to sell the gas abroad.

Yeldham contrasts the difficulties of 1987, when even making contact with the state company, PetroVietnam, was not easy, with his company's rapid progression from surveying to production sharing contract the following year after the foreign investment law had come into operation. 'We were very surprised at the speed with which detailed terms were agreed: 90% of the text was settled within a week', says Yeldham. Four years on, Yeldham is 'very positive' about the business environment in Vietnam compared with other 'difficult' countries where BP operates, although he does not pretend things are always easy.

When foreigners talk of the difficulties of doing business in Vietnam they invariably cite problems with the bureaucracy or administration. Efforts are underway to improve the speed at which investment proposals are considered and to ease regulations relating to the hiring of local staff. A more fundamental reform, which has implications for Vietnamese business as much as for foreign ones, is a United Nations-backed programme of administrative reform. Its objective is to improve the calibre of public servants by strengthening their training and generally to make government more efficient and effective. In the process, the project may bring about a fundamental shift in who wields power in Vietnam, as an official involved in the project explains: 'Previously the Communist Party had the main say in promotions and advancements; now it is expected that the government will have more say. With this project the government is expected to take over the management of high level officials, although it is not yet certain how high or whether the prime minister will be able to select his own ministers for the first time, without the Party telling him who to appoint.'

Another official is not so sure the reforms will go that far, although he believes it is still in the balance. 'In the final analysis this reform is about power; there is a constant struggle for power', says the second official. Both officials agree that the objective of the project is the creation of a much-needed class of civil servants who owe their positions to merit rather than connections or party membership. They believe the government is enlightened enough to recognize that the absence of a professional civil service is an impediment to the economic reforms, although they are not sure that all the Party leadership share that view. However, things are changing. 'Five years ago if you wanted to work in a senior position in a government department you had to be a Party member; now membership is almost irrelevant. It is qualifications and skills that count', say the officials. An administrator of the United Nations Development Programme, which is helping to fund the project, agrees that it is probably one of the most significant reforms underway at present, with enormous implications for the nature of power in Vietnam. 'Previously the government had no personnel policy, or posts, of its own. They all belonged to the Party. Now that is changing and the Party will not be able to intervene any longer', he says.[5] After bureaucratic delay and confusion, the next greatest obstacle encountered by potential investors is the deficient legal infrastructure. As with China, Vietnam just does not have the legal base necessary to build a modern, commercially-based society. In late 1994 a dispute in Beijing between the fast-food chain McDonald's, which said it had been given a 20-year lease on a valuable city centre site, and the city authorities, who wanted to redevelop it, served as a warning to potential investors of the dangers of doing business in a country with scant regard for the rule of law. In Vietnam there are complaints from foreign firms about trade mark theft, but none has so far wanted to tackle the issue head on by suing. Trade marks can now be registered, but first the registering party needs to have a presence in the country and to hire a local lawyer to handle the registration. Foreign companies know that a liberal foreign investment law means nothing if it does not include the means to enforce commercial agreements and protect investors. Economic courts are being set up to rule on trade and investment disputes. The test will be whether they take on the army and other state bodies who have been implicated in commercial piracy. The third problem area for foreign investors is the shortcoming in banking and accountancy services. Although foreign banks and accountants are proliferating in Vietnam, some companies still prefer to do their accounting outside the country.

Among the more obvious economic legacies of communism are the large number of state-owned enterprises, known as SOEs, as well as those operated by provincial and district governments and by national institutions like the police and army. They range from small-scale retail operations, transport enterprises and printing works to the banking, energy, communications and construction sectors. Even the Communist Party itself, encouraged by the legitimization of the profit motive, is heavily engaged in commercial activity although few people seem to know exactly what it owns. It is believed to control several tourism companies and hotels and to be engaged in the sale of land, while the army is thought to have significant interests in hotels, construction and transportation.

[5] Because of the sensitivity of the subject, neither of the government officials quoted, nor the UNDP administrator, wanted to be named. They were interviewed in late 1994.

Despite the enormous irony of the Communist Party making money through capitalist ventures, none of this is illegal. Some senior Party members have publicly warned of crossing the line of acceptability and of people or institutions 'making money by virtue of their position'. It has been argued that the Party has been corrupted by this exposure to capitalism and should now end its commercial activity and raise its funds from membership fees alone. The problem is that if all the perks of Party membership –such as preferment for government jobs and involvement in lucrative business – were to end, then recruitment would rapidly dry up. Indeed this appears to be happening already, although it is difficult to get accurate information about the level of Party membership. As one resident of Ho Chi Minh City put it: 'The only reason people are now in the Party is for personal advancement –it's not about ideology. Otherwise it is a disadvantage to be in the Party, at least here in Ho Chi Minh City, because nobody likes Party members.'

The government has withdrawn most of the subsidies that previously kept state-owned enterprises afloat. Now they have to find their own profitability or else go under. Privatization is encouraged, although the word is thought to have negative (or anti-socialist) connotations so the word 'equitization' (*co phan hoa*) is preferred. More of an obstacle than the name is the lack of clarity as to how equitization is achieved in a country without merchant banks or a stock exchange and with very limited supplies of capital. Even less clear is who will benefit from the sell-off and whether the administering government departments, like the Ministries of Construction or of Light Industry, stand to keep any proceeds from the sale of assets which technically belong to 'the people'. By the end of 1994, only two enterprises operated by central or regional governments had been successfully sold off. Such sales were not helped by the fact that the term 'state enterprise' had become a term of abuse, demonstrating the low esteem with which such ventures are regarded in newly capitalist Vietnam.[6]

The problem of what to do about SOEs is one of the more difficult challenges facing the government. There is nothing in Vietnam's economic reform textbook about how to handle the issue beyond the capitalist principle that subsidies should be ended. Subsidies were halted in late 1992. As a result of a process of re-registration completed in early 1994, many small SOEs simply

---

[6] See Laurence J Brahm and Hoang Ngoc Nguyen, 'Capital Vietnam: The Making of a Market', *Business Vietnam*, August-September 1994, pp 20-25.

disappeared, leaving debts in their wake which the government has been forced to meet. For those that remain, there is uncertainty as to who actually owns them and should be responsible for their debts, or for hiring and firing their executives. Company law is in a poor enough state in Vietnam, but the situation of most SOEs is even more parlous. If they aim to compete against the private sector they are finding that, with the removal of their monopoly position and the ending of government control over prices, they lack the managerial experience to be able to compete in the new, free marketplace.

The problem of SOEs may in due course solve itself thanks to the mechanism of market forces. Re-registration reduced the number of SOEs from 12,000 before *doi moi* to around 7,000, employing about one and a half million people. Compared with China,[7] where around 108,000 SOEs employ perhaps 108 million people, Vietnam's SOE problem is tiny. It will become smaller still as the numbers of private, foreign-owned and joint-enterprise companies grow to dwarf those still owned by the state. A small number of SOEs are profitable, helped by the injection of foreign capital and by the monopoly they continue to enjoy. Notable examples are those charged with exporting Vietnam's rice surplus. This explains the reluctance on the part of central and provincial governments to divest themselves of these sources of revenue. Ministries and many local authorities, notably those of Ho Chi Minh City and Hanoi, are actually earning considerable income from their SOEs, especially those which have formed joint ventures with foreign companies. Foreign firms like doing business with SOEs because they feel the enterprise comes with official blessing and any problems – for example, of land acquisition or of guaranteeing power supplies – are more easily overcome.

Even the Party looks at SOEs in terms of their profitability, as a source of state or Party revenue, rather than as a financial liability. Yet a conservative faction believes that the numbers of SOEs should not be reduced further for ideological rather than economic reasons. A healthy ownership of SOEs, it is argued, is a measure of the level of socialism in a country. Conversely, if only a small proportion of enterprise is state-owned, this signifies that capitalism has taken over – as for all intents and purposes it has in Vietnam. The Party faction believes that retaining a sizeable state sector will check any

---

[7] See *Far Eastern Economic Review*, 2 March 1995, from where the statistics on China are extracted.

further widening of the wealth gap, what Prime Minister Vo Van Kiet has called 'the confrontation between luxury and misery, between cities and country'.[8] Others believe the process has already gone too far. 'If the basis of our socialism is in our state-owned enterprises, then our socialism is in a lot of trouble', one reformer in the government told the *Far Eastern Economic Review*.[9]

This faction also sees the reduction in the state sector as symptomatic of a loss of control by the Party and is anxious that it should go no further. It is particularly opposed to the privatization of strategically-important enterprises, such as publishing, printing, banking, the defence and telecommunications industries and of prestige companies like Vietnam Airlines. Prime ministerial approval is in any case needed for foreign investment in the defence or media sectors. This same faction within the Party hopes to build up the remaining SOEs by grouping them into large engineering conglomerates like those of South Korea (the *chaebol*), over which the government retains considerable powers, and are promoting a new law to encourage this. Others doubt whether the government or the Party have the managerial or entrepreneurial know-how – or the power – to achieve this.

There is a Vietnamese saying that 'when you open the door to the breeze the dirt comes in too'. *Doi moi* has brought its share of 'dirt' although this is tempered by an overall feeling, which it is difficult not to share, that most people have benefited from *doi moi*. The way in which both rural agricultural communities and city dwellers seem to be busily engaged in economic activity is the main evidence for this. Production and export figures provide further evidence. Several years of sustained economic growth have helped people forget the bad times that preceded *doi moi*. There is a widespread feeling that *doi moi* has rescued the country and its people from fear of famine. Farmers seem relieved at being able to make their own crop-planting decisions according to local economic circumstances, and at being allowed to keep a higher proportion of their produce than previously.

However, there is a downside. Disparities are increasing, the gap between rich and poor is widening. This is most evident from the

[8] Quoted in Michael Williams, *op cit,* p 56.
[9] *Far Eastern Economic Review*, 2 March 1995, p 58.

numbers of *nouveaux riches* Vietnamese. Private residences are expanding upwards, a sure sign of wealth. Private car ownership, which simply had not existed since 1975, is on the rise too, especially in and around Ho Chi Minh City. Given the high import duty, a Vietnamese has to be seriously wealthy to own a car. While there is nothing wrong in the creation of wealth, according to the new thinking in Vietnam, there are plenty of Vietnamese who have not seen any improvement in their lot as a result of *doi moi* –for example landless peasants and lower level government employees. It is the entrepreneurs, those who have a skill or service to sell, who are growing wealthy. As prices go up in response to this new wealth and the demand for goods, those on fixed incomes are becoming poorer.

Another aspect of the downside of *doi moi* is the way social indicators are slipping. Vietnam boasts that 88% of its people are literate – a figure high by developing world standards, higher than some of its ASEAN neighbours and significantly higher than China. There are indications that this level is falling because teachers are being wooed to higher paid jobs. It is no wonder that a rural teacher, whose government salary is the equivalent of $10 per month, will migrate to the city where both foreign and Vietnamese companies are willing to pay up to $300 for someone with fairly basic skills. Teachers of English are in strong demand. The problem is compounded by the fact that, in order to hold on to their teachers, schools are paying higher wages from their own funds and the only way they can do this is by charging fees. Officially, only children from families that can afford to pay are charged. However, in Ho Chi Minh City all parents are now expected to pay for their children's education. Education, even at primary level, is no longer free.

As in education, so too in health: *doi moi* has brought with it the end of the welfare state. Even government hospitals and doctors now charge both for medicines and medical treatment. The government says this allows it to provide a better health service than was possible before, but it is a health service for the 'haves', those that can afford to pay, not for the 'have-nots'. Medical attention for the poor is still meant to be free, but limited resources of time and drugs can mean there are none left for those that cannot pay. The privatization of health and education services has gone further in Vietnam than in Conservative-ruled Britain, where primary services remain free. Health workers claim that, as a result of the ending of government subsidies into health-related activity, the incidence of communicable disease – notably of malaria – is rising.

For rather different reasons, AIDS has become a scourge in Vietnam. Prostitution, which had been under control during the austere years, is now rampant – a combination of the effect of looser political control of people's lives, an increase in demand resulting from the new money in the economy as well as the encouragement now given to private enterprise. In the prevailing free enterprise culture, women who have nothing else to sell are tempted to sell their bodies. Drug use is another growing problem, also fuelled by new money as well as by youth unemployment and frustration. While the levels of prostitution and drug use remain small by the standards of most other South East Asian countries, it is the rate at which they are increasing which is causing concern. The greed factor in private enterprise has combined with the frustration of those without jobs or the means to earn money to fuel an increase in crime. Another undesirable side-effect of *doi moi* is uncontrolled migration to the cities as the unemployed seek opportunities or farmers come to sell their wares. Migration in Vietnam is no longer strictly controlled: congestion and slums are the result.

With a country developing as fast as Vietnam there is inevitably a danger of 'overheating' – economic activity outpacing the development of the infrastructure. Similarly rapid expansion caused the authorities in China to apply the brakes to slow things down. Dr Oanh suggests 'overheating' is a matter of inflation levels; he recognizes that inflation is an inevitable accompaniment of high growth. 'As long as inflation is kept down to single digit levels we need not worry about overheating', he says. Wages are going up rapidly in Ho Chi Minh City and this is fuelling inflation, although intense competition as a direct result of *doi moi* has the effect of keeping some check on prices. Even so, by the end of 1994 inflation in Vietnam had risen to double figures again – still less than half the level in China.

Adverse consequences of *doi moi* articulated by ordinary Vietnamese include worries that the heightened influence of Western culture will dilute Vietnam's identity; that the Vietnamese people will become selfish through greed; that family life will be disrupted as the pursuit of wealth becomes the overwhelming imperative; that the environment will be neglected in the pursuit of commercial advantage and that there will be social disorder as economically strong people show less respect for authority. To an extent, all these thing are happening. They have to be balanced against the fact that the majority of Vietnamese are better off following the reforms. More fundamental concerns that are expressed openly by Communist Party leaders are that the gap between rich and poor will inevitably widen and that the poor will grow poorer as prices are driven up by market forces without wages following, itself rather an academic point for those who are jobless or unwaged.

In the eyes of the people, it was the Communist Party that ushered in *doi moi*, so there is no widespread challenge to the Party's view that its wise and generally benevolent leadership is needed to see it through. The people are ready to support the view that while economic liberalism will bring prosperity to Vietnam, Communist Party rule will ensure the political stability that is essential to build that prosperity. What is widely resented, though, is the corruption that has come with *doi moi* and particularly the way in which Party members and officials are seen to be enriching themselves by taking advantage of the new liberal economic climate. This, rather than its authoritarian insistence on its right to rule, is ultimately more likely to be the Party's undoing.

The ardour with which even the Communist old guard now defends *doi moi* is either an acute demonstration of hypocrisy, or belated recognition of the seriousness of the predicament that they faced by the mid-1980s. Men and women brought up to believe in the socialist transformation of the economy and other such communist orthodoxy have embraced *doi moi* with the enthusiasm of converts, making a virtue out of necessity. Party leaders have been able to boast that Vietnam's version of perestroika was launched a full two years before that of the USSR and may even have helped pave the way for the subsequent reforms in Russia. They have made less of the fact that they were in fact following an example set by China eight years earlier.

Party leaders go to great lengths to argue that the introduction of the market system does not spell an end to socialism or communism. A popular argument is that 'the market system does not belong to capitalism: it belongs to mankind, not to one particular ideological system'. According to this reasoning, there is nothing incompatible between market forces and socialism, although (it is conceded) some adjustments need to be made to the market system to ensure that it remains fair and socialist. No one in the Party or government seems ready to admit what is apparent to most people: that as far as its ordering of the economy is concerned

Vietnam has joined the ranks of post-communist nations, like those of Eastern Europe. The country is still ruled by a Communist Party, but it has shed its economic philosophy in favour of that once-damned capitalist device, market forces. Whilst it grapples to retain control of the state and its people through the paraphernalia at its disposal, it has surrendered control of the economy, whilst denying that socialism has been abandoned.

Nguyen Co Thach, who advises the government on economic policy (although he admits he is 'no economist') lists three characteristics which, he says, 'prove that Vietnam is still socialist'. First, there is the continued existence of state enterprises, which he says must no longer depend on subsidies but should compete against private companies to make money. Second, the state is not encouraging the exploitation of man by man, which he suggests is a characteristic of capitalism. Third, says Thach, 'we remain intent on organizing a just society'. Thach believes strongly that key sectors like banking and telecommunications should remain under government control. His only worry about some people getting rich out of *doi moi* is that they may be doing so 'by making use of their positions'.

Thach seems not entirely happy with the way the Communist Party has adopted capitalist methods to make money and says he has written a paper proposing that the Party stop its business activities. 'Corruption amongst cadres is the biggest problem facing the Party and government today', says Thach. 'The credibility of the state and the Party depend on our taking measures to eliminate corruption.' Explaining the difficult and crippling path which brought Vietnam to the brink of bankruptcy before *doi moi* was adopted, Thach says: 'We thought we could build socialism from our backward economy. But socialism only comes once the means of production are very developed and the country is productive. We misunderstood Marx, now we are on the right track. What we have today is market economics with a socialist orientation, or state capitalism.'

Dr Oanh has his own label to describe the system ushered in by *doi moi*: 'I call what we have now market socialism, a sort of hybrid. We have committed a grave error in labelling systems capitalist or communist. What's important is to create a hybrid which must meet the historical context of the country and the mood of the people.' Yet what Dr Oanh advocated and the government adopted are undisguisedly free market reforms of a kind that have the enthusiastic support of such capitalist institutions as the World Bank and International Monetary Fund. The World Bank was particularly impressed that Vietnam's 'Transition to the Market'[10] had been accomplished without significant support from outside the country in the face of a continuing trade and aid embargo from most of the non-communist world.

War hero and former deputy prime minister Vo Nguyen Giap, now in his mid-80s, was quoted a few years ago as saying: 'We don't know what socialism is about any more.' When the author quoted this remark back at him, he reacted angrily saying he had been misquoted. 'Of course we know what socialism is and it remains our objective. Never, never shall we abandon socialism', he said. Pushed to explain his understanding of socialism, General Giap says socialism means having clothes to wear and enough rice to eat. Giap defends the economic reforms as perfectly on course with what Ho Chi Minh had advocated, although his reasoning at times seems rather strained. He could have fallen back on Ho's own words to defend the Party's espousal of the profit motive since Ho once said: 'Managing a country is like managing a business. You must make profit... Everything has to be calculated carefully.'[11]

Asked whether Ho would have approved of *doi moi*, Giap has no doubt that he would, quoting him as saying that after the triumph of the war 'we have to build a new life'. He does not go so far as Nguyen Co Thach, who says: 'If Uncle Ho had outlived the war he would have implemented *doi moi* long before his successors actually did because he was so intelligent.' Deputy foreign minister Le Mai echoes General Giap's definition of socialism saying it means 'bringing better material and spiritual living conditions for the people as a whole'.[12] Vietnamese officials travelling overseas refer to Vietnam's frenetic economic activity as 'socialism at work' and explain the thrust of *doi moi* as 'trying to make the country strong, the people wealthy'.

This shift from a preoccupation with equality in favour of national wealth-creation is familiar from China. Just as Vietnam's reforms have been greatly influenced by those of China, so the ways in which Vietnam's communist leaders defend moves from central planning to market economy echo those of Chinese leaders. While

[10] The title of a 1993 World Bank report on Vietnam.
[11] From a speech made in 1953, when Ho was busy advocating land reform in Vietnam. The quotation is prominently displayed (in English and Vietnamese) in the Ho Chi Minh Museum, Hanoi.
[12] *Financial Times* (London), 8 December 1994, p 37.

neither communist hierarchy is ready or able to admit to having abandoned socialism, both have found ways of rationalizing the pursuit of wealth as being for the good of the nation, while downplaying the fact that the wealth is not shared equitably among the people. The most famous articulation in China came from Deng Xiaoping, regarded as the father of China's economic reforms. On a visit in January 1992 to Shenzhen special economic zone, a capitalist enclave adjoining Hong Kong, he gave this rationale for China's reforms: 'It doesn't matter whether it is called capitalism or socialism as long as it makes the people rich.' In China, many people have become rich as a result of the country's economic reforms; others have seen little or no improvement in their often desperate economic circumstances. In China, making money has become a national obsession, especially among city-dwellers. The same is becoming true in Vietnam. By way of denying that China has abandoned socialism in its national pursuit of wealth, Deng's wealth-pursuing philosophy has been officially dubbed 'socialism with Chinese characteristics'. One commentator has less kindly dubbed it 'market-Leninism'.

So where is *doi moi* leading Vietnam? Nguyen Co Thach is philosophical about what the future holds in store. As a former foreign minister he has had more opportunity than his contemporaries to see how far Vietnam was getting left behind economically. He says: 'In the past we condemned the market economy without really understanding what it was. Now we are applying it and we still don't know what it is!' Thach's joke echoes the views of those who are not quite sure that *doi moi* is here to stay and remain worried that economic reforms could be put into reverse. Their uncertainty about the future course of Vietnam's economic reform programme is summed up in an oft-quoted sentiment: 'Everyone agrees that Vietnam is in transition. They know what we are coming from. But nobody, especially not the government, knows what we are heading towards!'

6

The New Capitalists

Whatever the arguments over labels and ideologies, the reality is that *doi moi* has created a class of capitalists once more in Vietnam. Some are very wealthy. (The term 'millionaire' does not mean much in a country where exchanging US$100 puts more than a million dong in your pocket!) Vietnam's new capitalists have succeeded through their own efforts, often helped by their connections. Here are the stories of some of them.

Chi[1] is 26 and comes from a small-scale trading family in Hanoi. As the eldest child of a widowed mother, she dropped out of her law studies after only a few months to support her family. In the pre-*doi moi* climate, this meant trading in Hanoi's main market, where she tried her hand successively at selling sugar, milk and beer. Opportunities for making much profit were severely limited, although she earned enough to support her mother and two younger sisters. After *doi moi*, things became much easier. She borrowed money to open a small shop selling shoes. The business flourished and after a while she had enough money to invest in another enterprise, a slate factory around 300 miles to the south of Hanoi, in the impoverished province of Nghe An. This earned enough profit for her to be able to graduate from her ordinary motorcycle to every young Vietnamese's preferred means of transport, a Honda Dream motorbike which costs US$2,700 – more than many can earn in a lifetime. Her home life was by now fairly comfortable and, as her profits continued to grow, she bought herself a modest house.

In the boom period of 1993, when every Hanoian was looking for ways to make money, Chi discovered there was an easier way to

---

[1] All names and some minor details in this chapter have been changed to preserve the anonymity of the subjects. Their stories are otherwise as told to the author.

make it than running a shop, which needed constant attention and the services of an assistant. She sold the shop and her share in the slate factory, which had made her a lot of money, and turned her hand to money lending. It was modest amounts at first – the dong equivalent of US$500-1,000. At interest rates ranging from 4% to 6% a month, depending on the size and duration of the loan, she found enough clients to absorb her savings and to bring her a decent and regular income. Her 20 or so clients, all small market traders looking for money for stock or expansion, deposited the land certificate of their selling plot with Chi as collateral. There were setbacks, such as when fire swept through Hanoi's Dong Xuan market causing extensive damage to the plots of many of her clients. But she learnt to cope and to balance the risks. Rather than lose all her advances, she chose instead to extend the period and lighten the burden of the loans as the only means of ensuring she got at least some return.

Chi's business prospered. She took a loan of her own from the bank at the more favourable rate of 2% a month – for which she was required to deposit the land certificate of her own home – in order to take on more clients. Her profit was the difference between what she charged them and what she paid the bank. As a property owner, she was able to borrow from the bank whilst ordinary market traders could not. She capitalised on this advantage and transformed her initial savings of US$10,000 into around US$120,000 over a period of two years. Chi's story, which is not untypical, points up how *doi moi* has opened the way to free market profit-making. It also shows vividly how the lowest level of the economy can expand even without a sophisticated banking structure. The private money-lender fulfils the role of retail banker, just as jewellers function as exchangers of currency.

Whilst not everyone has Chi's capitalist flair, it is easy to get the impression that a high proportion of the inhabitants of Hanoi are 'on the make' in one way or another. How else can one explain the wealth and purchasing power that is in evidence? Chi herself ventures the opinion that at least 40% of government employees are trading in some form or another and probably most members of the government too! Whilst proudly proclaiming that she 'never was a communist or anything like that', she is honest enough to see the downside of the post-*doi moi* revolution in attitudes. 'In the old days life used to be gentle and much more straightforward; now all that everybody is interested in is making money.' It has its effect on social life too she says: 'Just look at the incidence of divorce resulting from women meeting men who are richer than their husbands.'

Minh, aged 37, thinks of himself as primarily an English language teacher; he speaks the language fluently and very precisely, ever eager to acquire a new idiomatic usage. Three years ago he was sent abroad to improve his interpreting, a skill the government badly needs. Shortly after his return he was transferred from his job teaching at the Foreign Language Teaching University in Hanoi to a key government department involved in implementing new economic policies. Foreign experts are attached to the department, so Minh's language skills are much used.

However, Minh has also taken a second job: as consultant to a joint-venture steel operation involving Australian and Vietnamese partners. His work there is occasional, paid on a piece-rate basis, and he knows the fact that he works for a key government department was an important factor in his selection for this second job. 'They wanted someone with government connections as well as my knowledge of English. My role there is as a consultant, helping in a number of ways including interpreting and translating. They also use my knowledge of public administration', says Minh. The phenomenon of government employees taking second jobs is not uncommon. They are recruited in particular for their language or computer skills, two areas of knowledge in heavy demand. It may seem as if Minh is working for state and private enterprise at the same time. In fact, it is not quite like that for the two Vietnamese partners in the steel project are companies owned by the Ministry of Heavy Industry and it was the ministry who approached him to join it. So in reality he works for two different arms of the state, which makes it easier for Minh to take time off from his first job to attend to the needs of the second.

But it does not end there. Like many educated Vietnamese, Minh has other part-time work which supplements his relatively meagre civil service salary, as well as broadening his experience. He continues to teach at his old university, which he much enjoys. Then he also does part-time work, mainly translations, for foreign law firms. Minh's wife is supportive of the long hours he puts in at his work, though it means he does not see so much of his four-year old daughter. She tries to compensate in that regard for they both recognize that Minh needs to take advantage of the opportunities while they are there.

Nga, 45, is a daughter of the Red River delta. She was born in a poor village just up-river from Hanoi. Her father was a train driver, but he died young leaving Nga's mother to bring up six children alone. Nga and her siblings went to the fields after school to help her mother in the cooperative farm, where 30 families worked together and shared the output. It was, says Nga, a struggle involving constant hard work. In 1967 Nga was selected by communist cadres for training at the foreign ministry training school. She does not know why she was selected – 'my family were not Party members' – but considers it her stroke of luck.

Much of her three-year training course took place in the mountains, because the Americans often bombed Hanoi at that time. After graduating as a secretary, Nga at first worked for the Ministry of Justice, as secretary to the minister, because there were no jobs available at the foreign ministry. Later, when the United Nations Development Programme (UNDP) opened offices in Hanoi, she was seconded to work there. She has worked for UNDP for 15 years, as telephone operator, communications clerk and administration clerk.

It was her contact with foreign UN personnel that gave her the idea to open a business to cater to their needs. She was so often asked for help in acquiring things – from fresh chickens to ceramics – that, supported by foreign UN staff, she opened a small shop in the foreigners' residential compound. Despite having a full time job, she made time to buy in goods and employed her brother and sister-in-law to sell them. Another sister brought fresh chicken and pork from an outlying village, while selling off the chicken feet, a Vietnamese delicacy, in the local market. As the shop flourished, Nga started to cater for special needs: for example, procuring geese and turkeys to help foreigners celebrate Christmas and Thanksgiving. (Hanoi has a growing population of Americans – employed by the UN, the US diplomatic mission and increasingly by business.) Nga is always open to special requests from her customers. When the state milk operation, Vinamilk, started producing well packaged yoghurts she was quick to add these to her stock at the shop. It also gave her ambitions to expand into food processing and packaging.

A side venture running a restaurant ran into difficulties when the state company from which she rented the land became greedy. She closed the restaurant, having demonstrated first that there was a demand for the service she provided. Now she hopes to re-employ the team of four, who include her husband's brother, by running a fast food delivery service. She sees fast foods as a growth area in Hanoi and a stepping stone to take her into food manufacturing or processing.

Nga's husband has a senior position in a state run organization and they have been allocated a good-sized apartment. Like his father, Nga's husband is a Communist Party member. They joke in the family that he is the communist whilst she is the capitalist. Nga has got where she is largely through her contacts, foreign and Vietnamese, as well as her business instincts. She has also made good use of her family, giving work to four immediate family members, and her village from where she brings the fresh foods she sells, as well as flowers. Whilst she was establishing the business, she kept pigs for a while at her Hanoi home, fattening them from 20 to 90 kilograms in three months by making use of food waste from the UN canteen. (Pork sells for about 1800 dong, or $1.70, a kilogram.) She is so busy with her job and shop that she sees little of her husband, 18-year old daughter and 12-year old son, who as a result have become very self-sufficient. Her daughter is starting in law school. Nga's story is that of a girl from a poor farming family who has done well for herself in the city and is now helping Vietnam to discover how to satisfy demand – the mechanics of market forces.

Luyen is a receptionist at a hotel in Vinh, which is owned by Nghe An provincial administration. At 40, he is older than the other receptionists and appears to be making good use of the additional experience of his advanced years. Born in Vinh, Luyen graduated in English from the city's university. In 1972 he became a guerilla fighter in the south, eventually ending up in Saigon as the city was 'liberated' in April 1975. As a fighter he played a role in administering the city for the new communist authorities. Part of that role was closing down capitalist enterprise but Luyen now says that he 'learnt capitalism' during that period between 1975 and 1980. He is adamant that Ho Chi Minh City never really stopped being capitalist, a fact he believes has become evident now that *doi moi* has unleashed private enterprise there again. Luyen went from Saigon to Cambodia shortly after Vietnam ousted the Khmer Rouge government; he was involved in helping administer the western cities of Battambong and Sisopon. In 1986 he returned to his birth place of Vinh, in time to take advantage of *doi moi*.

Luyen believes he has two particular advantages. He speaks passable English, which first gained him a job in the province's international relations department which runs the hotel. He has practised it at the hotel on the small but steady stream of foreigners – business people, aid workers and tourists – who have been staying at the hotel since the country started opening up. Second, he says he is used to dealing with foreigners from his Cambodian days. He believes he understands their needs better than most Vietnamese. He used this latter advantage to assume the role of middleman in helping traders from Laos to ship goods through Vinh's port, having first taught himself some Lao. Now that foreign visitors are coming to Vinh more regularly, Luyen has again capitalized on his advantages by opening a small travel business, which he runs from an office down the road from the hotel. He can organize a car for you which, given the difficulties of transport in a city where the Honda motorbike is the main means of transport, is an important role; he claims to have access to 24 vehicles of different sizes. In the process he is touting for foreign investment from visiting Taiwanese who have come to look at the export potential of frozen shrimps, marble or the possibilities for developing nearby Cua Lo beach as a tourist resort. Though this may appear to conflict with his job as a hotel receptionist, it does not since his employer, the province administration, is happy to encourage his freelance work. They will be especially pleased if he attracts investment. Luyen is not ashamed to admit that he has enriched himself in the process. Like other new entrepreneurs in Vinh and elsewhere, he has added new storeys to his home – a sure sign of prosperity that is now visibly marking out Vietnam's new capitalists from their single storey neighbours. In Vietnam, 'upwardly mobile' is a particularly apt expression for the new entrepreneurs!

Lam has excellent revolutionary credentials. Both his parents worked for the communist side in the south before 1975 during what he, like most southerners, calls 'the civil war'. Originating from Quy Nhon in the south, they had each migrated with their respective families to Hanoi after the Geneva accords of 1954 split Vietnam. His father studied medicine and became an army doctor, travelling south in 1967 to work in a 'liberated zone' near the famous tunnels of Cu Chi. His mother, having qualified in Hanoi as a teacher, journeyed south in 1968. They married in Can Tho in 1969 and Lam was born in Rach Gia in the delta a year later. Lam has distant memories of his mother taking him to Hanoi when he was about four years old – in 1974. 'We went via the Truong Son mountains', he says, referring to the route that outsiders call 'the Ho Chi Minh trail'. The Truong Son ridge marks the divide between Vietnam, Laos and Cambodia. The journey, he says, was by all forms of transport – boat, motorcycle, truck and sometimes on foot: 'We left Vietnam from Tay Ninh province and re-entered into Nghe An.'

Lam's father, a member of the Communist Party, now heads the health services in the Mekong delta province of Soc Trang. With such a pedigree, Lam might have been expected to join government or Party service. Instead, after graduating from Danang and Hanoi Universities in chemistry – one of his teachers was the wife of Prime Minister Vo Van Kiet – Lam applied for and received permission to further his studies in Singapore, where he stayed with some friends. The trip was half funded by the government. The visit gave him some good capitalist ideas and on his return he determined to set up in business. In Ho Chi Minh City he joined an advertising agency promoting brands of Western liquor.

Then an opportunity presented itself while he was visiting the hill resort of Dalat. He and a cousin put their $20,000 savings accumulated over the years into opening a Western-style bar specializing in cocktails and offering a wide range of imported spirits. It was an instant success with the large numbers of foreigners now visiting Dalat for business or tourism. 'The other bars in town offer very little competition because only my bartender knows how to cater for Western tastes', Lam boasts with confidence. He says it would have been much harder to open a bar in the more competitive atmosphere of Ho Chi Minh City, though that remains his ambition.

How has he done it? Apart from the savings, which were crucial to renting the site, he says the single most important ingredient is the bartender, whom he encouraged to move to Dalat from Saigon where he had learnt the trade. 'Without him I could not have done it', admits Lam. Other factors such as the location and the range of drinks he has managed to obtain – mainly smuggled from Cambodia thus evading high import duties – were important too. Among other essential ingredients Lam could also have listed are business acumen, which he clearly has, his knowledge of English – not strong but getting better – and promotion, at which Lam is an expert. He has a habit of handing around neatly printed business cards, which brought him customers from day one. Every night there were new customers at his bar who had been given a card or had heard about the place on the grapevine.

What do his parents think of the venture? He believes they would approve of him using his initiative and succeeding, since *doi moi* encourages initiative. Asked about his ideology he (perhaps deliberately) misunderstands, answering instead that his target is 'to make money and to become a big businessman, as opposed to a small one!' After opening a bar in Ho Chi Minh City or perhaps Hanoi, he wants to use his skills as a chemist to move into large battery production. Lam's father should approve: what he is doing is encouraged by the Communist Party, which is itself making a lot of money out of tourism in Dalat.

Before 1975 Sinh was a doctor in the South Vietnamese army. That earned him three years in a re-education camp after Saigon fell to the North Vietnamese army, plus an extra six months in prison for attempting to escape from Vietnam by boat. While he was in re-education camp his father, a lawyer, died in the camp to which he had been taken in northern Vietnam. Shortly after Sinh's release in 1978, his mother won the right to follow her other children into exile with a place on the UN-sponsored Orderly Departure Programme. This gave her the privilege of leaving Vietnam by plane rather than on a leaky boat. She settled in France with other members of her family.

Sinh returned to his job as a doctor under the new communist administration of Ho Chi Minh City. These were difficult times, particularly because, as a former servant of the so-called 'Saigon puppet regime', he was a marked man. Also because his wife and two children had fled by boat and settled in California. Then *doi moi* arrived and Sinh was allowed to open a restaurant – which he did in partnership with two others. In the new economic climate, the restaurant was a success and now employs around 80 people. A waiter earns about $50 dollars a month. The nightly cabaret includes a fire eating dancer who comes as close to performing striptease as 1995 Saigon allows. The restaurant is particularly popular with overseas Vietnamese returning to Vietnam from Canada, Australia or the USA, either for family reasons or to assess the feasibility of investing in post-*doi moi* Vietnam.

Sinh was lucky in one sense. He had both the money, which he says did not come from abroad, and the business acumen, to enter business and succeed in the new *laisser faire* climate that prevails. Besides the restaurant, he owns a sports good shop, runs a private clinic – something not allowed during the austere communist days – and retains his job as a government doctor at a major Saigon hospital. But in another sense his life has been bleak. Apart from losing his father while they were both in re-education camps, a particularly bitter blow, his wife and two children are living in California. The authorities in Vietnam will not give him permission to join them, though he has twice been allowed abroad briefly to visit his mother in Paris. She in return has revisited Vietnam. Sinh will not feel free until he knows he can visit his children in California, or even settle there if the whim takes him. His business success is little compensation for the splitting up of his family. He is bitter about the past while remaining positive about the future: 'Communism has gone, it exists in name only. Business-wise I can do anything I want – but the authorities still do not trust me because all the rest of my family are abroad. Yet they need the skills of people like me.' The irony of Sinh's story is that he is supporting his family in California by sending them money earned from his business enterprises in Saigon – the reverse of the normal flow of remittances into Vietnam.

Nam is one of Saigon's self-made businessmen. Now aged 44, he graduated from Hué University in central Vietnam in bio-chemistry in 1977. (He explains his non-involvement in the war by saying his parents pretended he was five years younger than he was, although they were under pressure from both sides – 'the VC came to our house'.) After graduating, Nam moved to Saigon where he joined a scientific research institute. During ten years there he experimented with yeast production, selling compressed yeast for the first time on to the local market. Previously yeast was imported. When the economic climate eased as a result of *doi moi*, he left the Institute and became a full time yeast producer making about 200 kilograms a day, which he sold in the market to Saigon's bread makers.

His big break came in April 1987. The city was desperately short of power and planned to turn off supplies to industry for seven days. He invested almost his entire savings of $20,000 buying up old refrigerators left behind by the US military. He then increased his yeast production massively by using a new technique and stored enough in his fridges to make a killing on the black market during the power shutdown, when the price of compressed yeast rose from 300 to 5,000 dong a kilogram. Others who had entered the yeast market could not compete. Nam made the equivalent of around US$ 500,000 during that one week, enough to finance much of his subsequent expansion, establishing his yeast as the market leader. From yeast he has moved into instant noodles, a popular snack food throughout East Asia. He now has two production lines in Ho Chi Minh City and joint-ventures in three other cities, Quang Binh, where he is in partnership with the People's Committee, Haiphong and Hanoi. He has also diversified into packaging, initially set up for his noodles but now run as a separate business supplying to outside companies too, and plant fertiliser, packaging a chemical imported from Germany into small sachets for the local market – an offshoot of his packaging enterprise.

Nam made most of his own production machinery from locally-available materials. He estimates the noodle production line cost less than a tenth what it would have cost to buy from abroad. But he is very conscious of the advantages of the latest technology and has imported machinery where it is necessary to stay ahead. Never slow to capitalize on an opportunity, Nam is now making noodle manufacturing equipment for other companies, just as he is selling packaging to other noodle manufacturers. He believes he has a strong market position and is making noodles more cheaply than almost anyone in East Asia: he sells 70 gram packets for the equivalent of 4 US cents, while export quality retail at 8.5 cents. His business philosophy from the yeast onwards has been to sell large quantities at low profit margins. He pays his workers well by local standards – US$70 a month. Labour in Vietnam is cheaper than in the more developed ASEAN countries, which gives him an advantage in the export market.

Nam's Ho Chi Minh City production lines produce about 10 million packets of noodles a month. He exports about 20 million packets a year, three-quarters to Russia. Key Russian markets are Moscow and Sakhalin in the Russian Far East, where they want to barter noodles for their locally-produced Kamraz trucks, which are popular in Vietnam. But Nam prefers the versatility of cash. Demand from Russia is so strong that in 1994 he teamed up with a former Russian diplomat in Vietnam to set up a production line in Moscow, exporting all the equipment from Saigon via Vladivostock and the Trans-Siberian railway. Demand remains high so he plans a second factory in another Russian city soon. Much of the rest of his exports go to Eastern Europe. Japan, Canada and Australia are also buyers; he hopes soon to break into the US market where he thinks his noodles will be popular with the overseas Vietnamese.

Nam seems so full of expansion plans that it is difficult to contain his enthusiasm. His next project, a logical offshoot of the packaging plant, is a new printing works. By buying equipment from South Korea, he boasts it will be 'one of the ten best printing presses in the country'. Another project, though just a dream at present, is a chicken farm and perhaps beef too, to be able to open a 'Vietnamese McDonald's'. He has visited the Philippines to see how their fast food outlets work. He believes he can make the necessary ovens and other machinery in Vietnam and came back from the Philippines with a promise from the operator of the first McDonald's-style restaurant there that if he succeeds they will place orders for such machinery.

Nam is clearly a good chemist and an exceptional businessman and has combined these talents with a good share of pragmatism when dealing with the authorities. He has friends on the Ho Chi Minh City People's Committee, which must have helped. His noodle factories are on land rented from the army, which is a usual way for new businesses to operate. Nam wanted to secure his right to stay put on that land, so he offered a half share in his second production line to the army on a profit-share basis. They do not interfere with the operation. By doing this he hopes he has ensured that the army has its own strong interest in his retaining the site. Most of his machinery was made from metal goods bought from the army, which still has warehouses full of former US army equipment appropriated at 'liberation'. He is conscious of the importance of staying on the right side of officialdom. He says that without *doi moi* he would be nothing like as big as he is by now – the Vietnamese equivalent of a dollar millionaire at age 44.

Ngon has had to play his cards cautiously. A southerner from Tay Ninh province now aged 43, he was completing his education as the war ended. He looked for opportunities to make money and became involved in the export of sandalwood from Hué and Quang Tri in central Vietnam, across the border of his home province to Cambodia. At that time one kilogram could fetch US$100, which was a huge amount. After a while he was caught and told the trade was illegal. He was given a three year prison sentence – a year for each kilogram found on him at the time. He spent his sentence partly in Saigon, firstly in a solitary cell then in crowded communal conditions, where the food rations were particularly sparse. 'We were very afraid of diarrhoea because it spread so fast in those conditions,' he recalls. Finally he was taken to the provinces to do hard labour in the fields. (Nowadays he says prison conditions are better and with corruption rife it is possible for those with money to buy their way out of prison.)

On his release, Ngon turned his attention to trading in seafoods. On a small scale, this was allowed. His great opportunity came with *doi moi*, which he was able to exploit to his commercial advantage. With his acquired business skills he has now won orders to export shrimps, crabs, eels, squid and fish to China, Taiwan and Hong Kong. His supplies come mainly from the southern province of Minh Hai. He arranges for them to be frozen, except for the crabs which are exported live by air and the squid which is dried. It is very expensive to set up a refrigeration plant, so he has contracts with existing province-owned plants to do the freezing. He then brings his produce to Saigon for export by ship, or by plane to Hanoi and thence across the land border to southern China.

Ngon's business has expanded fast under *doi moi* and he now employs 22 people, whom he pays the equivalent of US$40-60 a month. But he still has worries and feels that he is by no means free of government control. For a start he is not allowed to do his own exporting; this has to be done through a state corporation. Although some private companies have permission to export, one of the conditions is financial: they must have the equivalent of US$500,000 in a bank deposit. Ngon is not willing to deposit his savings in a bank because he lacks confidence in the country's political leadership. 'They might reverse their economic policy at any time and then I would lose all I have built up. It would be back to the old system under which my family worked hard as farmers, only to see Party or government officials come and take away the products of our labour. I do not trust them not to do that again, so I keep my money secret', he explains. For every shipment abroad of his perishable goods, Ngon has to pay customs officials to ensure the goods are not delayed – 'it's a sort of bribe', he says. He wanted to go abroad to meet his customers in China and it cost him US$300 to 'buy' a passport. According to Ngon, everyone is 'on the make' and it is important to do things the right way if you want to get results.

'*Doi moi* has certainly been good for my business', says Ngon. 'Without it I would never have entered the export market.' Two-thirds of his produce is exported. He plans to travel abroad soon in search of a market for frogs legs. Reflecting on the difficult years under communist rule, he says 'I respect Ho Chi Minh – he was a true patriot who only served the country – but not Le Duan [the Communist Party leader who followed him]. He kept our country backward.' The biggest change to have come with *doi moi*, he believes, is that 'we now have choice; there is a choice of newspapers to read and our children are no longer indoctrinated in communist propaganda at school. Now they are taught loyalty to the country rather than to the Party and they learn about other systems as well.' He thinks the most important outcome of *doi moi* is that 'the minds of people in the north have changed and nobody cares about communism any more; they want their lives improved.' He admits to what would still be regarded as a vice, though he regards it as an important means of keeping in touch with the world. He has an unregistered satellite dish with which he can watch Star TV broadcasts, which carry the news from the BBC World Service.

Ha is a self-made businesswoman of 27 living in Saigon. Coming from a poor background in Danang, she completed secondary school but received no further education, but had a passable command of English. This enabled her to get a job in Vietnam's fledgling hotel industry. She learnt the hotel business well – as a telephone operator, housekeeper and reception desk assistant. Two years ago, while working at one of Saigon's best new hotels, the Century Saigon, she asked to be transferred to the gifts counter, where she believed she could learn a new trade. In her spare time, she started buying handicrafts herself and selling them to gift shops at other hotels. It was hard work with little profit; what profit there was came from narrow margins between her purchase price from the wholesaler – on credit after they got to know her – and the price at which she sold the goods on. She trades mainly in stone and marbleware, with some brass and silk gifts too. She approached another new hotel and persuaded them to let her have the gift shop concession there, for a price of course. She then felt bold enough to employ a sales assistant and eventually started employing craftsmen to copy ornate marble boxes she had brought from the Marble mountains, near her home town of Danang. Now she needed only to bring the marble, the handiwork being done in Saigon, giving her a considerable advantage in cost.

Her gift shop was doing so well that she gave up her $100 a month job at the Century Saigon. She had by this time won the position of consignor at another new hotel; their gift shop bought handicrafts from Ha and paid her at the end of the month. After she has paid rent for her stall to the hotel and some unofficial 'tax' to the hotel director and auditor her overheads are low. She can make a profit of $1,000 a month in the high season, $500 in the quieter times. From this she has been able to afford to build herself a house in a smart area of Saigon. She also married. Her husband, Huy, is an engineer working for a state shipping company. In his spare time he does private construction work and also attends English classes. Both are so busy that they seldom eat at home together. Ha's parents and younger sister also stay in her home. Huy is nine years older than Ha and her main worry is that if she does not give him a baby he will leave her. But she does not want children yet, saying she would need to give a child her full time attention for at least two years.

Ha says businesses need two assets to succeed, capital and contacts, yet she says initially she had neither! Her capital was saved out of her hotel salary and she got where she is by being pushy – by making approaches to the hotels where she now sells her goods. She believes the assets which have helped her were her good command of English, her knowledge of the hotel business and the access that working in hotels gave to foreign visitors. It undoubtedly helped too that she is very smart in appearance and full of charm, which is important when you are trying to sell something. Her disappointment is that her employed assistant is not so good at selling.

Ha has now been offered a job by a German businessman making garments in Saigon, for $300 a month and is considering whether to take it. She does not feel she can leave her business yet, because she has not found the right person to run it for her. None of her brothers or sisters is as business-orientated as she is. If Ha does accept the German offer it would be with a purpose – to learn more about business, another business. Her ambition? She would love to open a petrol station – 'I look at the numbers of motorbikes and cars coming on to the streets of Saigon and feel that has to be the future' – but it would require much more capital than she feels she can raise at present.

———— ❖ ————

All these people have benefited from *doi moi* – perhaps because they are capitalist-inclined, or had the right connections to be able to take advantage of opportunities when they arose. In that sense they are the fortunate ones. Most are confident that there will be no turning back of the clock. They believe the future is bright, hence all have ambitions to develop their businesses. There are plenty of others who are less fortunate or well-placed to take advantage of the economic reforms and opening up; plenty of young people especially who describe themselves as 'jobless', who lack the means to go into business on their own. Although employment opportunities have blossomed with *doi moi* and wages have been forced up, there are still many people unemployed or underemployed. They will not see the benefits of *doi moi* until they have jobs. In the meantime they suffer the consequences of the market system as it creates a divide between the 'haves' and 'have nots'. The authorities recognize that the gulf is widening and that as some people get richer others are in danger of getting poorer.

The Communist Party had wanted to build a society of equality in which nobody was very rich and nobody was very poor. Belatedly they realized there was not enough to go around in the first place and that everyone was getting poorer. *Doi moi* represents an acceptance that wealth has to be created first before it can be shared equally and that the encouragement of private initiative, the creation of incentives and the legalization of the profit motive are the means of doing so. More questionably, the party believes that the objectives of socialism and social justice remain attainable. Thus they are hoping to apply capitalist thinking to develop a 'commonwealth', in which the prosperity of the nation is shared by all, rather than allowing its people to continue to share the equality of poverty.

7

One Country or Two?

Hanoi and Ho Chi Minh City are well over 1,000 miles apart by road or rail. It takes less time to fly from either city to Hong Kong or Bangkok than it does to fly between them. Distance helps explain how different the cities are. But it was the formal separation of North Vietnam from South Vietnam for 31 years, from 1954 to 1975, during which Hanoi and Saigon were capital cities of different countries, that really led to the divergence in lifestyles between the two. Then it was not possible to travel between North and South, nor even to telephone or trade between the two halves. The division was as absolute as those in Germany and Korea, even for families split between North and South. Yet the decision at Geneva to partition the country along the 17th parallel had provided only for its 'temporary division' pending elections within two years.

After the two countries were reunified in 1975, the government tried hard to reunite not just the twin capitals but the northern and southern peoples as well. It tried to heal the wounds of war as well as those of prolonged separation. Reopening the railway between the northern and southern capitals was one such attempt. However the 'Reunification Express' which linked them at first took more than two days to connect two cities whose pace is so different. This served only to demonstrate just how different north and south Vietnam and their inhabitants are. Even today, the railway journey takes 36 hours at least. The train seems to be bridging a time warp of many years.

Language, culture and religions – which broadly were shared between north and south – had been eclipsed by divergent social and political attitudes and, most of all, by the differences in living standards. Even 20 years on from reunification, average per capita income in Ho Chi Minh City is nearly one and a half times that of Hanoi. Ho Chi Minh City has tried to make up for its loss of capital city status by taking on the role of commercial capital. *Doi moi* has demonstrated just how deeply ingrained capitalist thinking was in the south, although the instincts of northerners towards business do not seem much less in evidence even if they have been suppressed for rather longer. The learning curve in the north is longer, but once the essentials have been learned northerners have been proving just as adept at making money.

Differences between north and south are not simply about business acumen and ability to make money. Someone wanting to prove their suitability for a particular role may claim to have the shrewdness of the northerner, the diligence of somebody from central Vietnam and the joy of living of the southerner –reflecting what are perceived to be the positive characteristics of people from each part of the country. There are no doubts in the minds of southerners that they are the 'true' Vietnamese; they are inclined to regard northerners as virtual foreigners. Northerners are equally sure that they are the purest Vietnamese, a notion reinforced by their feeling that the south was polluted during the 1960s and 1970s by too much American influence. They accuse southerners of corrupting the Vietnamese language by the dialect spoken in the south.

This mutual animosity with its associated sense of superiority has its origins in pre-1954 history. The deep divisions tend to be reinforced from abroad where South Vietnamese émigrés reject reunification as a bad thing and keep alive the notion that one day the south may secede again. People from the centre are caught in the middle, though they have the advantage of being more acceptable to southerners than northerners are – as business partners for example – and a great deal more acceptable to northerners than are southerners! Both northerners and southerners have a tendency to patronize their brethren from 'impoverished' central Vietnam and to allude to their reputation for parsimony.

Attitudes towards recent Vietnamese history mark an even clearer distinction between north and south, much clearer in a way than between communists and non-communists. Northerners speak of the American war whilst southerners prefer to talk of the civil war. The north commemorates 30 April 1975 as the 'liberation' (*giai phong*) of Saigon while southerners are more inclined to view that key date in history as the 'fall' of Saigon. Those who fled from the south at that time and settled abroad go one stage further and mark the anniversary as 'the day of shame' (*quoc han*). From that day onwards attitudes diverge even further as northerners regard it as the moment of reunification, the accomplishment of Ho Chi Minh's dream and the nationalist struggle, whilst southerners see it as the beginning of the colonization of the south by the north. The fact that the flag used by North Vietnam before 1975 (and before 1945 by the Viet Minh) – a yellow star on a red background – was adopted in 1976 for the unified country rather proves that it was a takeover rather than a merger; that is the southerners' interpretation. (During the war the communist leadership used to refer to the 'Saigon puppet regime'. Now, in a rewriting of recent history, the polite form is to talk of 'the former Saigon Administration'.) Southerners are resentful of the takeover of the South saying they never aspired to take over the North but were merely defending their independence.

Older southerners hanker after the days when Saigon was their capital. It is as if communism does not enter into it – that was just something between Washington and Hanoi. In any case, say southerners, there is a lot more to reunification than bringing the country under one flag. Sending people to re-education camps – as the Communist Party did to many southerners after 1975 – is hardly a gesture of reconciliation, they say.

Southerners point to the large number of northerners who came south from 1975 onwards, with almost nobody going in the opposite direction. Northerners have been encouraged to settle not only in Ho Chi Minh City but in underpopulated southern regions, such as the Central Highlands, as well. Southerners believe they became second class citizens after 1975, which is part of the reason (together with a fear that they may suffer retribution and the pursuit of a more appealing lifestyle) that so many attempted and many succeeded in leaving the country. Continuing discrimination against those who served the former southern regime or the Americans tends to reinforce this view. The system of requiring a *ly lich*, or curriculum vitae, when applying for jobs prevents those with a tainted past from being appointed to government jobs. (In 1970s Indonesia a 'certificate of non-involvement' in the abortive communist coup of 1965 fulfilled a similar purpose.) Top jobs in Vietnam today are reserved for those who are trusted, which gives a distinct advantage to northerners, whether or not they are Party members, or indeed are best qualified. At least these days southern communists are well represented in government, which has not always been the case.

Nga, a 24 year old from Danang, is deaf in one ear as the result of an American bomb exploding during her childhood. Despite four years studying book-keeping she has been unable to find a job because, she says, her family have been discriminated against.

Nga's father worked for the Americans before 1975. Now he rides a *cyclo*. Her mother, who is too ill to work, used to be a market trader. Both *cyclo* riding and market trading are jobs associated with having an unsatisfactory *ly lich*. Nga herself tried selling lottery tickets but that does not bring much income. She knows that with her qualifications she could be earning a decent income. She lives with her parents and other family members, totalling seven, in a one-roomed house. They have no television. While agreeing that *doi moi* is a good thing, Nga has not herself been able to capitalize on the reforms and complains that the government is still 'too communist', a familiar southern refrain. She feels that she and her family have been the victims rather than the beneficiaries of the communist era – and that as southerners they have borne more than their share of punishment for losing the war.

Southerners may secretly smile at the way the north has now come round to the south's way of economic thinking. They joke that it is now the northerners who are going through re-education – to learn what the southerners know already! But they cannot help questioning why they had to go through so much hardship and family separation before reaching this point. As with the separated peoples of Germany, China and Korea, it will take more than a generation to erase the bitter feelings of resentment felt in Vietnam by southerners towards the north and its leadership – although the deepest feelings of bitterness have gone into exile abroad with the boat people and other émigrés. Most former inmates of re-education camps have emigrated, but those remaining are bitter about their treatment, if a little bemused by the turn of events that now has the Communist Party all but admitting that the southern way was the right way after all.

One ironic consequence of *doi moi* is that it has created a need for skills that northerners tend not to have. Much in demand, for example, is knowledge of English, which became the main foreign language in the south after 1954 and is now the second language throughout the country. Proficient speakers of English are in such high demand that even rehabilitating the former southern élite cannot provide enough to meet current demand. As a result there is an incredible hunger to learn in both north and south, a hunger satisfied to some extent by evening classes. The Ministry of Education has estimated that as many as 300,000 people are studying English at evening classes. In 1994 the Prime Minister decreed that all senior government officials below the age of 45 must learn English to stay in their jobs, although other relevant foreign languages, like French or Chinese, are acceptable alternatives. Russian, more understood in the north than the south, is not particularly relevant these days, so once again southerners tend to be better equipped with the relevant needs of the moment.

Southerners inevitably see Ho Chi Minh in a rather different light too. The older generation do not venerate or respect him because they see him as the inspiration for the north's colonization of the south. They are disinclined to pay homage to Ho, for example by visiting his mausoleum in Hanoi. They do not necessarily see him as the patriot of Party propaganda, as communism was in any case an import from the West, although they respect his role in getting rid of foreign domination. Even southerners pay lip service to the notion that Vietnam is better off without foreign rule although, as already observed, they have plenty of reservations about northern rule.

Animosity between northerners and southerners is all-pervasive, but this is not the only way the country is divided. *Doi moi* notwithstanding, Communist Party membership still identifies the élite that wields power, although it is no longer invariably the case that senior officials belong to the Party. Members of the Party tend to be less well educated. Because of the war they lacked opportunity and, conversely, the less well educated, especially from poor rural areas, are more inclined to join the Party. Communist Party membership has been something of a passport to a good job but that is changing and skills and qualifications are counting for more in the new Vietnam. That process, with its inevitable corollary of the reduction of Communist Party power, is happening faster than many people realize – hastened by the strong demand for well educated and trained workers from both foreign and domestic enterprises under *doi moi*. The Party's justifiably proud boast that Vietnam has a pool of literate and highly disciplined workers is no longer enough. Businesses want language, computing, managerial and commercial skills as well. Even the 'disciplined' bit is becoming less true. Workers are less afraid to go on strike for more money than in the past, especially against foreign employers.

A foreigner working in Vietnam tells of a meeting at a hotel in Vung Tau, the southern beach resort and oil industry town. He was dealing with the local People's Committee, which administers the town on behalf of the Party. The catering was in the charge of the hotel catering manager, who had been trained in the USA before 1975 and has now been allowed to return to his field of expertise after years in the wilderness doing something he was not very good at. The foreigner describes it as very much a meeting of two cultures: the suave, highly professional catering manager anticipating and meeting his clients' needs, whilst the unsophisticated and uneducated People's Committee chairman looked on with evident disapproval, trying to absorb the lessons of the episode. These are that if you want foreign collaboration and cooperation, as Vung Tau does, then you have to meet your prospective partners on their terms and that service is a key ingredient of a business relationship. The catering manager understood these facts but the People's Committee chairman was having considerable difficulty doing so – and yet he knew that he must try. The vignette provides a powerful example of the distrust and tension that still exists between those brought up according to radically different ideological traditions.

While Communist Party members still wield power, they are increasingly under challenge (even siege) from those whose power comes from their economic muscle. The entrepreneurs are wise enough to know that the Party matters and that they need to support it and look after it if their businesses are to prosper. This does not mean they have to join the Party, but that they have to win its favour in other ways. Helping them carry on their own businesses is one obvious way. In fact the wise businessman will ensure he has friends in both the local Party organization and the army before setting up a new business. What complicates the issue is that close relatives of Communist Party members often belong to the new commercial class, because they have had the contacts to get the necessary permission to engage in business. It is a classic case of power corrupting, since Party members have been best placed to exploit the new opportunities presented by *doi moi*.

For example, the son of former Communist Party General Secretary Le Duan (who died before the onset of *doi moi*) is a successful Hanoi businessman controlling, among other things, the supply of spare parts for Russian aircraft operated by the airlines of Vietnam, Laos and Cambodia. He also owns a food processing plant whose output is mainly exported to Eastern Europe. In both trade dealings he was helped by contacts he made while studying in Eastern Europe, as the privileged son of a senior Party member. The so-called 'red capitalists' are now as strong in southern Vietnam as they are in the north. Their strength derives as much from their connections within the Party, which is of course nominally in power everywhere, as from their business acumen.

Though the Communist Party leadership in Hanoi today may look like an oligarchy, it is as factionalized as any group of leaders anywhere. A more open atmosphere in the country makes it easier for outsiders to identify the factions. In power at present are the non-intellectuals: President Le Duc Anh is a former rubber plantation worker; Communist Party General Secretary Do Muoi was a house painter, while Prime Minister Vo Van Kiet used to work as a porter at a cement factory in the extreme south-western district of Ha Tien. He was the victor in a power struggle during 1991 which led to the ousting of the architect of *doi moi*, Nguyen Van Linh, who leads a quiet life in Ho Chi Minh City these days. Today's leadership is at least more open than previously to the views of intellectuals, several of whom have exerted important influences on government policy. However, Prime Minister Vo Van Kiet is believed to favour another uneducated man of peasant stock, vice speaker of the National Assembly Nguyen Ha Phan, to succeed him, which has angered some of the so-called 'thinkers' within the Party.

National Assembly elections are due in 1997, preceded in 1996 by the eighth congress of the Communist Party. Jockeying for position is underway between hardliners and moderates, as well as between northerners, central Vietnamese and southerners and between intellectuals and non-intellectuals. No one doubts that the Communist Party will still be powerful, or expects any more than token non-members to be elected to the Assembly, even though the influence the Party wields over government is in decline. The challenge for the present leadership of the Party is to usher in a modicum of political reform although not enough to threaten its hold on power. 'As long as most of the people are happy with the progress of reforms they will not rebel against the Party's monopoly of power', runs the argument of the enlightened wing of the Party. They need no convincing these days, after the crisis years of the early 1980s, that the Party has to earn the people's respect and support. It is true too that the Party's future is inextricably tied up with the satisfactory progress of *doi moi*.

One southern intellectual believes the challenge to the Party leadership will come not so much from a demand for political pluralism as out of a sense of injustice as people see the sons and daughters of Communist Party members getting the best jobs, opportunities to study abroad and preferment in the granting of business licences. He says the Communist Party professes to be committed to social justice, yet its members are themselves taking advantage of their positions, either directly or through relatives. That at any rate is how it is seen by outsiders. He says foreign companies are especially guilty of hiring 'red capitalists' because they believe that in doing so they are buying government support. This new élite, most of whom have no ideological commitment or interest in the Party whatsoever, are resented in both the north and the south. In Ho Chi Minh City, antagonism towards them is stronger than towards northerners.

The Party in Ho Chi Minh City is in any case deeply factionalized. The forthcoming Party congress provides a focus of competition and there is constant rivalry for seats on the People's Committee, which runs the city on the Party's (rather than the people's) behalf. Some people see Ho Chi Minh City People's Committee as the most powerful institution in the country, so great is its power in deciding who gets permission to open what business enterprise. It is also rich with interests in many of the city's commercial activities, including hotels, the Phu Tho race track and the Tan Thuan Export Processing Zone, a joint venture with a Taiwanese company. Just as the Governor of China's Guangdong province is thought to wield more power than the political leadership in Beijing by virtue of the province's economic strength, it may be true that the Ho Chi Minh City People's Committee wields more power than the central government in Hanoi, by virtue of its economic muscle. Such matters are difficult to judge other than hypothetically since the two bodies are unlikely ever to oppose each other.

However, it is undoubtedly true that the leadership in Hanoi are wary of the leadership in Ho Chi Minh City, its power, its wealth and its connections. This is manifest in the slowness in approving business ventures in the south and the unwritten rule that foreign companies and banks should have an office in Hanoi before opening representative offices in the southern city. The same sort of hesitation has characterized Hanoi's attitude towards opening a stock exchange in Ho Chi Minh City. Commentators say the southern China parallel is particularly relevant. Hanoi apparently wants to avoid what happened there, where Shenzen and Hainan allegedly 'jumped the gun' in opening capital markets while Beijing was trying to establish one in Shanghai to serve the whole country. Hanoi wants first to establish a proper regulatory system before allowing financiers in Ho Chi Minh City to begin share trading. There has also been a certain amount of commercial rivalry between the two centres over control of state operated enterprises. For example, Saigon Brewery 'belongs' to the Ministry of Light Industry, which benefits from profits made on its popular '333' beer.

Ho Chi Minh City authorities receive no benefit from this state enterprise within their domain and are unable even to enforce local regulations against this organ of central government.[1]

What one foreign journalist describes as 'paranoia towards the south' is even more evident with overseas news organizations which have not been permitted to open offices in Ho Chi Minh City, or even employ local journalists as 'stringers' there. This illustrates the leadership's determination to hold on to the reins of power, which are in any case slipping. Local news organizations too are very much beholden to the Ministry of Culture in Hanoi, which regulates the press and in effect controls whom they hire and fire. Despite the 'opening up', all newspapers and magazines need a licence to publish and are in effect under fairly tight state control. How tight varies according to the political atmosphere, but the press (especially in Saigon) feels less free in the mid-1990s than it did during the first flush of *doi moi*.

The city of Hanoi is built around more than 20 lakes, of which the central one is Ho Hoan Kiem, or the Lake of the Restored Sword. Legend has it that the 15th-century king, Le Loi, having found a sword which he used to defend the city against Chinese domination, gave it to a golden turtle who appeared in the lake and carried it off in his mouth. The King believed that the sword had been sent to him by the gods and, when he had accomplished the task for which it was intended, the turtle had been sent for him to restore the sword to the gods. Thus he gave the lake its name. Another lake is called the Lovers' Lake, while the large West Lake, which marks the northern extremity of the city, is also a favourite outing spot for lovers. The Red River provides the eastern boundary to the city.

Hanoi is more like a series of villages, some of which have grown into towns but without destroying the trees which are one of its most appealing characteristics. The expansion of the city outwards has been especially rapid during the early 1990s. Old Hanoi, to the north of the Restored Sword Lake, remains village-like – a series of 36 narrow streets named after the merchandise formerly sold there: Hang Gai was the street of the jute sellers, Hang Bun for rice noodle merchants, Hang Bac for the jewellers

---

[1] This section has benefited from Laurence J Brahm and Hoang Ngoc Nguyen, 'Capital Vietnam – the making of a market', *Business Vietnam*, August-September 1994.

and so on. This area is renowned for its 'tube houses' that stretch a long way back from the street providing shop front and family accommodation on one level, or sometimes two. Some such houses are less than two metres wide. It is a characteristic of Vietnamese building these days, not just in Hanoi, that buildings expand upwards. A two-storey dwelling becomes a three- or four-storey one as soon as funds permit, providing a visual indication of the wealth of the owner.

One of the most distinctive and attractive features of Hanoi is its French colonial architecture, although much is in a run down state after years of neglect. Diplomatic missions and foreign firms have taken over some of the best property and restored it. For example, the Australia New Zealand Bank has beautifully restored the lakeside former residence of the French deputy governor general of Tonkin which, until the bank acquired it, had been a Communist Party printing press. In that capacity its physical appearance had not been a priority. Finding people with the skills to restore the building was not easy, according to a senior bank official. Government-owned villas are much less well maintained and many now provide homes for several families.

Hanoi is probably the least spoilt capital in South East Asia. Some might say that is the consequence of being the least modern, or most backward. Now there are worries amongst some Hanoians and foreign residents that the rapid opening up of the country and its 'invasion' by foreign business people risks destroying the city's charm for commercial interests. Indeed, they joke that what American B-52 bombers failed to do, commercial warriors are now attempting! As a result of *doi moi* the economic imperative has suddenly become very strong in Vietnam. The mini-hotel is a typical example of what one foreigner concerned for the city's heritage describes as 'short termism'. He describes what happens: 'They expand their property upwards with no regard to skyline or aesthetics and without getting permission, then advertise themselves as a mini-hotel. Given Hanoi's shortage of hotel rooms, the investment will pay for itself within a year and cover any fine levied for unapproved building. Once costs are paid, the owner is likely to invest his profits into developing more mini-hotels, perhaps even two or three at once.'

To combat uncontrolled building and to try to restore some of the city's former grandeur, a group of foreign residents of the city has formed the Friends of Hanoi. The former Australian prime minister, Gough Whitlam, is its patron. The Friends are working closely with the City Architect to try to ensure that any city development is planned and controlled rather than spasmodic and unauthorized. They are particularly anxious to preserve ancient areas like the 36 streets of old Hanoi. They have a hard task on their hands as restoration and preservation do not feature on government budgets. The difficulty of their task can be gauged by the scandal of the Yen Phu-Nhat Tan dyke, just outside Hanoi. In early 1995 it was found that many well-connected families had built themselves villas on and under the dyke over several years, despite it being a protected area where building was not permitted. The buildings weakened the dyke which had started to crack in a number of places, threatening to breach and cause flooding in the rainy season. As questions were asked in newspapers about how the owners had acquired the rights to use the land – which remain tightly controlled – the Prime Minister ordered that up to a thousand illegally constructed homes be demolished. The episode was considered an important test for the rule of law. In Hanoi it was said that two dykes needed shoring up: one against the water and another against those who break the law! On this occasion the rule of law won.

The UN Educational Scientific and Cultural Organization (UNESCO), was approached to help with the preservation of old Hanoi, but declined – possibly because it is already funding extensive restoration work at the former imperial capital of Hué. However, private foreign firms have seen preservation of the city as a worthy cause and have helped to sponsor the Friends and their activities. American Express has promised funding for restoration work at the Temple of Literature, the city's ancient seat of learning dedicated to Confucius, founded in 1070 – well before Oxford or Cambridge. One of the most attractive buildings from the French era is the Opera. Built in 1911, it was modelled on the Paris Opera but is two-thirds its size. Nowadays it is used for concerts of Western classical music and, in another sign of changed times, also hosts fashion shows and beauty pageants.

Hanoians are proud of their characterful city and its reputation as a seat of learning. It may not have been Vietnam's first capital, but they will constantly remind you that the Red River valley is the cradle of Vietnamese civilization. They seem to be making a point aimed at their southern countrymen. But Hanoians are not immune from commercial imperatives and there are plenty of plans afoot for developing the city, mostly involving foreign investors. A Singapore development company, for example, planned to build a block with two 20-storey towers, combining a hotel, shopping mall, offices and a convention centre, on the site of the 'Hanoi Hilton' – as American prisoners of war jokingly called the prison in central Hanoi where they were held during the war. Earlier, Hoa Lo prison (as it is properly called) had been used by the French to incarcerate nationalists, many of whom were guillotined within the prison walls. Aside from the issue of whether that particular piece of history should be preserved, the Friends were concerned at the proposed height. They had succeeded in blocking one high rise hotel project and subsequently helped bring about a ruling by the city authorities that no central Hanoi development should be taller than the city post office. The Friends are battling against commercial imperatives as developers know the taller they can build the higher their profits will be. In an effort to preserve the city's skyline, the Friends have proposed building a 'mini-Manhattan' of skyscrapers away from the city, further into the Red River delta.

At rush hour Hanoi's streets are a swarm of bicycles and motorbikes transporting Hanoians to and from work. The city seems to have been built for two-wheelers and the arrival of cars is causing the planners considerable problems. (There are estimated to be around 3 million motorbikes but only about 300,000 four-wheeled vehicles, although the latter figure is growing quickly.) Public transport is virtually non-existent, which may be the reason Vietnamese in Hanoi and elsewhere are used to depending on their own two wheels for getting around. It would take a great deal of persuasion (or bribery) to get them to try any other way.

Hanoians tend to dress more conservatively than people in the south, probably as a result of many years of austerity. Northern women are less inclined to wear the *ao dai*, Vietnam's attractive female national dress, than are southern women. Women in the north wear a short tunic over the near universal slacks or trousers. It is rare to see women in Hanoi wearing a dress, though not uncommon in Saigon. In all respects, Vietnamese women 'wear the trousers'. However, *doi moi* has revived an interest in fashion and cosmetics in both north and south and new, trendy fashion magazines carry a mix of traditional and Western designs. Such fashions remain for the time being the preserve of the relatively wealthy. Some people deplore the influence of foreign fashions in a country which prides itself on its traditional apparel, considering it to be a dilution of national identity and one of the less savoury side-effects of *doi moi*.

Early morning is the time for mature Hanoians to do their

exercises in public, at a street corner or on the shores of one of the lakes, while others are going to market to buy or sell produce. Young Hanoians are more night orientated; drinking draught beer (*bia hoi*) at a pavement bar is a popular, mainly male pastime, whilst both sexes enjoy café life, the taste of an iced coffee and live Western pop music, these days including singing after years during which Western lyrics were banned. Several hotels have live bands or discotheques which are frequented by young Vietnamese and foreigners alike. Such entertainment centres are often financed with money from Saigon and run as joint ventures with the Hanoi People's Committee, giving them a level of official approval.

Karaoke bars are enormously popular as they are throughout South East Asia. Ironically, many of the Vietnamese language karaoke video tapes are recorded by the Vietnamese community in California and smuggled into the country. There are strict controls on imports of video tapes because the authorities are said to have intercepted subversive messages or statements from overseas groups allegedly bent on overthrowing Vietnam's communist government. Paranoia or not, the flow of karaoke videos from California is another example of Vietnam's links with its overseas communities. Video cafés, where customers can watch feature films while drinking coffee, became popular in the city after *doi moi* and now are popular in rural areas too. Though hard to obtain, American Vietnam war movies are especially popular. *Doi moi*, with its less prescriptive lifestyle, has definitely made Hanoians more relaxed, more outward going, more natural. It has also unleashed a new spirit of enterprise in which the pursuit of money has become the overriding preoccupation.

Motorbike riding is strictly regulated by the police, although a foreigner visiting Hanoi may not believe it. Insurance is compulsory for all but the least powerful bikes. However a phenomenon which arrived in the capital in the mid-1990s from Saigon is causing the authorities some anxiety. This is motorbike racing on the city streets on Saturday or Sunday nights. One such race during the mid-autumn festival in 1994 caused the deaths of a number of bystanders. The most worrying aspect for the authorities was the way the bikers ignored the police and even engaged in brawls with them. According to some sources, the owners of the most powerful motorbikes are the children of senior Communist Party officials who apparently feel they are inviolate. Other sources say the sport is born out of the frustration of unemployed youth, though clearly participants in the racing are rich enough to own fast motorbikes.

This apparent breakdown of authority and lack of respect for those trying to enforce it is viewed by people close to the centre of power as the major law and order challenge of the moment, the most visible sign of social unrest and another adverse consequence of the relaxation of controls brought about by *doi moi*.

Saigon is an altogether brasher city where it is said 'anything goes'. So the prospect of a foreign consortium bidding to build Vietnam's tallest building 36 storeys high in downtown Saigon raises few eyebrows. The city was developing madly and seemingly with few controls before 1975 and is now doing so once more. Of course there are controls, but somehow it seems easier for developers to get permission to proceed than in Hanoi. Saigon together with Cholon, its adjoining twin city (a 'Siamese twin' as writer Norman Lewis rather incongruously called it[2], have always been bigger and more bustling cities where making money and enjoying oneself are ways of life. Nowadays, both Saigon and Cholon show evidence of having returned to their rather debauched night life of pre-1975 days.

Saigon is larger than Hanoi and its streets are wider. If the city lacks the character of the northern city it does have more of the air of a capital city about it. The grand French-built town hall – now occupied by the Ho Chi Minh City People's Committee – provides an attractive centre-piece, although there is currently some amusement (and even anger) that the planners failed to anticipate how a new office block would tower over it. Nearby Doc Lap (Independence) Palace, the former residence of the presidents of South Vietnam through whose gates North Vietnamese tanks burst on 30 April 1975, lacks a proper role. Renamed Reunification Hall, it is preserved as a museum and exhibition centre. The organizers of a trade show of US products in late 1994 failed to see the irony of using this symbol of the US 'puppet government' for such a purpose. The museum was closed for several days as US businessmen rode in their cars through those same iron gates to display goods that they hope to be allowed to market in Vietnam.

The new prosperity of Saigon is apparent from the neon advertisements, the rapidly increasing numbers of Japanese cars and the speed and extent of new building projects – especially hotels, office blocks and housing for foreigners across the Saigon river in the affluent Thu Duc suburb. From a mere three international standard hotels a few years ago, which were then sufficient for the

---

[2] In his 1950s travel book, *A Dragon Apparent*, Jonathan Cape, London, 1951.

small numbers of foreign visitors, the city now has well over 20 with more opening by the month. Saigon's streets are struggling to cope with the increased flow of vehicles. As in Hanoi, four-wheelers are uneasily accommodated alongside two-wheelers, creating a much more serious problem than yet confronts Hanoi because there are so many more of all types of vehicle in Saigon. Both cities are bursting at their seams, underlining the inadequacy of housing, roads and other utilities like electricity and water supplies. This is an undoubted consequence of *doi moi* with its economic opportunities and the associated relaxation of controls on internal travel. Saigon does retain strict conditions for migration into the city, but these are widely evaded and the revived economic activity of the city serves as a magnet to the rural unemployed. Its population is thought now to be in excess of 4 million, while even that of 'sedate' Hanoi has topped 3 million. It is the slums on the edges of the city that are expanding most rapidly, as well as the salubrious suburbs most attractive to foreign residents.

Saigon is clearly the commercial capital. Its outskirts accommodate many factories and through its port passes the vast majority of Vietnam's imports and exports. Close to Saigon port, on the south side of the city, is Vietnam's first export processing zone, where tax incentives and guaranteed electrical power are designed to attract foreign, export-orientated, companies. To the north, the former US base at Bien Hoa is being turned into another industrial zone. Heavy trucks ply the route between Bien Hoa and Saigon; much heavy industry is located in the area. Saigon itself has a commercial feel about it, from the street hawkers to the numbers of shops, the billboards and the foreign business visitors. The city is almost unrecognizable from the austere communist-run city of the 1980s, which was in turn a poor shadow of its pre-1975 self. Nowadays, it seems to be making up for lost time in trying to emulate Bangkok, Jakarta and Manila and other chaotic but commercially prospering South East Asian capitals.

One means of doing so is to encourage tourism, with an unashamed attempt to cash in on the relics of war, an 'advantage' Vietnam has over its neighbours which it is quick to exploit. The city's War Crimes Exhibition is a popular if propagandist destination for visitors. The word 'American' has been dropped from its name in the interest of cultivating links with the USA! The most popular tourist attraction is the former US Embassy building from whose roof evacuating helicopters carried American diplomats and senior figures of the former South Vietnam regime, an episode immortalized in the musical *Miss Saigon*. Returning GIs can take a drink at the Apocalypse Now bar, buy a Ho Chi Minh T-shirt or a toy American jet fighter fashioned out of a Coca Cola can. Not far from Saigon, tourists are guided around the tunnels at Cu Chi from which the communists infiltrated Saigon. Tourists including Americans are eager to buy as souvenirs samples of the hammocks on which communist guerillas slept. A particular tourist 'attraction' at the tunnels is the deadly 'Viet Cong' spiked punji trap.

A southern professional in his forties visiting Hanoi for the first time was struck by the poverty of people in the north. 'Outwardly they are smart and proud', he said, 'but go into their homes and you realise they have much less than we do; their poverty shows.' He exhibits feelings of compassion towards the north and self-satisfaction towards his own circumstances. He displays some resentment too at the way northerners have moved south since reunification to take advantage of opportunities there. He seems to be comparing the northerners who have settled in the south with the 'economic migrants' from southern Vietnam now living abroad.

The north is poorer than the south as a result of intense pressure on the land, the quality of the soil and years of socialism. The climatic and geographical differences cause northerners to think of southerners as lazy because 'they do not have to work hard for things to grow, yet they are always eating and drinking and never save; they make money and spend it.' The southern professional agrees that northerners are more hard-working and thrifty, characteristics he feels are born of necessity, but feels they do not have much to show for their labours.

A northern professional of similar age, who first went to the south in her twenties after reunification and has regularly been back since, was surprised to find how aloof and self-sufficient people are in the south. She says it was easy to imagine she was in a different country: 'In the north we are much more socialist and we care about each other. If you have a problem the word gets around fast and people come to help. In the south, you have to ask for help; it does not come otherwise.' She believes the fact that northerners have not been able to own property has made them more 'collective' and more used to sharing things, including time and companionship. Southerners spend more time on their own. 'They seem to relish their own company', she says. On her first visit to Ho Chi Minh

City in 1976 she stayed for three months in the house of her father's brother. She felt ignored and very lonely at first and was sad at the lack of attention paid to her. Communication with her cousins was difficult – not a matter of language so much as understanding.

She believes there are advantages and disadvantages in what she calls 'the southern way'. The north may be a more caring society, but it is more gossipy and there is less privacy for the individual, who is brought up not to expect privacy. 'In the north your business is everybody's business', she says, 'the south is a less caring society, but on the positive side there is less interference, less gossip, more personal independence.' She believes the pursuit of equality has had bad consequences in the north: 'For example, relations between adults and children are such that children do not respect or obey their parents or teachers.' She prefers teachers to be more severe and children to respect adults. Overall this daughter of Hanoi, who has also travelled abroad to both communist and non-communist countries, favours the atmosphere in the south. 'It is closer to foreigners' style', she says. But she has too many friends in the north and would not dream of moving south.

8

Down Highway One

Only a small proportion of Vietnam's 72 million inhabitants live in Hanoi or Ho Chi Minh City. Around 65 million live in towns and villages elsewhere, the greatest concentrations in the fertile Mekong and Red River deltas. Otherwise, the narrow coastal strip of land through which road and rail links between Hanoi and Ho Chi Minh City pass is the most heavily populated, reflecting both the fertility of the soil and the access to the rich pickings of the sea. The debate about differences between northern and southern Vietnam tends to overlook the 'third' Vietnam outside the two main cities: the countryside, where 80% of Vietnamese live.

The best way to discover that 'third' Vietnam is to travel the length of the country along Highway One. A route rich in history and immortalized by war, Highway One bears witness to the economic and social life of Vietnam today.[1] It is the physical link between Hanoi and Ho Chi Minh City – the proof that they are of one nation if distant from one another in space and time. In a significant rewriting of history, the government has recently acknowledged that it was the first emperor of the Nguyen dynasty, Gia Long, who first united the country in the early 19th century. He sealed that unity by building the road linking its two halves together. During French times, the road was known as the Mandarin Way. Emperor Gia Long transferred the capital from Hanoi to the city of Hué, which lies at roughly the mid-point on the north–south route.

Highway One actually begins at Lang Son, close to the Chinese border and 107 miles north of Hanoi. Lang Son was badly damaged during the Chinese incursion of 1979, but is now fast recovering following the normalization of Sino-Vietnamese relations in 1991.

[1] Two other books tell in greater detail of the journey through Vietnam: Justin Wintle, *Romancing Vietnam*, Viking Press, London, 1991 and Sue Downie, *Down Highway One*, Allen and Unwin, Sydney, 1992.

The growth in cross-border trade has caused the city to prosper and helped to compensate for the poverty of the province, which has only one harvest a year and has to bring rice from elsewhere. The northern border is the most mountainous part of Vietnam although Lang Son province does not reach the altitudes found further west, where Vietnam borders Laos and where few people live. Forest cover is sparse in the mountains, a result of slash and burn agriculture and the use of firewood for cooking rather than the defoliation of war which did not have any impact this far north.

This mountainous border region that separates China from the Red River valley is called Viet Bac. It is sometimes dubbed 'the cradle of the revolution' because it was within these mountains that the Viet Minh were formed in 1941 to resist Japanese and French rule. The region is home to many of Vietnam's minority ethnic groups, who provide an 'ethnic buffer' against China. Around 88% of Vietnamese are ethnically classified as *kinh*, the remainder belong to 53 other ethnic groups. These tribes are assimilated with the majority, imbued with a Vietnamese identity and have little in common with members of the same tribes on the Chinese side of the frontier.

The inhabitants of this northernmost region of the country are more inclined to regard the Chinese as their 'enemy' than the Americans or French, for Vietnamese history is dominated by episodes of resistance to Chinese incursions across the 700-mile border. The 1979 conflict was only the most recent and briefest such incursion. Now China and Vietnam are at peace once more although, with the unresolved maritime dispute, it is a somewhat uneasy peace. There is a high level of trade across the frontier, much of it illegal. The Vietnamese believe the Chinese are dumping cheap goods in Vietnam, in the process undermining its own manufacturing capacity. Besides the road, the railway line from Hanoi crosses into China, although the gauges are different necessitating a change of bogeys if trains are once again to connect the two countries. As yet there are no through services from Vietnam to Nanning, the nearest Chinese city.

Leaving Viet Bac, Highway One enters the Red River delta, the densely-populated northern rice growing region criss-crossed by an elaborate system of dykes and canals that nourish the rice paddy. The traveller becomes aware of men and women working in the paddy fields, wearing the distinctively Vietnamese *non* or conical palm leaf hat for protection against both rain and sun. On the map the country's two main deltas, the Red River and the Mekong, give

Thien Mu Pagoda in the imperial city of Hué is regarded as a centre of Buddhist opposition to the government – as it was to the former Saigon government in the 1960s.

Lenin presides over a park in Hanoi though his economic legacy is no longer in evidence in Vietnam.

Hanoi's charm derives from its mix of traditional Vietnamese and French colonial architecture. The Opera House, modelled on the Paris Opera, is adorned by Communist Party slogans but most often used nowadays for classical Western music concerts or for fashion shows.

Vietnamese immigrant workers control the fishing industry along the coastline of Texas – a tradition they brought from Vietnam.

Little Saigon is a thriving business district of Orange County, Southern California – home from home for the region's large Vietnamese community.

For 21 years, from 1954 to 1975, Vietnam was divided into two countries along the 17th parallel. The frontier crossing at the Ben Hai river is now open but the peoples of the south and north remain divided by their differing levels of prosperity.

General Giap, hero of Vietnam's May 1954 defeat of the French at Dien Bien Phu, Commander in Chief during the 'American' war and an important political figure in post-war Vietnam, talks to the author in November 1994 about doi moi *and the nature of socialism.*

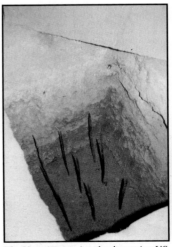

The Vietnam war involved massive US bombing and the use of napalm; communist tactics were just as brutal if less sophisticated. An example is the deadly punji *trap.*

This church alongside Highway One stands as a memorial to the devastating fighting for control of Quang Tri province which followed the peace accords of January 1973.

A fashion show at Hanoi Opera House. Fashion is now big business, spawning magazines and expensive clothers which only an élite can afford. Before doi moi *this show would not have been permitted.*

War veteran and author Bao Ninh whose book Sorrow of War *seems to question whether the war was worth it, Its publication signified a more relaxed official attitude to literature.*

Newly wealthy inhabitants of Hanoi build their houses upwards, perhaps opening a 'mini-hotel', one of the easiest ways to make money.

the country an appearance of symmetry. But the deltas are as different in appearance and in the life-styles of the peoples that inhabit them as are the cities that dominate them. What they do share is high fertility and consequent high population density: 40% of Vietnamese live in one or other of the deltas which between them constitute just 17% of the land area. Hanoi is reached by crossing the relatively new Chuong Duong road bridge across the Red River's main channel. No longer does Highway One have to share the old Long Bien railway bridge which was much bombed during the war. Nowadays three bridges connect the capital with the north, facilitating trade with China and linking Hanoi with the north eastern coal-mining region of Quang Ninh.

From Hanoi, the road southward passes through flat agricultural countryside with few distinguishing features. Soon mountains appear in the west which will continue to shadow the road until just before Saigon. To the east the sea, never far away, is sometimes close enough to view. Not far from Hanoi the road joins up with the railway line, the companion that accompanies it for most of the journey to the southern capital. The French called the railway 'le Trans-Indochinois'; nowadays the fastest train is called the Reunification Express. The line was a particular target of US bombing in the north and of communist sabotage in the south. Bringing it back into service after the war required the rebuilding of 1,334 bridges, 27 tunnels and 158 stations. The railway is under-utilized, which is just as well as there are an enormous number of road–rail crossings and road traffic is brought to a halt when a train is due. Being single track, trains have to wait at stations to pass one another, slowing them down considerably. The train straddles the enormous distance between Hanoi and Ho Chi Minh City, but taking at least 36 hours to do so at an average speed of 30 miles per hour it is one of the slowest railway journeys between major cities anywhere. Flying takes only one and a half hours but is much more expensive.

There is always the bus, the cheapest form of travel. Buses come in many vintages from the oldest Russian-made models to the latest Japanese. They are always packed tight with people: since fares are regulated by government, the only way to make more money is to cram more people inside! Not many people make the whole journey in one go. That takes three day because of the poor condition of the road. Heavy trucks carrying goods between the two halves of the country also use the road. Like the buses, they are dangerously overloaded and not infrequently leave the road, or axles buckle under the excess weight! The trucks bring Chinese goods south and carry textiles, shoes, processed foods and drinks and plastic household goods northwards. Highway One is Vietnam's main trade artery. Without this important link, north and south would still be two countries. Traffic moves at the pace of the slowest vehicles, slowing in towns to the speed of motorbikes, bicycles and pedestrians. Bicycles, the main means of transport in the countryside and small towns, are often heavily laden with vegetables bound for market and it is common to see a pig or a goat carried on the back of a motorbike! Colourful markets take place along the roadside. For those buying and selling, Highway One is nothing more than the main street of their town, lacking any greater significance as an artery connecting the north and south of the country. Highway One serves these twin roles. The Highway doubles up in another respect when it carries the railway track over river bridges. Road vehicles wait as the train takes priority.

The countryside changes but the homes that line the road are remarkably constant: stone or brick built, faced with concrete painted pastel green, blue or ochre and roofed with neat terracotta tiles. Even homes built of mud are usually topped by tiles. Some houses have marbled fronts, marble being produced in central Vietnam. Homes are strong enough to withstand the sometimes severe coastal weather. Inland in the highlands, wooden houses with thatched roofing are more common. Vegetables are grown in neat rows between the house and the highway. The Vietnamese are good at using all available space to grow food.

The first sizeable city after leaving the Red River delta is the port city of Vinh, capital of Nghe An province and gateway to Annam, as the French called the central part of the country. Vinh was the first place to be bombed by the Americans, a response to the Gulf of Tonkin incident. Vinh was previously bombed extensively by the French in their fight against the Viet Minh and later by the Americans who believed the port was being used to ship arms to communist guerrillas in the south via the infamous Ho Chi Minh trail, so hardly a building of the old city remained undamaged. It was subsequently rebuilt by East Germany and has an austere, functional air about it. (Vinh used to be 'twinned' with East Berlin.) High rise apartment blocks hardly seem appropriate in this spacious coastal city. Nowadays Vinh is not an important port except for land-locked Laos for which it provides access to the sea. Two roads across the Truong Son mountain range connect Vinh with Laos – bringing down its timber for export and taking up all manner of imported consumer items. Neither road is open to ordinary travellers, though there are plans to develop one of them as part of an Asian highway network.

The former French protectorate of Annam – modern day central Vietnam – is the least foreign-influenced region of Vietnam, being furthest from the two main cities. It is steeped in history, most recently because its capital, Hué, was the imperial seat during the 19th and first half of the 20th centuries. Annam is also the poorest part of Vietnam, the least developed and the birthplace of several important revolutionary figures. Not far from Vinh is Huu Lien village where Ho Chi Minh was brought up. His father was the village schoolmaster and the family homes have been preserved. Together with a museum dedicated to the founder of the nation, they form the centre of a local tourist industry. Vietnamese from all parts of the country come visiting on a sort of pilgrimage, much as they visit Ho's mausoleum in Hanoi.

Either because of its connections with Ho Chi Minh or else because it is Vietnam's poorest province, Nghe An is said to have a higher proportion of Communist Party members than anywhere else. It is also one of Vietnam's most populous provinces. Like other provinces, Nghe An is competing for foreign investment which it sees as the means of diversifying away from rice growing, at which it is not very good because of poor soil and worse weather. Instead the people grow tea, coffee and rubber or engage in Vietnam's fastest growing industry processing shrimps and squid for export. They are also concentrating their efforts on exploiting the province's mineral resources: marble, limestone (for making cement), bauxite and gold. Nghe An's 60 miles of coastline give it hopes of competing for investment in tourism. In these ways Nghe An is hoping to shed its reputation as Vietnam's poorest province.

Leaving Vinh southwards, road and railway enter the thinnest part of the country. For the next few hundred miles the country is seldom wider than 40 miles and just 31 miles from coast to the frontier with Laos at its narrowest. The Truong Son mountain range, or Annamite cordillera as the French called it, is constantly in sight. At several places it thrusts its way to the shoreline, causing the road to climb. One such point is the Ngang pass which marks Highway One's entry into Quang Binh province. After crossing the Giang river by ferry, the last river between Hanoi and Ho Chi Minh City yet to be bridged, there is a more tropical feel to the countryside with palm trees all around. Later, after crossing into what used to be South Vietnam, the spectacular Hai Van pass, whose French name translates as 'gateway to the clouds', sits above Vietnam's fourth largest city, Danang. As the railway here hugs the coast in a spectacular feat of engineering, the road with similar ingenuity leaves behind the Hué lagoon and sandbanks as it climbs towards the clouds to offer the traveller (cloudbase permitting) a view of Danang city and the Marble mountains to the south. The pass is littered with US fortifications. Danang, with its naval and air bases, had one of the largest concentrations of US forces. The retreat from Danang during the final weeks of the war in 1975, with refugees hanging on to the undercarriages of US military aircraft, was one of the more humiliating demonstrations of US impotence in the face of the advancing North Vietnamese army.

Before reaching Hué and Danang the road crosses the bridge over the Ben Hai river, which marks the 17th parallel. Here the country was divided into two by the Geneva accords of June 1954 until the surrender of Saigon on 30 April 1975. This frontier is an important part of Vietnamese history – as the Berlin wall was for German history and the 34th parallel remains for still divided Korea. The area is rich in war remnants. A five-kilometre wide demilitarized zone (the Dee-Em-Zee!) was supposedly enforced on either side of the Ben Hai river. In fact, communist forces found little difficulty infiltrating the south across the DMZ. The USA responded by dropping bombs within the DMZ.

At the northern edge of the DMZ, there is a remarkable network of tunnels at Vinh Moc. Running on three levels, they provided a refuge to as many as 2,500 villagers during US air raids and were probably guerrilla hideouts too. They extend for one and three quarter miles and have a total of 13 entrances and exits, some on the sharp escarpment overlooking the sea into which the excavated red clay soil was thrown. The tunnel complex contained a hospital where 17 children were born during air raids. Bomb craters in the vicinity testify to the need for such a retreat. One bomb made a direct hit on the tunnel complex killing many people inside. Some accounts suggest Vinh Moc was used to store arms brought from the offshore Con Co island in transit for forces in the south, which suggests the Americans knew what they were after. This may have been a more strategic target than Vinh.

South of the DMZ, Quang Tri province witnessed some of the heaviest fighting in the latter part of the war. After US forces withdrew and the 'Vietnamization' of the war had taken place, communist and Saigon forces fought each other for control of the area, damaging the city of Quang Tri so badly that the provincial capital was transferred to Dong Ha, a bustling frontier town, even though the 'frontier' no longer exists. A badly damaged church beside Highway One bears witness to the heavy fighting in the area.

Dong Ha does still command a frontier though it is 65 miles to the West for this is the start of Highway Five to the border with Laos and eventually to the town of Savannakhet on the Mekong River border between Laos and Thailand. This route too is littered with reminders of the war, mostly US bases or hills which US forces commanded in an attempt to prevent the infiltration into the south of communist men and arms. This was the theoretically impenetrable 'McNamara Line'.

One of the most famous US bases in the area was Khe Sanh, in the north-west corner of former South Vietnam. Here, in 1968, a 77-day siege of US forces by communist guerillas who controlled surrounding hills was one of the longest continuous engagements of the war. Around 250 Americans and many times that number of communists lost their lives in a battle that grates deeply with US military strategists, who felt it was not a wise location for a base. Khe Sanh was abandoned shortly after the siege was broken. The attentions of both US army teams searching for the bodies of those unaccounted for from the war and of local bounty hunters searching for scrap metal have ensured that little remains to be seen of this now overgrown base. The trade in scrap metal through Danang port to Japanese smelters has helped clear the landscape of military remains and provided local employment. Treasure-seekers risk death or serious injury from unexploded arms as they dig for scrap knowing that a 105mm shell can earn them the equivalent of $3.50. The aluminium 'ramps' which provided the landing strip at Khe Sanh were used to make tableware, such as the coffee filtration devices that are popular in Vietnamese cafés.

Just below the DMZ lies Hué, Vietnam's elegant former imperial capital and capital of the French province of Annam, the central part of Vietnam. As the last imperial capital, Hué has a strong claim to be the most truly Vietnamese city. Although French architectural influence is apparent, Hué does not have the feel of a French colonial city as both Hanoi and Saigon do. Hué exudes charm to which the Huong Giang or Perfumed River is a major contributor. The city's place in Vietnam's long history is assured by the 17th century citadel, modelled on that in Beijing and complete with its own 'forbidden city' of around two square miles. Highway One passes between the citadel and the Perfumed River, which is said to derive its name from an aromatic plant which grows near its source.

Hué's long steel bridge was designed by Georges Eiffel. Hué is Vietnam's 'jewel in the crown', its major tourist attraction. Since the country opened up, bus-loads of European and Japanese visitors have been coming to see the historic sights. Young European, Australian and American back-packers are arriving too, hiring bicycles and boats to visit the imperial tombs, or Thuan An beach at the mouth of the Perfumed River. Hué is a centre of learning: both Ho Chi Minh and his arch opponent, Ngo Dinh Diem, attended the city's Quoc Hoc, one of the leading schools in French ruled Vietnam. So too did General Giap.

Hué is also the best demonstration of the 'third' Vietnam. Its people show no obeisance to either of the capitals, Hanoi or Ho Chi Minh City. Their city, after all, had been the imperial capital for a century and a half and remains Vietnam's most attractive city. During the war, the people of Hué earned a reputation for supporting neither the communists nor the Saigon government, especially not under Diem whose pro-Catholic policies did not go down well in strongly-Buddhist Hué. In 1963 monks from Hué's Thien Mu pagoda poured petrol over themselves and set themselves alight on the streets of Saigon in protest at what they said was President Diem's harassment of the country's Buddhist majority. Seven monks burnt to death. This brought to worldwide attention the so-called 'third force' in Vietnamese politics which the USA refused to acknowledge because it did not fit into their simplistic view that all Vietnamese were either communist or anti-communist.

The people of Hué were as strongly nationalistic as any Vietnamese. They just expressed it in a different way, considering both the communists and the southern regime to be tainted by foreign influences. They blamed the USA for preventing the holding of the elections promised at Geneva and for corrupting the military leaders of the southern regime. In 1966, they erected barricades against South Vietnamese troops flown to the city by US aircraft, opening fire on them. Two years later during the 1968 *Têt* offensive, the old city suffered heavy casualties and severe damage as American and South Vietnamese forces fought communist forces, who occupied the citadel for 24 days flying their flag from its 37-metre flagpole. The battle for Hué has been described as one of the most bitter of the entire war. Comparing Hué to other ruined cities like Warsaw and Budapest, the correspondent of the London *Observer*, Gavin Young, wrote that 'the people have been raped by two forces which they have come to distrust and fear'. According to Young, 'the Americans... regained Hué at the cost of destroying it'

whilst the communist forces needed to understand that they could
not assume the loyalty of people 'simply because they have opposed
the Saigon government'. Young wrote that 'neither side has won
any appreciable number of hearts and minds'. For Young, the battle
of Hué demonstrated clearly that 'there are three political forces in
South Vietnam, not two, and that third one... rejects the big stick
images of Hanoi and Saigon.'[2] Subsequently, because of the
hostility of its people towards Americans, Hué was off bounds to
US troops for much of the war.

What was true in 1968 remains true today. The people of Hué are
as proud as ever of their beautiful city and what they see as their
independence from Hanoi and Ho Chi Minh City. Thien Mu pagoda
is once again the centre of protest at government policies towards
Buddhism. Several of its monks have been imprisoned for public
order offences. Church leaders say they are again being persecuted
as they were under Diem. In 1993 there was another case of self-
immolation at the pagoda and the following year 49 monks
threatened to burn themselves if the government did not lift a ban
on their church organization. Hué's Buddhist leaders are proud of
their independence, which they believe is being threatened by the
government. Because Hué is so staunchly Buddhist its people are
most sensitive to constraints on their religious observance including,
as in the current case, the government's attempt to control the body
which manages Buddhism in Vietnam.

Vietnamese Buddhists have altars in their homes at which they
commemorate their ancestors; the practice incorporates elements of
Confucianism and Taoism. A walk after nightfall through the
residential area of Hué (or any Vietnamese town or city, north or
south) and a peek into the homes where incense burns on lighted
altars affords evidence that religion is an important part of daily
lives. The ritual has changed little whatever complexion of
government is in power. Following Buddhist practice, Christians too
have home altars. Christianity in Vietnam has had its ups and downs
too but the evidence of newly-built churches as the road nears Ho
Chi Minh City seems to be that it is enjoying a revival, or that a
period of intolerance by the authorities has come to an end. In every
town, government buildings and many private homes fly Vietnam's
flag. Loosely copied from that of China, it is bright red with a large

---

[2] Young's reports from wartime Hué are republished in Gavin Young, *Worlds Apart*,
Penguin, London, 1987.

golden star in the middle and is said to represent the communist revolution. Years of war have instilled into the Vietnamese people a strong sense of patriotism. It is common to see posters or monuments to Ho Chi Minh, or an inscription of one of his sayings. There are frequent war memorials, sometimes commemorating a particular battle or 'liberation'. Some have graves around them, others stand alone. The vast majority of the estimated 3 million Vietnamese war dead (fighters and civilians) are buried where they fell.

As the mountains force road and railway towards the coastline, the traveller becomes conscious of another north–south artery. This is the newly-built national grid, the transmission system, which carries electricity from the Soviet-built Hoa Binh power station in the Red River delta to power hungry Ho Chi Minh City. The grid was a source of controversy because of its huge costs and a feeling that the north itself will soon need the surplus electricity being carried to the south. A government minister was imprisoned for corruption in connection with the import of steel for the gantries. The transmission line mars the countryside somewhat. Also alongside the road are telephone lines; even small villages have roadside post offices from which you can – according to the sign at one on the Hai Van pass – call any number in Vietnam or abroad! Together these communications arteries indicate just how vulnerable Vietnam is to any sabotage of its road, railway, electricity grid and telephone lines. They are the cords which bind together the complementary economies of north and south along the country's isthmus-like middle. However, occasional microwave towers demonstrate that nowadays not all communications need physical land lines. Satellite dishes in the cities and television aerials everywhere make the same point, though television ownership in Vietnam is not as widespread as in most other South East Asian countries.

Just south of Danang is China Beach, where US forces used to enjoy 'R and R', or 'rest and relaxation' breaks. The beach is a popular resort among young foreign visitors and is regaining the reputation it once enjoyed amongst GIs as a surfing centre. In 1993, Californians organised an international surfing tournament there, pronouncing its surf 'some of the finest'. The welcoming of Americans as surfers rather than as warriors is as potent a symbol of peace emerging from war as that of beating swords into ploughshares. (They may soon be welcoming more, since a corporation based in Maryland is hoping to build a $250 million resort and golf complex there. The prospective Vietnamese partner company is headed by a former Viet Cong officer.)

China Beach is one of the many fine beaches along Vietnam's long coastline. From the developed resorts of Vung Tau and Nha Trang in the south, to Halong Bay in the extreme north, there are dozens of beaches. A beach lover could spend a month travelling the country and swim at a different beach each day. Seaside resorts are favourite targets for foreign investment, so the 'package' beach tour may yet come to Vietnam, to rival those to Thailand's Pattaya and Phuket resorts. For the time being, one of the chief attractions is the absence of people – but then there are few hotels or refreshment facilities either. International snorkellers and skin divers have also found locations to their tastes.

South of Danang, the town of Hoi An marks an earlier settlement of Vietnam. Traders from China and Japan and later from Europe, beginning with the Portuguese, set up trading bases in this port, which thrived between the 17th and 19th centuries. In the days of sail, Hoi An was part of a great seafaring network that embraced Goa, Malacca, Batavia (present day Jakarta) and Ambon in the Spice Islands as well as more distant European ports. The town retains its old world charm and its mix of oriental and European architectural styles. In the past few years it has become a popular destination for back-packers. As a result the town has geared itself to accommodate young foreign travellers to a greater degree than any other Vietnamese town – with some loss of identity, but considerable enhancement of earnings in the process.

The countryside truly is the constant of Vietnamese life. Farmland is divided between rice growing and other subsistence crops like vegetables and various sorts of fruit. Rice is dried on the side of the road and rice straw even across the road, another example of the Vietnamese putting to the best use or uses every available bit of land. East of Ho Chi Minh City, the road passes through rubber estates planted by the French. Cash crops such as peanuts, coffee and tea are concentrated in the inland highland regions where coffee beans rather than rice are dried on the road. Coffee is one of the country's most successful cash crops, its cultivation encouraged by the high world price of more than $2,000 a tonne. Vietnam is already the world's eighth largest coffee exporter. Given current expansion in the area under cultivation, coffee is likely to become an even more important earner of foreign exchange. It has already brought cash into some of the poorer regions of the country and caused an economic boom in the coffee capital of Buon Ma Thuot.

In these upland areas, the defoliation of war is most evident, although deforestation for economic reasons has also taken place. The government has now banned the export of unprocessed timber – to help Vietnamese industry as well as to preserve the country's jungles and the wildlife within them. These include tigers and elephants as well as some new species of mammal like the Vu Quang ox discovered in 1992, one of the largest new land mammals to have been found anywhere in the world for 50 years. Since trees can still be felled for domestic use, the ban is having only limited effect. Water buffaloes, cows and the pot-bellied pig, which has curiously acquired cult status in the West as a domestic pet, are farmed. A particularly Vietnamese sight is that of the farmer escorting his flock of ducks along the road or across the fields. Duck farming is especially popular in the Mekong delta where water-filled bomb craters have taken on the role of duck ponds. Rivers are more plentiful in southern Vietnam and bigger, providing yet more means for people to make a living. The waters they bring from the Truong Son mountains provide nourishment for the coastal plains – but can also be a hazard when they flood. The rivers have little role as transport arteries except very locally. In that sense, like the railway they are an under-utilized resource. Severe monsoon flooding also cuts the road and railway.

Being close to the coast, Highway One offers plenty of opportunities to sample Vietnam's seafood. Prawns and squid are ubiquitous. Around Nha Trang, prawns are harvested in large sea-water ponds. Towns tend to have local culinary specialities, such as the pork and noodle *cao lau* of Hoi An which, it is said, can only truly be made with the water of a particular Hoi An well. The people of Vinh eat their local delicacy, eel soup, for breakfast while Nha Trang is renowned for the distinctive dragon fruit with its speckled black and white flesh. The town of Phan Thiet further south, where Ho Chi Minh worked briefly as a teacher, is the centre of the industry which makes fermented fish sauce, or *nuoc mam*, an essential ingredient of Vietnamese cuisine. Vietnamese rice noodles, or *pho*, would not be the same without the pungent, slightly fishy flavour of *nuoc mam*, the aroma of which hangs over Phan Thiet. Some attribute the generally slim and healthy appearance of Vietnamese to the high protein content of *nuoc mam*. Vietnamese will tell you that one of the more positive relics of French colonialism is the *baguette* of bread, a favourite snack food available from the Chinese frontier to the Mekong delta. It is sold warm at the roadside filled with Vietnamese-style patê, or with imported French processed cheese.

The changing brands of beer mark the passage down Highway One. Ten years ago Vietnam had breweries only in Hanoi and Ho Chi Minh City. Nowadays even small towns have their local brews. Danish technology has helped Hanoi produce Halida beer, Vinh produces its Vida brand, Hué makes Huda beer while Song Han (Han river) is the brew of Danang. Other joint-venture beers like Tiger from Singapore, Heineken from the Netherlands, BGI from France and San Miguel from the Philippines are available throughout the country – all made possible by *doi moi*! In Vietnam the motto seems to be: 'It's never too early in the day to open a can.'

Family planning posters down Highway One exhort families not to have more than two children. A more severe warning comes from graphic billboards depicting the dangers of AIDS in an attempt to educate the people about this new and spreading scourge. More than 2,000 cases of AIDS causing 50 deaths had been recorded by early 1995. Prostitution is increasing in today's less repressive atmosphere, as is drug taking. Both are blamed for the spread of AIDS, which is no longer blamed entirely on foreign visitors. Public information posters about AIDS are replacing faded exhortations to work harder for a greater Vietnam or for the glory of the revolution. Presumably such exhortations are no longer needed now that the incentive system is achieving these objectives.

By the time the road reaches the seaside resort of Nha Trang it has become quite crowded. There are more of everything – trucks, buses as well as private cars, which are mainly used by foreign tourists. The road is in no better condition but is much busier. Nha Trang has an air of prosperity which is only partly explained by its tourism, its port and its seafood industries. It is said to have benefited from an inflow of funds from overseas Vietnamese – perhaps because a significant proportion of its inhabitants earlier left Vietnam as 'boat people'. The Nha Trang to Ho Chi Minh City section of the Highway – around 600 miles – is a priority for improvement with loans being provided by the World and Asian Development Banks. A US company has won the contract to supervise the work.

As well as being a resort and thriving port, Nha Trang is the gateway to what South Vietnam called the Central Highlands, but which are now called the Western Highlands. Highway 26 leads up to the coffee-growing province of Dac Lac and on to Gia Lai and

Kontum. The rapid fall of this area to advancing North Vietnamese forces in early 1975 precipitated the capture of Saigon and the end of the war. Highway 20 connects Nha Trang with the hill resort of Dalat, the market garden of the south famous for its fresh fruit, vegetables and flowers. Developed by the French, Dalat became the summer retreat of the last emperor, Bao Dai, and of the French governors general. It remains a favourite Vietnamese holiday destination. Foreigners are flocking there too, some on tours, whilst back-packers go trekking in the surrounding valleys. Some foreigners, including a firm of British knitwear makers, are coming to invest and work. They have been encouraged by the opening of a brand new golf course overlooking the lake which is the town's main attraction. Dalat has more hotel rooms than any other Vietnamese towns – including in the former palaces of both Emperor Bao Dai and the French governors general. Further big new hotels are planned with foreign partners.

Highway One passes close to the former US headquarters base at Bien Hoa before finally reaching Vietnam's bustling commercial capital of Ho Chi Minh City. With billboards for Coca Cola, Pepsi, Kodak, Castrol and BP much in evidence, it is easy to forget that advertisements and foreign firms were almost non-existent between 1975 and the late 1980s. A public information poster explains how to observe traffic lights, a reminder that there have been none since leaving Hanoi! Ho Chi Minh City is trying hard to be a modern city. Its latest acquisitions include paging and cellular telephone networks. Yet, like many big South East Asian cities, Ho Chi Minh has its slum dwellings at the side of its fetid rivers and canals, especially on the rapidly expanding southern side of the city near Saigon port. Ho Chi Minh City – the metropolitan district of which Saigon is but one part – has expanded fast in recent years; it seems to go on for ever. Even its suburbs are a hive of life and commercial activity. One cannot help wondering if this is what Hanoi will become in time.

Highway One has travelled 1,070 miles from Hanoi to reach what is supposed to be the country's second city. Saigonese do not see it that way; for them this is the seat of power that matters. Decisions taken all those miles away in Hanoi have less impact on their daily lives than decisions taken here in Thanh Pho Ho Chi Minh, its mouthful of a name in Vietnamese. Because the Vietnamese are so little travelled, very few residents of Ho Chi Minh City have ever ventured north, especially not as far as Hanoi, and fewer Hanoians have set foot in the southern capital. Most have no inclination to do so. Ho Chi Minh City is as far from Hanoi as Naples is from London or as Singapore is from Bangkok.

Continuing its journey to the Mekong delta, Highway One leaves Ho Chi Minh City westwards through Chinatown, or Cholon, which is even more bustling than downtown Saigon. It passes through the expanding slum area which is still drawing migrants in from the delta region. Beyond the city limits, the road turns southwards and heads straight towards the delta. (Saigon is sometimes mistakenly thought to be in the delta; it lies on the Saigon river, which is not strictly part of the delta.) The road here is crowded by the delta traffic, most of the delta's surplus produce being brought by truck to be traded in Ho Chi Minh City. Highway One reaches the delta at My Tho, a pleasant riverine town 100 miles from Saigon. Nearby is Ap Bac, site of one of the first major victories by communist forces over the South Vietnamese army, in January 1963.

On the outskirts of My Tho Highway One diverts inland for the ferry crossing into the heart of the delta. The road crosses the main channels of the massive Mekong River in two ferry boat 'leaps'. Firstly the mighty Tien Giang, or Northern Channel; 20 miles further south flows the even mightier Hau Giang or Southern Channel, known to Cambodians as the Bassac River for the Mekong's division into these two great branches takes places upstream from the Cambodian capital, Phnom Penh. Downstream from the ferry crossing point, the rivers split again, emerging eventually into the South China Sea through eight 'mouths'.

The Vietnamese call the Mekong 'Song Cuu Long', or the River of Nine Dragons, leading to the conclusion that there are nine rather than eight river mouths. In fact, in both Chinese and Vietnamese mythology the symbol of 'nine dragons' is associated with prosperity and good fortune, which suggests the river may have been named for auspicious reasons rather than for the number of its estuaries. The Mekong's waters are Vietnam's single most important natural resource for both the daily challenge of feeding its people and for earning foreign exchange – through rice, fish and other exports – with which to develop their land. Virtually all Vietnam's exported rice is grown in the Mekong delta. With the right planning, investment and development, it could become an even more important resource, as we shall see in Chapter Eleven. Pouring an estimated 500 billion cubic metres of water into the South China

Sea each year, the Mekong is one of the world's greatest rivers. Were it to enter the sea without first splitting, the Mekong would have the widest estuary of any great river except the Amazon.

Ferries carry trucks and buses, cars, motorbikes and bicycles as well as pedestrians on a regular and continuous shuttle service. Stall holders on both sides make their living selling snacks, newspapers, lottery tickets and trinkets to waiting travellers. The lower Mekong has never been bridged, though there is talk of bridging its two channels now that the upper Mekong has been bridged near the Laotian capital, Vientiane. Cambodia has rebuilt its bridge across the Bassac, which was destroyed in fighting more than 20 years ago. Without bridges, transporting the delta region's surpluses by ferry is a sophisticated and efficient operation. The ferries are run by the provincial governments.

The second ferry crossing brings Highway One directly into Can Tho, the delta's capital and centre of commerce and a university city. Can Tho's economic activity is entirely agricultural, or concerned with processing farm produce, rice milling in particular. Nearly half of Vietnam's rice comes from the Mekong delta, which is fertile enough to grow two or three crops in a year. The dykes and canals built originally by the French have successfully irrigated the entire delta and reduced the dangers of flooding, although floods still occur. Apart from rice, sugar, coconut palms (providing copra) and just about every variety of tropical fruit are grown in the delta. After dark, men with torches strapped on their foreheads, looking rather like coal-miners, can be seen searching the hedgerows for frogs, whose legs are eaten as a delicacy in restaurants in Ho Chi Minh City and throughout East Asia.

One sign of prosperity in the delta is the large number of motorized vehicles: trucks, buses and cars as well as motorbikes. There are motorized rickshaws, or *cyclos*, which are not found elsewhere in Vietnam, and motorized boats, small and large, ferrying people and goods. Only in the southern delta are the rivers and canals important arteries of travel and trade. Much farming produce begins its journey to market by boat. Small ships dock at Can Tho and My Tho river ports, which are not deep enough to accommodate larger, ocean-going vessels. Hence the continuing, indeed growing, importance of Saigon port for transshipment.

Housing in the Mekong delta tends to be simpler than elsewhere: less stone and brick, more wood and thatch. Climate has much to do with this because the standard of living in the delta is certainly higher than in most other agricultural regions. There are brick houses too and the main cities of the delta – My Tho, Ben Tre, Can Tho and Long Xuyen – are all prospering with upwardly mobile dwelling places! The real give-aways are the television aerials of which there are a higher preponderance in the delta than anywhere else. Through mile upon mile of rich farmland, where paddy fields and fruit trees occupy all available land space and settlements hug close to the rivers and roads, the people of the delta appear to be a self-contained community, distinctive from the inhabitants of other parts of the country. They are self-sufficient in food. Many of their other supplies, including liquor, are smuggled across the border from Cambodia to evade steep import duties, which further lessens dependence on Ho Chi Minh City. The delta people seem to relish the fact that the ferry crossings keep the rest of the country at bay!

Southwards from Can Tho, Highway One makes a 'dog leg' towards the coast before resuming its journey south, eventually petering out at Ca Mau, capital of the southernmost province of Minh Hai. Ca Mau is 217 miles from Ho Chi Minh City, 1,286 from Hanoi and nearly 1,400 from Lang Son on the Chinese border. Ca Mau is as far from Lang Son as Athens is from London, or as Miami is from New York. The people of Ca Mau seem to be living in another country, almost another world, from their compatriots in Lang Son, so different politically and climatically are the two towns. The Ca Mau peninsula is mangrove swampland, the least fertile and populated part of the delta. It suffered some of the worst napalm defoliation of the war and is only very gradually recovering. However, the low fertility of the soil is compensated for by the province's burgeoning industry in aquatic produce – shrimps, crab, squid and various sorts of fish – most of which is frozen for export. The country does not end at the Ca Mau peninsula. Vietnam also lays claim to the Spratly islands, several degrees latitude further south towards the coast of Borneo, as do China and most other South East Asian nations.

The journey down Highway One demonstrates Vietnam's backwardnesss. Transportation shortcomings are a major obstacle to the development of trade, both internal and export. They are also one of the reasons the Vietnamese are a relatively untravelled people. The railway system is in bad need of upgrading – some would say replacing – if it is to be a competitive means of moving people and goods in the *doi moi* age when everything is to be judged by its competitiveness. The line would benefit considerably if it were fenced off, or if the gauge were to be broadened, but such costly investments do not seem feasible at present. The line crosses the street so much within Hanoi that the city authorities are considering running it through a subway.

Investment is being made to improve the country's roads (not just Highway One) which will make them a much more attractive means of travelling, especially if *doi moi* allows private bus services to take advantage of a smoother surface, and if the prosperity riding on *doi moi* increases car and truck ownership. Curiously for a communist country, public transportation is grossly inadequate, so individual transportation has flourished. Bicycles and motorbikes remain the main mode of transport everywhere, whilst three-wheeled *cyclos* provide taxi services. The government has an ambitious target to convert up to 50% of bicycle and motorbike users to bus by the year 2000 – mainly for economic reasons but also to check fuel pollution. In Hanoi they hope eventually to follow the example of all other ASEAN capitals (except for Bandar Seri Seri Begwan in Brunei) where mass transit railway systems are being built in response to congestion, fiscal and pollution pressures; 90% of journeys in Hong Kong and 66% in Singapore are made by public transport. But Vietnamese are used to being dependent on their own transport for their short, daily journeys and are unlikely to give up this freedom willingly.

The newly rich Vietnamese are inevitably attracted to the private motor car, a post-*doi moi* phenomenon. Still relatively rare, cars are slowly taking their place in Vietnamese city life. Japanese car-makers have ambitious sales target for Vietnam while prestige car-makers from Europe and the USA are also showing an interest. BMW, Chrysler and Ford are investing in car assembly plants – mainly to take advantage of cheap Vietnamese labour to assemble cars for export. The market for private cars in Vietnam is around 10,000 a year, compared with more than 500,000 in neighbouring Thailand. Daimler-Benz may have a bigger local market for the output of the truck plant they are building.

The motorized two-wheeler is an important part of Vietnamese social life in at least three ways, observable in a provincial city, like Nha Trang for example. First, there are the motorbike girls, successors to the bar girls of the 1970s, seeking customers with the unoriginal line: 'You like massage?' Second, men on motorbikes seek a different sort of customer as they offer a faster means of getting around than by *cyclo*. They are trying to earn enough to repay the loan with which the motorbike was bought in the first place. Third, both boys and girls use their motorbikes in a sort of courting ritual – side by side on different bikes at first, driving or pillion; subsequently riding together on the true *xe ôm* or 'hug vehicle'. Any attempt to supplant the two-wheeler from Vietnam's city streets risks upsetting these social customs. Another complicating factor is the quantity of goods that are transported on *cyclos* or two-wheelers, which are often dangerously unwieldy. *Cyclos* are already banned from parts of Ho Chi Minh City. If the ban is extended, it would have an impact on the price of goods at the market in the centre of the city.

Ports are a government priority for improvement since at present only three – Haiphong, Danang and Saigon – can take sizeable ocean-going vessels. The government is seeking investment to upgrade and dredge many smaller ports which would enhance the ability of provinces to export their produce direct, and relieve pressure on the major ports. Can Tho and Vinh's port of Cua Lo are two ports that have enormous potential but are as yet under-utilized.

Most recent investment in transportation has been directed towards air services. The creation of a second state-owned airline, Pacific Airlines, has provided competition for Vietnam Airlines, which has bought new Boeings (through intermediaries to evade the US embargo) and Airbuses and hired foreign pilots, to improve its service. As yet only 14 cities nationwide are served by the air network. Ambitious expansion plans are said to require 80 new aircraft by the year 2005.

It is possible after completing the long journey through re-unified Vietnam to draw certain conclusions about the country. One is that there is still a north–south divide, an economic one, and that in terms of buildings, vehicles, shops and economic activity in general it does seem as if the south won the war – the economic war. Everything is more plentiful in the south. Another conclusion is that rural development has been nowhere near as rapid in recent years as that in the towns and cities, although prosperity has not only come to the two major cities. Mekong delta cities are prospering as are northern provincial cities like Haiphong and Vinh. Indeed, one interesting facet of *doi moi* – visible from buildings and vehicles – is the emerging northern capitalist class. Such people were first to take advantage of the opportunities *doi moi* provides.

Another overall conclusion is that while life is changing more slowly in rural areas it is changing and serious poverty is not evident. Villagers in northern or central Vietnam are visibly poorer than those in the more developed south. Yet the slum dwellers of Ho Chi Minh City are worse off than villagers in even the poorest provinces. Poorest of all are the hill dwellers in the extreme north and in the inland central provinces, especially the minority ethnic groups who still carry out slash and burn farming. Highway One has at least brought a measure of well-being to those through whose communities it passes.

A final conclusion is that, despite big differences between north and south that seem to put years between them, there are also big similarities. There is a sameness about life throughout Vietnam, notwithstanding differences in climate, level of development, dress and wealth. Vietnam, as viewed from its main arterial highway, does appear to be one nation – in terms of language, life-style and a myriad other characteristics.

9

Vietnam's Diaspora

The exodus from Vietnam which followed the end of the war was one of the largest mass migrations of modern times. Around 2 million people left Vietnam, most by small boat in an attempt to find a new home in a richer country. Many were not accepted for resettlement and were subsequently repatriated to Vietnam – on occasions by force. But most of the 2 million have made new homes for themselves in more than 25 countries. Before 1975 very few Vietnamese lived abroad, except for small communities in the immediate neighbouring countries and those who had settled in France during colonial times. Now, the Vietnamese diaspora straddles the world, embracing even distant and unlikely countries like Iceland, the Ivory Coast and New Caledonia!

The Vietnamese government itself contributed to the mass migration by sending plane loads of workers to Eastern Europe and the Middle East. This had the twin purposes of helping to pay off the country's debts to those countries – the host governments took a share of the workers' earnings – and providing employment for demobilized soldiers, which eased the social effects of the reduction in the size of the northern and southern armies following the end of the American war. When communist regimes in the USSR and Eastern Europe collapsed, many of the workers stayed on and set themselves up in business. This has created problems in reunified Germany where the government has had difficulty sorting legitimate immigrants who have been granted asylum from illegitimate 'workers' of the former East Germany who have overstayed their welcome. Many of the Vietnamese in the Netherlands first came to Eastern Europe as indentured labourers and have migrated across Europe's porous borders. Both Germany and the Netherlands have asked Vietnam to take back its unwanted *Gastarbeiter*, or guest workers.

Other emigrants from Vietnam who are not regarded as refugees (according to the definition of the UN High Commission for Refugees, UNHCR) are those Vietnamese who walked across the northern border into China, or westwards into Cambodia. These are the spontaneous migrants, many of them Vietnamese of Chinese origin. They do not appear on official statistics because they have not sought and do not need help, but they have found homes and work outside Vietnam. It is often forgotten that the second largest number of emigrants from Vietnam, after those in the USA, have settled in China: UNHCR estimates that 280,000 now live there. More prosperous Chinese Vietnamese have gone abroad by air to live in Taiwan or Hong Kong. Less fortunate would-be refugees left Vietnam by boat in search of 'the promised lands' of California or Australia only to be incarcerated in camps around South East Asia – in Hong Kong, the Philippines, Thailand, Malaysia and Indonesia – for several years pending a decision on their future.

Easily the largest numbers of émigré Vietnamese are those classified as refugees who have been accepted for resettlement in the West: more than 1.5 million fall into this category. They are not expecting, or expected, to return to Vietnam, except perhaps for short visits. Around 1 million have found new homes in the USA. Most of the rest have settled in Australia or Canada which each took about 150,000 Vietnamese. The UK took in around 25,000 refugees, Germany 30,000 and France 45,000 bringing its ethnic Vietnamese population to around 400,000. (Vietnam's last emperor, Bao Dai, had made France his home since 1954.) Most other Western European nations accepted between a few hundred and a few thousand Vietnamese settlers. Those granted asylum were a combination of boat people, who were interviewed and chosen in first asylum camps, and Vietnamese who were allowed to leave by air on the Orderly Departure Programme (ODP).

The story of the boat people is a tragic one that has had some surprising consequences. The initial exodus was triggered by the 'fall' of Saigon on 30 April 1975 and the evacuation by the USA of members of the South Vietnamese armed forces and their families. Other employees of the Americans and high ranking members of the South Vietnamese government simply fled into exile by whatever means, fearing the 'blood-bath' that it was predicted would follow the communist takeover. In the chaos that ensued, there was no careful selection process: it was every man, woman and child for him or herself. Many of those who found themselves on US warships in the South China Sea and subsequently in camps on the Pacific island of Guam would not have qualified had there been such a procedure. A total of 150,000 people left Vietnam at this time as part of what was known as the 'first wave'.

There was no blood-bath in Vietnam but there was a programme of compulsory re-education for all former employees of the Americans and senior officials of what the communists called 'the Saigon puppet regime'. Those who had fled were glad they had done so and others started to leave the country in small, often unseaworthy boats. By evading or bribing the authorities many thousands set sail from Vietnam's long coastline. A significant proportion of Vietnam's fishing fleet was appropriated for the purpose of fleeing the country. Refugees did not always succeed in evading pirates and there were numerous tales of rape and robbery on the high seas. Sympathetic Western organizations arranged for ships to position themselves outside Vietnam's territorial waters to pick up the escapees. Others were picked up by passing merchant vessels on the high seas and taken to the next port of call. The vast majority of boat people landed in what were called 'countries of first asylum', all of which made clear they would not offer permanent asylum. Vietnam became famous for its 'boat people', an expression that became familiar even in the non-English speaking world: they are known in French, for example, as 'les boat-people'. Newspaper photographs of distressed refugees in barely seaworthy boats with accompanying stories about them falling victim to pirates on the high seas painted a sorry picture of a repressive country from which people wanted only to flee. That picture was sharpened after 1980 when those fleeing came mainly from the north, demonstrating that communist Vietnam was not exactly a socialist paradise.

To complicate the story, as communism began to bite in the south, there was a deliberate policy of repression towards the Chinese community which had dominated commercial life before 1975 and which was now intimidated into leaving the country. The government did nothing to discourage the vendetta against thousands of ethnic Chinese or *Hoa* who had been born and brought up in Vietnam, spoke the language and were more closely integrated than in most South East Asian countries. Some provincial administrations even facilitated their departure in exchange for gold. While many *Hoa* journeyed overland to China and others flew off to new homes in Hong Kong and Taiwan, others fled by boat ending up in Western countries having been resettled like their ethnic Vietnamese brethren.

The boat people phenomenon touched the hearts of the people of

Western Europe, Australia and North America. Governments there took a welcoming, humanitarian attitude towards them – in contrast to the South East Asian governments which insisted from the first that they must all leave. But as time went on and the exodus failed to slow, attitudes in some countries changed. It was argued that the 'refugees' were no longer fleeing as a result of a fear of persecution by the Vietnamese government, but out of a desire to benefit from the higher standards of living and economic well-being in the West. Given the ease with which those fleeing were offered new homes in the West, it was said that a 'pull factor' had replaced the 'push factor'. In 1981, when the US government voted funds to resettle 144,000 refugees, more than the then population of the South East Asian camps, it was accused of preparing places for refugees who did not yet exist!

Indeed, by the mid-1980s a whole complex of motives lay behind the exodus of boat people of which fear of persecution was the least. Hardship at home was probably the major factor. Some boat people, especially unaccompanied youngsters, fled simply out of a spirit of adventure. Some fled to escape a commitment – a wife or a bad debt – or to start a new life with a new partner. Others left to avoid military service or being sent to fight in Cambodia. Many young men fled as the 'advanced guard': they hoped to be resettled in the West and then to arrange for family members to join them there. Others fled to be reunited with those who had gone ahead. Large numbers of fishermen fled, indicating that opportunity played a key part in the exodus. All were taking major risks – of capture and imprisonment by the Vietnamese authorities or of falling victim to piracy or other perils of the high seas –and most paid a high price in gold for their place on a boat that was suited for use only in coastal waters. Unknown numbers perished at sea, but most made it to neighbouring countries often after being rescued by larger vessels.

South East Asian governments screamed louder as the populations of 'first asylum' camps grew while resettlement offers from the West shrank. A crisis meeting in Geneva in June 1989 under the auspices of the UNHCR agreed a Comprehensive Plan of Action (CPA). This had a number of strands including an increase in the programme of family reunions by orderly departure from Vietnam by air in the hope of discouraging the illegal exodus by boat. But the major plank of the CPA was a programme to return to Vietnam all those asylum seekers who were not accepted for resettlement elsewhere. A process of screening was introduced in the South East Asian camps to determine whether the refugees' fears of persecution were genuine or not. Those 'screened out' were deemed not to be genuine refugees, merely asylum seekers.

The principle of returning to Vietnam boat people who had taken big risks and spent large amounts of gold was controversial. The USA took the view that anyone fleeing communism was a genuine refugee and deserved to be offered asylum. However, like other countries, it was much less willing than previously to take in the inhabitants of the South East Asian camps. Also, people were still putting to sea, often encouraged by sympathetic comments from the West. A statement by a Californian congressman in 1991 that the Vietnamese inhabitants of camps in Hong Kong should be used to rebuild Kuwait after the Gulf war encouraged as many as 20,000 people to put to sea from northern Vietnam. They had interpreted his remarks as heralding a more welcoming attitude from the USA.

However, the philosophy of repatriating those not categorized as refugees prevailed and a programme of voluntary repatriation began. Even the USA assented when it came under pressure over two further exoduses of 'boat people' – from Haiti and Cuba: the Caribbean onslaught onto the coast of Miami had the effect of changing American public opinion towards the Vietnamese boat people. It took rather longer for Washington to acquiesce in the more controversial involuntary, or forced, repatriation. Newspaper pictures of Vietnamese being forcibly carried on to aircraft in Hong Kong for return to Vietnam provoked uproar from human rights organizations. The vast majority went voluntarily with more agreeing to go back as it became apparent that 'returnees' were being rewarded for returning rather than punished for fleeing in the first place. It was a deliberate and largely successful attempt to bribe them back, made easier by the unappealing conditions in the camps. At first only Hong Kong backed its encouragement of voluntary return with the sanction of mandatory repatriation. Later, as world public opinion (even in the USA) changed and UNHCR agreed to support what it preferred to call 'non-voluntary repatriation', Indonesia, Australia, the Philippines and Thailand all came to accept the need to use force to back up the considerable inducements being offered.

Initially UNHCR offered incentive payments to returnees of $400 or more – twice the average annual income in Vietnam. This was successively reduced – to $360 then (in October 1994) to $240, mainly to encourage volunteers to apply before the reduction came into effect. The European Union (EU) pioneered a programme of resettlement which provided for various types of assistance to those returning. Most popular was the credit scheme under which loans were given to enable returnees to stand on their own feet economically once more. Returnees used these loans to set themselves up in business. Some went back to fishing, others became motorcycle mechanics, hairdressers and sewing machine operators or set up small factories making *nuoc mam* or processing timber. The EU programme also provided training in various skills and assistance in finding jobs. Children, some of whom had spent several years of their childhood in camps, were given special educational help to catch up. Most returnees feel they have done well for themselves.

EU support was deliberately targeted at the entire community into which returnees were resettled to avoid giving preference to returnees. Such villages are markedly more prosperous than those which have not benefited from aid, demonstrating that even fleeing and failing to be accepted as a refugee has helped make people richer – the so-called *nouveaux riches* returnees. Both the UNHCR and the EU have monitored the programme closely and pronounced themselves satisfied that returnees were not being persecuted by the government or anyone else and that the programme of support was assisting their rehabilitation. Interestingly, the orderly return programme brought aid for Vietnam's villages from the US government, directed through the World Vision charity at a time when the USA and many other countries were not otherwise giving aid to Vietnam because of the continued presence of its troops in Cambodia.

By the end of 1994, around 70,000 Vietnamese had been repatriated, leaving around 44,000 in camps in Hong Kong, Thailand, Malaysia, Indonesia and the Philippines – out of a total exodus by boat since 1975 of nearly 800,000. A year later, by which time UNHCR hoped to have closed all first asylum camps, there were still about 38,000 inmates, of whom fewer than 2,000 had been 'screened in' as refugees. The remainder were expected to be repatriated to Vietnam; a process of persuasion was a key part of the programme. As word got around the camps that early returnees had not been punished and were prospering it became easier to recruit volunteers for repatriation. However, assurances from UNHCR were not always believed because the organization clearly had an interest in repatriation. Some camp inmates were allegedly discouraged from volunteering by disinformation from Vietnamese settled in California about the fate awaiting them in Vietnam. Those 'screened out' or denied refugee status who subsequently lost their appeals were said by the Vietnamese to have 'two chicken wings' (*hai canh ga*) – no chance of flying anywhere! Their only hope of getting out of the camp was to accept the repatriation deal.

Vietnamese resettled in the USA have benefited from a long tradition of immigration. They rapidly qualified for US citizenship and then sponsored family members to join them. Not until the mid-1990s did the inflow to the USA slow significantly as the harsher immigration conditions introduced after 1989 started having some effect. The USA has got over its open door policy, which some saw as a means of punishing Vietnam for inflicting defeat on the world's most powerful nation. Chapter Ten examines the impact Vietnamese Americans have had on their new homeland.

Australia, another country made strong by immigration, has given homes to around 150,000 Vietnamese. Most have settled in Sydney and Melbourne, with smaller groups in Brisbane, Adelaide and Perth. Many Australian Vietnamese occupy professional positions, suggesting the country pursued a policy of selecting the best educated when interviewing refugees in first asylum camps. Being among the first countries to offer asylum it had first choice! Australia's Vietnamese settlers are predominantly from the former South Vietnam. As in the USA, there may have been an element of guilt in the initial open door policy since Australia also sent troops to fight alongside South Vietnamese forces. Australia has its Vietnamese ghettos of which the Sydney suburb of Cabramatta is the best known. (It is sometimes nicknamed 'Vietnamatta' in recognition of the way the Vietnamese have come to predominate in an area that has absorbed all complexions of immigrants from Europe and Asia since the Second World War.) The Vietnamese specialize in restaurants and general trading. Cabramatta has some of Australia's highest levels of both unemployment and crime, especially drug use and dealing. Vietnamese gangs have been implicated in the heroin trade. In late 1994, the area's MP in the New South Wales Parliament, John Newman, launched a campaign against organized crime threatening those convicted with deportation. He was shot dead outside his home. The killing, the country's first ever political assassination, shocked Australians.

The UK's agreement to take refugees from Vietnam was forced on a reluctant government by the fact that the largest numbers of boat people were arriving on the shores of Hong Kong, for which the UK was responsible. The government agreed to resettle a small number to encourage other European nations to follow suit, which they did. By the time the quota was filled and family reunion cases had been accommodated, the UK had a Vietnamese population of around 25,000. Because they came mostly from Hong Kong camps, a high proportion of Vietnamese in the UK are northerners who set sail from Quang Ninh and Haiphong. Many are of fishing or peasant stock. Having lived under communism for more than 20 years they have had much bigger problems adjusting to Western life than most of those in the USA and Australia.

An early policy to disperse the refugees around the country was unsuccessful, not least because of language problems and the generally low level of education of the immigrants, compounded by the effect of many months living in overcrowded camps in Hong Kong. This was followed by the opposite phenomenon of concentration. At one time a twelfth of all UK Vietnamese lived on the run-down North Peckham estate in south-east London. The vast majority continue to live in the London area. Those in work have gravitated towards traditional Vietnamese areas like sewing and bakery work. Many of the refugees have become known to the police for one reason or another, including crimes which were unheard of in Vietnam like wife battering and child abuse. Also unknown in Vietnam, but prevalent among UK Vietnamese, is unmarried motherhood. Social workers report that the incidence of depression is high within the community. Many have learned to take advantage of the social welfare provisions. For example, couples have chosen to live apart to qualify for a second council house. Unemployed youngsters have become involved in gangs, some of which have clashed with London's much larger Chinese community. The community maintains close links with Vietnam as the high incidence of family visits there demonstrates.

The Vietnamese diaspora is widely dispersed because ships of many nationalities had rescued the refugees from small boats, or because many countries had wanted to play a part in one of the largest humanitarian rescue operations of recent times. Several Muslim countries gave homes to a thousand or so refugees, as did Israel and a number of Latin American countries. Yet Vietnam's immediate neighbours, the first asylum countries, refused to take any for permanent resettlement. They strongly support the repatriation programme and aim to close all remaining camps –Sungei Besi in

Malaysia, Bataan in the Philippines, Si Khiew in Thailand, Galang in Indonesia and the Whitehead and High Island camps in Hong Kong – as soon as possible.

The programme to persuade inmates to be repatriated to Vietnam suffered a setback when the US House of Representatives signalled its willingness to give homes in the USA to 20,000 more Vietnamese. The proposal was certain to be vetoed by President Clinton but the damage had been done. Would-be refugees in camps in Hong Kong and Malaysia rioted. UNHCR officials, who said the proposal had severely curtailed the numbers volunteering for repatriation, accused Congress of unreasonably raising expectations that were unlikely to be realized and of setting back the repatriation programme in the process. In an attempt to counter-balance its effect, the administration offered asylum interviews in Vietnam to those camp inmates who agreed to return there.

The fact that so many Vietnamese have successfully settled in the West has brought a steady flow of remittances back to Vietnam. Most of it has travelled by hand or via some complicated transaction made necessary by the absence of an effective bank transfer system. For example, *Viet kieu* (as the overseas Vietnamese are called) would deposit Australian money with a tailor in Sydney who would arrange for equivalent funds to be paid to relatives in Vietnam, minus a commission. A travel agent in London performed a similar function. Money was not necessarily physically transferred since there were people wanting to send funds out of the country too. Because of these unconventional means of transfer, it has been difficult to estimate the net flow of currency into Vietnam, but from the early 1980s onwards it was significant. By the time *doi moi* made such things easier (and the US Western Union Bank started to offer a money transfer facility) the government estimated that around $700 million was flowing in annually. The extent of these remittances reveals how successful the *Viet kieu* were, relatively speaking, although experiences varied significantly between resettlement countries. A poor village in Vietnam today is one which neither has any returnees in receipt of UNHCR and EU grants nor family members in the West providing regular remittances.

As Vietnam opens its doors, it is the *Viet kieu* who are heading back in the largest numbers. Those who earlier fled the country claiming persecution are now heading back on visits to the country from which they fled, though it is the 'economic' migrants who have the fewest inhibitions about returning. There can be few more telling illustrations of just how completely 'heaven has changed' than that of the *Viet kieu* trying to take advantage of the newly-introduced effective right to own land by buying back property previously confiscated, or new property being sold off by Vietnam's communist rulers, as if they were doing so through an American-style real estate agent. Since mid-1994, foreigners can buy the right to use land – virtually land ownership – almost as easily as Vietnamese. The government itself touts among foreign residents of Hanoi for buyers for desirable plots on the northern banks of the Red River. In Ho Chi Minh City, overseas Vietnamese have been encouraged to buy plots in the desirable Thu Duc suburb across the Saigon River.

In a speech which marked a turning point in the government's attitudes towards the *Viet kieu*, Prime Minister Vo Van Kiet told a conference of overseas Vietnamese in Ho Chi Minh City in February 1993: 'Our country is currently in want of many things which can be provided by overseas Vietnamese in the forms of their knowledge, their investment capital and their assistance in establishing relations between overseas organisations, individuals and the country.' He told the conference, which was timed to take advantage of the large numbers of *Viet kieu* visiting Vietnam for *Têt*, that his government was committed to changing people's attitudes and reducing bureaucracy to ensure that the formerly suspect *émigrés* were welcomed back to Vietnam and encouraged to play a part in helping develop the country. Towards this end, the government has set up a Committee for Overseas Vietnamese (COV) which has its main branch in Ho Chi Minh City.

It is no longer taboo to talk about those who fled the country, though officials display some sensitivity in how they talk about them. The official line is that 'they went to live abroad at diverse times for many social and economic reasons'. No reference is made to their political allegiances. In listing their virtues and qualifications – and the government in Hanoi is proud at how well the *Viet kieu* have fared – official spokesmen never fail to mention 'their love for their motherland' as if this will make them more acceptable to those who find it difficult not to harbour feelings of distrust towards the *Viet kieu*. While some returnees undoubtedly feel a close bond with the land of their birth, others remain strongly anti-communist. If they return for *Têt* or on family visits it is not out of any fraternal feeling. Most refugees have no intention of visiting.

Some of those who have paid visits have gone to help the country rather than just their families – to support aid projects for example. Overseas Vietnamese groups have been quick to offer aid in response to flooding or other natural disasters. This is especially true of those who left Vietnam before 1975 who may feel an added degree of guilt at having evaded the war.

One of the most prominent Vietnamese *émigrés* in Europe is Tran Van Thinh. He left Vietnam as long ago as 1947 and admits that his Vietnamese language is now rusty. He married a French woman and rose through the ranks of French and then European Union officialdom to become a senior trade negotiator and latterly the European Union's ambassador to the General Agreement on Tariffs and Trade in Geneva. Returning to Vietnam in 1988 on his first visit since leaving, he resolved to help Vietnam emerge from poverty and take its rightful place in the world. 'My ambition is to ensure Vietnam's integration into the world economy', he says, 'not through classic methods like heavy industry but by introducing computers'.[1] He set about collecting money by holding exhibitions of photographs of Vietnam to buy computers for Vietnam to 'liberate the brain', as he puts it. He also raised funds to support an orphanage and a polio centre in Ho Chi Minh City and to restore a pagoda in the Red River delta. Thinh says he is 'a European with his heart in Asia' and regards himself as a natural bridge between the two cultures. He believes he had some influence in encouraging the EU to take a more generous attitude towards Vietnamese textile imports during the years they were effectively 'blacked' by the USA and Japan.

The government in Hanoi welcomes all returnees whether they come with money or not, although it hopes to persuade as many as possible to invest in Vietnam's development; that is the main function of the COV. Official figures showed that overseas Vietnamese had invested nearly $80 million in more than 50 approved projects by early 1994. While the claim that *Viet kieu* are largely responsible for Ho Chi Minh City's boom-time is exaggerated, they have played a role in helping *doi moi* take off by both direct and indirect investment. The government is keen too to harness their experience in management and business, according to Dr Nguyen Ngoc Ha, who heads the Ho Chi Minh City Committee for Overseas Vietnamese and is himself a returnee from France. He drew up the invitation list for the 1993 conference. Among those

---

[1] Quoted in the *Far Eastern Economic Review*, 11 November 1993, p 82

who came were professors, doctors, experts in the fields of informatics, electronics, biochemistry, construction and communications.

The government regards the *Viet kieu* as a 'brain bank' to be lured back to help the country. It is intent on removing obstacles in the way of their doing so, but is conscious of the public relations challenge to convince them that Vietnam today is not the austere and undernourished country where political persecution is rife from which they fled. One sign of its determination to change attitudes is that *Viet kieu* visiting Vietnam are no longer solicited for money by underpaid customs and immigrations officers, as they were previously. Most *Viet kieu* now report no harassment during their return visits. In return they accept that as foreigners they must pay higher charges in hotels and public transport, according to the prevailing two-tier pricing policy.

Dai Chau left Vietnam by boat with his parents and younger brother in 1980, when he was 24. It was not that the family felt persecuted, just that it was 'the fashion'; everyone was fleeing and they were afraid to be left behind! They left from Ca Mau, near Vietnam's southernmost tip, and landed safely in Malaysia. Being amongst the first boat people, they had no problem gaining acceptance as refugees by Australia, where they arrived two months later. They settled in Brisbane. Chau, who already had an engineering degree from Saigon Polytechnic, found a job as a draughtsman despite his rather inadequate English. He also enrolled for further studies and qualified as a quantity surveyor. The family enjoyed a good life in Australia, though Chau admits they were lucky. Not all boat people fitted in as well as they did, or found it as easy to get jobs. He says it helped that Brisbane had hosted the Commonwealth Games in 1982 generating opportunities in the construction business.

As he grew older, Chau started to yearn to return to Vietnam. His opportunity came when he was offered the chance to work in Saigon for the Hong Kong-based New World company which was building a big hotel there. The company was attracted by the fact that he combined professional qualifications with the language and local knowledge. He had been born and brought up in Saigon. He returned there to work exactly 10 years after fleeing by boat. After his contract with New World ended, Chau decided to take a much more hazardous plunge. He set himself up in Saigon as a freelance consultant in the construction business operating out of a small office in *Dông Khoi*, the old French Rue Catinat. He recalls: 'The country was just opening up and I could see the potential. The Vietnamese were lacking management skills, lacking quantity surveying skills and lacking construction skills. As both an engineer and a quantity surveyor I knew I had something to offer – something that was needed in Vietnam at that time.'

Business did not come easily and Chau realized he had made a mistake in thinking his professional qualifications would get him work. 'It was all Asian businessmen here and for them connections are everything. Networking is very important in Asia. I did not have connections so I did not get work', he says, 'I got the system totally wrong.' Fortunately, as he was despairing of making a success of things, the large UK construction firm, Maunsell, entered the market and appointed him its local representative. That relationship blossomed and Chau is now director and chief executive of Maunsell's local subsidiary, as well as keeping his consultancy going. 'I was very, very lucky that Maunsell came along, because they have a big name. Now the Asian business groups respect me and come to me, so I get work on my reputation', he says. The building business in Vietnam is booming and Chau enjoys a share of it. Eight years on from the start of *doi moi* and after some very difficult years for his business he now has more work than he can handle. He believes he could not have achieved either his professional reputation or his level of income in Australia. He attributes his success to his qualifications and his knowledge of Vietnamese – but he knows it was a close run thing. So has he any regrets about moving back? 'Not really, though there was a time when business was so bad that I nearly changed my mind and moved back to Australia', he confesses. 'If Maunsell had not come along at the right moment I might have left.'

Chau's parents still live in Brisbane and have been back to Saigon several times to visit him. They are not afraid to do so, but are content with their life in Australia. Chau, as yet unmarried, has a girlfriend in Saigon. Though retaining his Australian passport, he plans to stay in Saigon 'as long as there is work'. He has various projects in the pipeline. He insists there is no discrimination against the *Viet kieu* these days. So how important does he believe *Viet kieu* investment in Vietnam is? 'Not particularly important, but it could become a significant force if the government pursues the right strategy', says Chau. He thinks the *Viet kieu* working in high-tech industries, like computers and telecommunications, have a lot to offer – but the government has to attract them back. He estimates that at least 200 *Viet kieu* have already come back to work in Vietnam, most of them motivated in part by a desire to help Vietnam develop. He is very positive about the way the country is developing and has no doubt that the changes are permanent, insisting 'there will be no reversal of *doi moi*'.

David Phan Thanh, as he now calls himself, is another returnee. He left to study hotel management in Canada a few months before Saigon fell to communist forces, at the age of 30. Coming from a wealthy Mekong delta rice-trading family, David avoided being drafted into the South Vietnamese army. His parents and the rest of his family stayed in Saigon. In Canada he enjoyed a good life, opening two restaurants in Montreal, but the climate did not suit him and provided an incentive to return.

He did not come straight back to Vietnam but moved in 1985 to Singapore, which was and remains Vietnam's main trading partner. He had sold his restaurants and with the proceeds set up a company, Lee Quan Trading, to try to enter the Vietnamese market. This was before *doi moi* when doing business with Vietnam was much riskier than it is now. His move back to Saigon was gradual: 'After 1989 I came more often; I saw the market developing very fast.' He admits it was a struggle at first, but now his trading company is prospering. These days it supplies airport, construction and factory equipment – 'even turnkey factories'. He is not a licensed importer so has to operate through a state trading company. Since moving to Saigon, he has expanded his business interests and has shares in two hotels, one in Ho Chi Minh City and one being built in Hanoi. His partners are from Singapore and Vietnam. David has retained his Canadian nationality which means his investments have to be approved by the State Committee for Cooperation and Investment (SCCI). He also has shares in a ruby mine in northern Vietnam and in a construction company.

David entertains visitors at his ranch in Thu Duc on the eastern bank of the Saigon river, ferrying them there from the Saigon promenade by speedboat. This area favoured by foreign residents of Saigon is rapidly sprouting luxury homes as well as golf courses and driving ranges and the price of land is rising fast. He knows at least 300 Singaporeans live there as do plenty of other foreigners. David plans to develop the ranch into a sport and fitness centre.

During the war, the South Vietnamese army sometimes exchanged fire with communist guerillas on the river's east bank. Now the part of Thu Duc facing downtown Saigon is bedecked with the neon billboards of Asian multinationals like Toshiba, Fuji and Samsung. David believes it will not be long before Thu Duc becomes 'the centre of town'.

Why does he like operating in Vietnam? 'Vietnam is a very nice country to invest in. They keep their word and their security is good. Although I'm a foreigner, I can do anything I want. I have a house and car. Contacts are important and you can do business faster if you have contacts', he says. Reflecting on the qualities that have helped him succeed, he believes foreign firms have confidence in him because he has been trained in foreign business management. 'They trust me', he says. Also, there is no language problem. Most of his partners are state enterprises; he feels more secure doing business with state enterprises because, he says, 'if they fail the government bails them out!' David's current ventures are with companies owned by the Ministries of Trade, Construction and Heavy Industry. He believes the future lies in exploiting Vietnam's natural resources, like the rubies he is already trying to extract.

David is happy to be back in Vietnam – to be among his family and because it is his motherland. He feels he cannot lose, because whether or not he makes a profit he will have helped the people of Vietnam in the process. So far David has not lost money and the profits from his initial ventures have been reinvested. Living in Canada was fun and enabled him to make money – around $12 million which he brought back to invest in Vietnam. He often visits Canada where his wife and two children live, but prefers to stay in Saigon. He knows about 30 friends who have come back from Canada to do business. Many others come on visits. 'Not everyone can do business', he says, 'but many want to come back. My 92-year old aunt wants to come back to die in Vietnam. A lot of people want to die in Vietnam.'

———— ❖ ————

Giang Tran left Vietnam by boat in 1977 with his parents. After spending some time in a holding camp in Indonesia, they were accepted for resettlement in the USA, where they made a new home in San Diego, southern California. Giang studied law there, but started up in business before completing his studies. Now he heads San Diego-based Vietnam Investment Information and Consulting

(VIIC) whose objective is to promote trade with and investment in Vietnam. Until the US embargo was lifted in early 1994 it was a waiting game since no trade or investment was allowed. Giang is proud that his firm was the first to win the endorsement of both the USA and Vietnamese governments to carry on trade between the two countries. He is prouder still to have provided the means for several US companies to 'dip their toes' into the Vietnamese market through two trade shows held in Vietnam within nine months of the lifting of the US embargo; a third show is planned for late 1995. Another show in San Francisco aimed at winning Vietnamese goods a place in the US market provoked a demonstration by Vietnamese Americans opposed to the restoration of trade links with Vietnam.

Giang does not believe connections are important in his business, although clearly he has had to win the trust of the Vietnamese government to be allowed to operate in Vietnam. VIIC now has offices in Hanoi and Ho Chi Minh City. In the USA the company also has non-Vietnamese working for it. Giang says many US firms hoping to sell to Vietnam have Vietnamese Americans working for them. This was evident at his 'VietnAmerica' trade shows where some Vietnamese Americans came to represent US firms, their first visits back to Vietnam since emigrating. Other participating firms were run by American veterans of the Vietnam war. Some were just looking for an opportunity to revisit the country in more favourable circumstances than before, others genuinely wanted to help Vietnam with its development. Giang himself is not motivated solely by his blood ties with Vietnam. He says that 'from a purely commercial point of view now is the time to invest in Vietnam.' He speaks with conviction when trying to encourage US firms in that direction. Nor is he solely an intermediary. 'My two offices represent an investment of half a million dollars, so they show I am serious. Next I would like to set up a *Viet kieu* bank, rather as Chinese Vietnamese have set up the Viet Hoa Bank', he explains.

Nguyen Duy Binh[2] had lived in the USA for more than 13 years when he first came back on a family visit to Saigon in 1989. In the USA he had worked for the international air delivery service, Federal Express, for many years, latterly as operations manager at

---

[2] Nguyen Duy Binh's story is taken from *The Saigon Times*, 8-14 September 1994, p 20.

Washington DC's Dulles airport. Seeing a sign in the Saigon post office for DHL, one of Federal Express's competitors, Binh recommended to the group's chairman that Federal Express should be in Vietnam too. Federal Express liked the idea and asked him to return for further exploratory visits to assess the feasibility of entering this new and relatively unknown market. Federal Express, which has offices in 188 countries, is a relatively young company having started business just about the time Binh was starting his new life in America. When the US trade and investment embargo was lifted, Binh was despatched to Saigon to open an office, which he did two months later in April 1994.

Binh says that returning as Federal Express's country manager for Vietnam is 'like a dream come true'. One of the most challenging parts has been to train local Vietnamese staff, imparting the professionalism and integrity that he believes have helped both him and Federal Express to succeed. He says the average mark attained by Vietnamese trainees in their final exams was significantly higher than those achieved in other countries which he says show 'that Vietnamese workers are amongst the best'. Binh says it has been 'an emotional experience' for both him and his Vietnamese-born wife moving back to Saigon. He feels he is doing his bit for his motherland – participating in the economy and helping bring a quality service to Vietnam. He also believes he is helping to end Vietnam's isolation and bring it closer to the rest of the world. Next he hopes to open a Federal Express office in Hanoi, with Danang and other provincial cities to follow.

When Thuy Ngo[3] first arrived in California, she found part-time work as a receptionist in an optician's shop. After rising to a management position, she left to set up her own chain of opticians. On a family visit to Vietnam in 1990, she realized she had a skill that was needed there. During several subsequent visits, Thuy Ngo set up 'Euro Vision' on Ho Chi Minh City's Tran Hung Dao Street. A few years on, Thuy Ngo and her sister, who is based in Vietnam, run four stores in Ho Chi Minh City and Hanoi, with plans to open branches in other cities. Their spectacles use mainly French and Italian frames with US lenses and cost up to $100 a pair – expensive

[3] Thuy Ngo's story is extracted from *Vietnam Economic Times*, September 1994, p 39.

for a country with an annual per capita income of around $200. But Thuy Ngo's stores have shown there is a demand. She puts her commercial success down to a combination of advanced techniques – computer eye-testing and lens grinding – and fashionable frames. Also her American selling techniques, guaranteed quality and price, although her knowledge of the language and market were important too. She says Vietnamese are demonstrating a preference for paying more and getting the latest fashions and technology, rather than settling for second best.

Vietnamese *émigrés* in Eastern Europe, of whom there are around 260,000, face an uncertain future. Like Vietnam, the countries of Eastern Europe have changed very considerably and very rapidly. Originally seen as the East's equivalent to the *Gastarbeiter* of West Germany, the Vietnamese workers arrived in Russia and its component republics, East Germany, Poland, Hungary, Czechoslovakia, Romania, Bulgaria and Albania under labour contracts between governments. Part of their wages was used to repay Vietnam's debts to those countries. When communism began to crumble, many lost their jobs as factories closed down. Most tried to find other work. Some had their work permits extended, others stayed on illegally. Before long they were teaching their host countries elementary capitalism. Some set up restaurants, others were more ambitious, opening garment factories. Some followed the Poles and the Ukrainians into a role as the trades-people of Europe, journeying from country to country with their wares, making a speciality of smuggling.

One particular talent of the Vietnamese has been much valued in Russia. Most Vietnamese know how to make alcohol out of rice by distillation and fermentation; it is a basic peasant skill. So when former President Gorbachev imposed restrictions on alcohol production, the Vietnamese were able to make large sums of money catering to the Russians' thirst for alcoholic beverages. An offshoot of this was the restaurant business. Emulating the Chinese in an earlier age (and the Italians and Indians in the UK), the Vietnamese *Gastarbeiter* opened restaurants catering to their host communities. There are now thriving Vietnamese restaurants in many Eastern European cities.

Workers sent by their government teamed up with a more privileged élite from Vietnam: the sons and daughters of senior

Party members and officials who had been sent there to study. Their connections and superior education gave them advantages in their host countries. Some learned to meet market demand by importing goods from Vietnam, taking advantage of the greater availability of certain goods there. In the early 1980s it was second-hand blue jeans that were bought from foreign travellers in Ho Chi Minh City and sent for sale in Moscow; now it is new jeans. In the 1990s the most lucrative item is the computer. In order to encourage computer literacy, Vietnam allows computer imports at very low duty. Many are then re-exported to Russia at a handsome profit. Well-known American brands like IBM and Compaq – which under the embargo should never have reached Vietnam in the first place – are reaching Russia and other Eastern European countries from Saigon!

Around half of the estimated 80,000 Vietnamese in Russia live and work in the Moscow area. On the western outskirts of the city is the Vinaco Trading Centre, the largest clothing distribution centre in the Russian capital. In a building rented from the Moscow city authorities, hundreds of Vietnamese men and women run stalls selling jeans and other low-cost clothing made in Vietnam and Thailand. A staggering 2 million pairs of jeans are sold at Vinaco each month, a significant proportion of the total trade between Vietnam and Russia, although this trade is unofficial and does not show on either government's statistics. Most Vietnamese in Russia will face deportation as their work permits expired in 1995 unless they can convince the authorities that they are providing a necessary service. Although they are good at what they do and manage to undercut the price of locally-made clothing those facts are unlikely to persuade their host government that they should stay on – especially now the state no longer benefits from their presence as it did when they were indentured to state enterprises.

Russia seems an unlikely place to go to make US dollars through private enterprise, but many Vietnamese have followed the contracted workers there for precisely that purpose. The opportunities to make money are so good in Moscow that middle men in Hanoi charge about $4,000 to 'ship' a Vietnamese there. Unlike those heading for the West, however, the Vietnamese in Russia have every intention of returning to Vietnam to spend and invest their dollars there. Amongst those engaged in this massive Vietnam-Russia clothing business is a diplomat who used to be based at Hanoi's embassy in Warsaw. He says he came to Russia 'to make US dollars, because with dollars I can buy anything anywhere!'

In another part of Moscow, a former Russian diplomat previously posted in Vung Tau is partner in a Vietnamese–Russian enterprise importing instant noodles. This low-cost food has become popular in a country used to food shortages. Each year the Saigon factory sends around 15 million packets to Russia, its most profitable overseas market. In 1994 the partners opened a manufacturing plant at Sladimir, not far from Moscow. It is doing well but cannot satisfy local demand, so further factories are planned – possibly one in the Russian Far East to meet demand there. Noodles and jeans have made some Vietnamese in Russia quite wealthy, which in turn has led to resentment and harassment against these immigrants. A Vietnamese-run department store in Moscow was raided by police in mid-1994 and many items confiscated because the Vietnamese had allegedly 'forgotten' to pay their taxes. The tale was the talk of Hanoi, although it was not reported in any Vietnamese newspapers. Undeterred, some Vietnamese businessmen in Russia have diversified into other businesses, including aircraft leasing and transportation. Another is trying his hand on the new commodities market!

Harassment by the police is the major problem faced by Vietnamese in the Berlin, Bernau and Leipzig areas of Germany, though poverty comes a close second. These former workers in the state factories of East Germany tried to find other jobs after reunification and the collapse of many of the factories where they previously worked; their former employers could not even afford to meet their contractual obligations by providing an air ticket back to Vietnam. But there were no jobs in a country coming to terms with over-manning in its eastern wing, at least not for immigrant workers. Some Vietnamese set up 'Chinese' restaurants only to fall prey to Chinese or Vietnamese extortion gangs. Other favoured businesses are food shops and clothing stalls, but the most popular trade is the lucrative business of smuggling duty free cigarettes from Poland and selling them on the streets of German cities. The highest profit is on Marlboro; ironically, smuggling cigarettes is also big business in Vietnam, where foreign cigarettes are officially banned but Marlboro and other popular brands have been available throughout the period of the embargo. Cigarette-toting Vietnamese in Germany have fallen foul of the police trying to crack down on the trade in cigarettes which they call 'organized crime'. A Berlin-based immigrant aid organization has taken up their cause and helped around 50 Vietnamese bring cases of assault against the police. Berlin's new Vietnamese ghetto is the industrial suburb of

Ahrensfelde, nicknamed 'Little Hanoi'. Many of those out-of-work live there in impoverished dormitory-style accommodation.

Vietnamese workers in East Germany applied for resettlement, like their compatriots who reached West Germany via the refugee camps of South East Asia, claiming with some justification that they and their children would have difficulty settling back in Vietnam after years of working in Germany. They were turned down. As far as the German government is concerned, they are *Gastarbeiter* who have outstayed their welcome and whose very presence has provoked anti-foreigner sentiments and violence. So while the former boat people are well integrated and enjoy comfortable lives in the west of the country, secure with their residents' permits, their brethren in the east live a precarious and illegal existence trying to make money by trading, but fearing assault by the police and deportation. The main difference between the two groups is that the latter, who number around 40,000, were invited by the former communist government of East Germany, while around 30,000 'refugees' were invited in by the Bonn government.

During 1994, the illegal Vietnamese workers became an issue between the governments in Bonn and Hanoi when the latter apparently refused to accept them back. Germany suspended its programme of development aid to Vietnam. Later agreement was reached to repatriate 40,000 'over-stayers' to Vietnam and for the German government to resume its support for forestry, health care and railway rehabilitation projects in Vietnam and to provide credit guarantees for German firms wanting to sell goods there. Aid from the German government is more valuable to Vietnam than the remittances of workers living there.

Many Eastern European *Viet kieu* have entrenched their positions in their host country, presenting something of an economic threat to the indigenous peoples. Their fear is that, if the local economies encounter hard times, they will become victims of persecution, as other successful immigrant communities have done elsewhere – including, for example, the Chinese in Vietnam during the late 1970s. This is already happening in Germany where the Vietnamese regard themselves as victims of the collapse of communism, which has cost them their jobs and even their means to return home. Eastern European Vietnamese tend to have close ties with their motherland, because they are products of a communist upbringing – not exiled like those in the US and Australia – and they have invested a lot of their earnings back in Vietnam. Indeed, Vietnamese *émigrés* living in Russia and Germany are blamed for the skyrocketing house prices in Hanoi as they re-divert their business skills back home.

Back home in Vietnam, the Eastern European *Viet kieu* and their relatives have become a powerful economic clique who are dubbed 'the red capitalists' – the Vietnamese equivalent of China's *gaoganzidi*, sons and daughters of high officials who are benefiting from that country's new economic policies. Many family members of senior Vietnamese Communist Party officials control important businesses. Prominent amongst them is the son of former Party Secretary General Le Duan, who married a Russian during his time as a student in Moscow. Now he runs an import–export business which, among other things, imports spare parts for the many Russian-built aircraft operating in Indochina. Just as former Russian diplomats are involved in this import-export trade between Russia and Vietnam at both ends, former Eastern European diplomats can be found in Ho Chi Minh City heading 'freelance' organizations promoting trade links between their countries and Vietnam. This is a reminder that capitalism is not just the preserve of the capitalist countries and that former communists can be just as successful when they turn their hands to private enterprise!

10

The American Connection

By far the largest number of Vietnamese *émigrés* have settled in the USA. Vietnamese Americans were estimated to number around 1 million by mid-1995, approximately the population of Haiphong city, or double that of Danang. The first Vietnamese evacuees, some 130,000, were brought to the USA by the US armed forces in the immediate aftermath of the war, mostly within days of the 'fall' of Saigon. Many had worked for the US or South Vietnamese governments, or at least had a family member who had. Others had just seized opportunities to get out during the chaotic mass exodus from South Vietnam as communist forces rolled south.

The USA also accepted the largest numbers of the subsequent exodus which came in three further waves. First the boat people, the largest wave; then, from around 1978, the Orderly Departure Programme (ODP) refugees; finally, after the 1989 Comprehensive Plan of Action (CPA), came the so-called 'H.O.' or humanitarian operations *émigrés*, who included former inmates of re-education camps, family reunion cases and Amerasians – children fathered in Vietnam by American soldiers. All joined the long tradition of immigration to the USA. The land of opportunity beckoned and the Vietnamese came literally by the boat and plane load.

Vietnamese Americans dispersed through all 50 American states as the result of a deliberate government policy. It wanted to avoid a Vietnamese concentration, like that of Cubans in Miami, although such concentrations have come about despite the initial policy of dispersal. Later arrivals tended to follow family members, while the job market caused internal migration. In Alaska and Texas they found work in the oil industry, while in northern California they gravitated towards the computer industry. The airport taxi rank at Honolulu in Hawaii is dominated by veterans who jokingly call themselves the Second Armoured Brigade! Washington DC has some of the more politically-orientated Vietnamese. Their children are more likely to study at one of the East Coast's 'Ivy League' universities. Washington is also the home of Vietnamese 'yuppies' – young, upwardly-mobile professionals – and of organized youth groups.

At least 2,000 Vietnamese restaurants have opened around the country. The commonest Vietnamese family name, Nguyen, is to be found in telephone directories from Alabama to Washington state, often with long lists of names. More than 300 Vietnamese newspapers and magazines keep the community in touch with each other, around the same number of publications as serve the entire population of Vietnam, which is 70 times greater. Cities with large concentrations of Vietnamese, like Houston and San Jose, also have their own Vietnamese-language radio stations, which play an important role engendering community spirit as well as advertising Vietnamese businesses. Those cities also have their own community 'yellow pages' offering a range of businesses from ethnically-distinct ones like restaurants, hairdressers, acupuncturists and astrologers to mainstream professions and trades like doctors and pharmacists as well as builders and plumbers. The same directories also list Vietnamese Americans associations embracing everything from cultural and religious activities to the fishing community, journalism and scouting organisations.

In San Jose, you can buy your American car from a Vietnamese dealer and have it repaired or re-sprayed at another all-Vietnamese business. You can buy your house from a Vietnamese estate agent and hire all manner of building and decorating services from within the community. Weddings may be carried out by a Vietnamese Buddhist or Catholic priest and the wedding dresses and cake would be provided by Vietnamese too. Another Vietnamese would take the photographs, probably in the city's Japanese gardens where Asian brides, grooms and their entourages follow one another in quick succession at weekends. Gay Vietnamese Americans can subscribe to a San Jose-published magazine which recognizes a lifestyle which does not exist in Vietnam itself – according to the authorities there.

Young professionals in San Jose are likely to be employed in the computer or electronics industry – Silicon Valley links the city to its northern neighbour, San Francisco. Some Vietnamese settled in the area after being hired by one or other of the computer giants with headquarters there, who include Apple and Hewlett Packard. Sunnyvale, a suburb of San Jose, is home to an interesting sideline to the Internet; Vietnet, a Vietnamese-language network within the

Internet which young Vietnamese Americans use to communicate with each other throughout the USA and beyond. They use it to exchange technical information, or just to chat. One bulletin board within Vietnet is for 'singles' only – a potential marriage bureau. In an intriguing cross-cultural phenomenon which observes neither political or economic embargoes, young Vietnamese in Washington DC use the Internet to talk with their contemporaries in Vietnam via a terminal at Hanoi's Institute of Cybernetics.

Around half of all Vietnamese Americans live in California. They call the state 'Cali' and refer to its appeal with the saying *'Cali di de kho ve, Trai di co vo, Gai ve co con'*: 'It's easy to go to California, difficult to leave. Boys find wives there, girls have children there.' In fact it was job opportunities and the state's sub-tropical climate that first attracted those brought up in the steamy heat of Saigon and the Mekong delta. Other enticements included generous welfare benefits (now discontinued) and a welcoming local community. Some see themselves as followers of a tradition that began in 1849 when the first recorded Vietnamese immigrant to the USA, Le Kim, joined prospectors searching for gold in California. Later he returned to spend his fortune in his home town of My Tho in the Mekong delta. Apart from a few students of the 1950s and 1960s who stayed on, there were very few Vietnamese in America before 1975, although, as already pointed out, the ship on which Ho Chi Minh was working his passage is believed to have put into San Francisco harbour in the early 20th century! Both Ho and his contemporary, Ngo Dinh Diem, who is the apotheosis of Vietnamese Americans, spent some of their formative years in the USA, but on the East Coast – in New York and New Jersey respectively.

California already had substantial Chinese and Korean communities in the San Francisco and Los Angeles areas before the Vietnamese arrived. They were a magnet to the new arrivals since both these nationalities use some (though by no means all) of the same cooking ingredients. Camp Pendelton near San Diego was one of three US military camps to which the first wave of Vietnamese were brought after the evacuation from South Vietnam in April and May 1975. Many moved to Orange County, between Los Angeles and San Diego, where job and housing opportunities were good at that time. Orange County had been a favoured resettlement area for American veterans of both the Second World War and the Vietnam war. Vietnam veterans did their best to make the evacuees welcome and to sponsor them in new homes. For some Americans it was a way of assuaging the guilt they felt at having lost the war and the country to communists.

Vietnamese Americans on the whole have fitted in well in their adopted country. Many have taken advantage of their new homeland's natural encouragement to private enterprise by establishing themselves in business – with loans from within the community or from US banks. Others have found employment with US technical, computing or engineering corporations, while doctors, dentists and pharmacists have set up in practice – mainly serving fellow Vietnamese. Less well educated émigrés have been absorbed into the labour market. Even in recession-hit California of the 1990s, unemployment is no higher among the Vietnamese than among other Americans. Fewer than 10% Vietnamese Americans (mainly the elderly who benefit from pension provisions) remain dependent on welfare. Most states have cut back drastically on their earlier support. Some refugees cite the harsh resettlement regime, under which welfare support ended a few months after their arrival, as the major factor in encouraging Vietnamese Americans to stand on their own feet. 'In other countries welfare has run on too long, making the Vietnamese immigrant community highly dependent on the state', observes one.

Vietnamese American children have been 'high achievers' in school and have grown up as 'good American kids'. They demonstrate a pronounced leaning towards technical options in college rather than the arts. At this level they find the competition to graduate top of their class much stiffer. Parents without any higher education are especially keen to ensure that their children take advantage of educational opportunities they never had. It is not uncommon to find children of Vietnamese manual workers who may not speak much English graduating as doctors, pharmacists or engineers, careers much favoured amongst the Vietnamese.

There is inevitably a problem of children feeling more American and rebelling against Vietnamese family and cultural traditions. (By the early 1990s, around 20% of Vietnamese Americans had been born in the USA.) Some parents regard television as particularly dangerous in breaking down traditional Vietnamese culture and speak of what they call 'the answering back phenomenon'. They regard it as the least happy consequence of their new lives in the USA. As one parent explains it: 'Our kids live between two cultures. We spend every weekend with our families, the grown-ups socializing in Vietnamese while the kids play with each other in English. We're trying to bring them up as Vietnamese but we're not succeeding. What we require is obedience and respect. There's no talking back in our family; it's the Vietnamese way.' The divergence between traditions becomes more apparent as children become teenagers. As another parent put it: 'American culture is stronger than their [Vietnamese] culture.' Their teenage children have minds of their own and an inclination to argue with their parents who, they say, don't understand American mores – for example that American dating rituals are far removed from those of their motherland. The incidence of inter-marriage between Vietnamese and other American communities is rising, to the consternation of some parents, although marriage within the community remains the norm.

If the alienation of children from their parents' culture and traditions is one community-wide problem, the predicament of the elderly has given rise to another. Some Vietnamese families have readily accepted the US solution by depositing aged parents in old people's homes. More often, though, an aged parent comes to live (according to Asian practice) with one of his or her married children. This has caused strains between married couples who have had the chance to relish the freedom of the small American-style family unit. Families have broken up as a consequence of arguments over what to do about a mother or father-in-law, or because a parent comes to live in a family home. For this and other reasons, the incidence of divorce amongst Vietnamese Americans is high, although not as high as the American average. 'It seems high', explains one who has felt the strains but held his marriage together, 'because in pre-1975 Vietnam divorce was virtually unknown.' He may unconsciously be recognizing another truth: that in the USA, Vietnamese wives feel liberated and more entitled to a say in family matters than they ever did in Vietnam. What is true of the children is as true of mothers too, which calls to mind a line in the Le Ly Hayslip novel and movie *Heaven and Earth*, when the American husband tells his Vietnamese wife after they set up home in the USA: 'You're answering back just like an American wife'. The Vietnamese American who despairs at the rising incidence of divorce in the community is surprised to learn that divorce is now commonplace back in Vietnam, following the introduction of *doi moi*.

Asked about success stories among the community in the USA, Vietnamese Americans have difficulty thinking of anyone who has 'made it big' in American society. There are no major political leaders, movie stars, novelists or even captains of industry who stand out. There is an Alaska-based artist whose paintings of Indian and Alaskan scenes have been much in demand. Another figure mentioned is Nguyen Viet, who wrote one of the first software programmes for the Vietnamese script and went on to develop programmes for the Arabic and Hebrew languages as well as a Russian programme which was bought by the Ministry of Defence in Moscow. Mostly, though, the figures who come to mind as having 'made it' in terms of fame or fortune or both have done so by serving their own community. In the political arena, few have emulated the example of Tony Lam, a restaurateur in Orange County, who has three times been elected to a seat on Westminster City Council – depending, it has to be said, not just on Vietnamese votes but on the support of the Hispanic community too. One of Tony Lam's claims to fame – apart from his elections victories – is to have persuaded the city council to erect a sign on the Garden Grove Freeway directing motorists to the turn for 'Little Saigon'. 'It has put this centre of the Vietnamese community in southern California on a par with nearby Disneyland', proclaims one community leader with pride.

Little Saigon is a phenomenon deserving of pride. Located to the south of Los Angeles in Orange County, it is the business and social heartland for the one third of all Vietnamese Americans – more than 300,000 – who live in Southern California. Originally a two-mile stretch of Bolsa Avenue dominated by Vietnamese shops and businesses, Little Saigon has grown into a business district embracing several square miles of the neighbouring cities of Westminster and Garden Grove. Here a self-sufficient and reasonably self-contained Vietnamese community runs its own supermarkets, clinics, pharmacies, hairdressers, travel agencies, car dealers, real estate businesses, legal practices, building and financial services. Little Saigon community advertisements offer the services of teachers of English, musical instruments, dancing and secretarial skills as well as retailing services of all varieties. Every conceivable ingredient needed in Vietnamese cooking can be found in Little Saigon's many supermarkets although, because of the previous embargo, almost none of it comes from Vietnam. (Since the embargo was lifted, Vietnamese beer, coffee beans and instant noodles have begun to be imported while a state enterprise in Vietnam is importing American grapes!) Little Saigon has almost as many gold dealers as the whole of Hanoi and its music shops have a wider variety of Vietnamese music, all recorded in America, than any store in Saigon. You can live in Little Saigon and avoid doing business with any non-Vietnamese speaker!

At weekends, Vietnamese from as far afield as San Diego to the south and Studio City to the north of Los Angeles drive to Little Saigon for their shopping and entertainment, or just to meet friends. The elderly come to visit the pagoda or consult a doctor or acupuncturist. The young come to enjoy the *karaoke* bars with recorded-in-America Vietnamese videos, to go dancing or to watch Vietnamese movies. All age groups come to eat. Probably the finest Vietnamese cuisine anywhere, including Vietnam, is to be found in Little Saigon, where Vietnamese recipes are combined with American standards of service and cleanliness – and served in American-sized helpings! The joy for the Vietnamese is the wide range of foods from the Hanoi specialities of *pho* and *banh cuon* to Saigon's *cha gio* spring rolls and the Mekong delta delicacies of *hu tieu* and *bo kho* and every other local speciality in between. Here, no one seems to worry that the dishes are made with American water!

It seems strange to find a shopping mall named after the Vietnamese hero, Le Loi, and to find Vietnamese businesses trading under hybrid names like Cathy Nhung, Johnny Giang and Tina Pham, or behind all-American facades like Bridgecreek Realty. (Most businesses in Little Saigon make few concessions to American society and retain their Vietnamese names in full.) It is stranger still to hear the communist theme tune, the *Internationale*, playing in a Vietnamese coffee shop whose proprietor can have no idea of the tune's significance! Vietnamese from around the state choose to get married, divorced or buried in Little Saigon because all the necessary facilities are there. The community sustains several newspapers and magazines. For the comprehensive service it provides, Little Saigon is the envy of other ethnic groups in the area, including the Chinese and Koreans.

The man mainly responsible for Little Saigon is Frank Jao, who built the first shopping malls in a district which now has dozens. A Chinese Vietnamese from Saigon, Jao raised the finance from Hong Kong and Taiwan, in the same way as Lo Ky Nguon did to build his shopping mall in Cholon. Jao was following a long-established tradition that has brought 'Chinese money' into retailing in many Californian cities. Los Angeles itself and its Chinese-populated suburb of Monterey Park (where a woman of Taiwanese origin has been mayor) have benefited greatly from ethnic Chinese investment, which has given rise to something of a power-struggle between pro-

Taiwan and pro-Beijing interests. By the mid-1990s, Beijing, with its Vu supermarket group, was thought to be more powerful. Both Vu and its Taiwanese rival, the 99 group, have opened supermarket branches in Little Saigon, recognizing the purchasing power of the Vietnamese Americans, who are inclined (like South Vietnamese back home) to spend what they earn immediately rather than to save. So just as investment from ethnic Chinese sources is playing a major role in developing Saigon itself, Little Saigon is also growing big on Chinese money. Traditionally, Chinese in East Asia have channelled investment into South East Asia, including Vietnam, through the local Chinese community and now they are doing just the same in California. As they pursue new economic policies heavily dependent on foreign investment, both the Vietnamese and Chinese governments seems to be competing for investment from Taiwan with *émigré* Vietnamese businesses in southern California.

The Little Saigon community recognize that their self-containment is both a strength and a weakness. Some are attempting to diversify from services aimed specifically at Vietnamese to serve other Americans – notably through restaurants – but their limited command of English is an obstacle. One ambitious scheme is to promote Little Saigon as a tourist attraction to rival Disneyland ten miles away, which already attracts thousands of American and foreign visitors to the area each week. Other Little Saigon traders are quite content to serve their own community and not to integrate too much, reassured by the knowledge that Southern California's Vietnamese community is still growing.

Little Saigon is home to *Nguoi Viet*, the main Vietnamese language daily newspaper in the USA. It circulates widely among the community in Orange County and the adjoining counties of San Diego and Los Angeles and has syndication agreements with papers in San Jose and other US cities as well as with newspapers in Montreal and Toronto in Canada and Sydney, Australia. It makes its money through a lively classified advertisement section. Publisher Do Ngoc Yen stresses the importance of its distribution system and the fact that it contains the sort of news Orange County Vietnamese want to read. Though aimed primarily at Vietnamese who do not speak English and thus cannot read US newspapers, it is read too by English-speaking Vietnamese who want to be kept in touch with the Vietnamese *émigré* community in the USA and elsewhere. 'Nguoi Viet aims to be a newspaper of record for overseas Vietnamese', says Yen, 'just like the New York Times is for Americans.'

'The paper also tries to provide a window on Vietnam,' says Yen.

News about Vietnam is extracted from Saigon newspapers, like *Lao Dong, Saigon Giai Phong* and *Tuoi Tre* as well as by de-briefing travellers returning from visits there. Yen himself is a fount of knowledge about Vietnam. *Nguoi Viet* is the main way in which the Vietnamese of Orange County (or Quân Cam as it is literally translated into Vietnamese!) keep abreast of development in their homeland, together with transmissions from London of the Vietnamese Service of the BBC, which are re-broadcast by a local Vietnamese language radio station. Yen himself favours reconciliation with Vietnam but is cautious about advocating this in the columns of his newspaper. He knows it is all too easy to arouse the indignation of those of his readers who oppose such moves. He has already been accused of 'going soft on communism'. As a commercial enterprise, his paper has to respect the views of its readers.

A magazine published from the same Little Saigon street as *Nguoi Viet* sets out to strengthen ties between Vietnamese writers in the USA and Vietnam. The publisher of *Hop Luu*, Phan Tan Hai, tried to reach agreement with a publishing house in Saigon to exchange writers' manuscripts. Negotiations broke down when the publisher in Vietnam published stories by overseas Vietnamese without their permission. Nonetheless, Hop Luu's publishers maintain contact with Vietnamese writers through intermediaries in France and have published their works alongside those of contemporary Vietnamese writers abroad. They see this as an important channel of communications between intellectuals which would not necessarily have the approval of the authorities in Hanoi. 'It is one way of keeping Vietnamese culture alive', says publisher Hai, who also believes it is a means of promoting reconciliation between Vietnam and its diaspora.

Vietnamese American culture is promoted by a large output of books, music and *karaoke* videos produced in southern California and sold throughout the USA. (CDs and *karaoke* videos are also on sale in Vietnam, fuelling what seems to be a national obsession with *karaoke*, despite strict government restrictions on the entry of cultural material into Vietnam. Young Hanoians and Saigonese sing along to Californian-recorded Vietnamese music videos just as young Vietnamese Americans do – another example of culture straddling the political divide!) The publication of novels by Vietnamese Americans is itself a lively industry, although their reputation for quality is not high. One editor sees the proliferation of book, magazine and newspaper publishing as a consequence of the tight controls on publishing which prevailed in Vietnam before 1975. 'Since the first French newspaper appeared in Vietnam in 1865, no private Vietnamese was allowed to publish. In that sense Vietnam today is no different from South Vietnam under Diem or Thieu', he says. When the *émigrés* reached the USA they found that permits to publish were not needed so Vietnamese publications blossomed. 'Much of it was very poor', says the editor, 'and very few publications make any money.' He sees this as one more way in which Vietnamese Americans are enjoying a freedom they never had at home and which their compatriots in Vietnam still do not enjoy.

Kieu Chinh was well-known as a film actress in Saigon and around South East Asia before 1975. She is now a minor Hollywood star with roles in television series such as MASH and 'Asian' movies to her credit, though she says she has not had a good Vietnamese part yet. A Hanoian by birth, she is, she says, 'a refugee twice over'. In 1954, she was separated from the rest of her family and sent south to begin a new life in Saigon as Vietnam was divided. As she puts it: 'I became a refugee within my own country.' In 1975 her second displacement brought her to the USA as a refugee with her three children. 'That makes twice that I have run away,' she explains suggesting a deliberate choice on her part. 'Even now', she says, 'it remains extraordinarily difficult to talk about the events which brought me to California.'

Apart from her screen successes, Kieu Chinh owns a film studio and a publishing company and is a prominent figure in the Vietnamese community of southern California. She describes herself as a 'social activist' and is as committed to the cause of resettling her country-people in their new homes as she is to her career as an actress. Lately she has become a leading light in the Vietnam Memorial Association, one of the many US–Vietnam reconciliation organizations, which seeks ways to commemorate the estimated 3 million Vietnamese who lost their lives in the war. In 1993, Kieu Chinh took part in a memorial ceremony in Washington DC at which the names of all 58,183 Americans killed in Vietnam were read out. As part of what it calls 'a living memorial', the Vietnam Memorial Association has already built a school at Quang Tri province in central Vietnam, scene of some of the heaviest fighting.

Although she supports reconciliation and the normalization of relations between Vietnam and the USA, Kieu Chinh has not herself been back to Vietnam. She says her memories are still too painful. The Second World War allies bombed Hanoi as her mother was in hospital giving birth to a younger brother; both mother and new born baby were killed, when Kieu Chinh was five. She last saw her father and elder brother in 1954 when she was 15. Her father, who she knows spent five years in jail after she left the North, died in 1978. 'I never even heard his voice again though we did exchange a few letters', she says. In recent years she has managed to talk on the telephone to her only brother in Hanoi. Now he is asking why she does not come back to be reunited with him 'before it is too late'. He is over 60. On the one hand she yearns to return and feels that, having known both the north and the south, it should be easier for her than for others. But she is apprehensive as to what she will find and the effect it will have on her, especially to meet her long-lost brother after more than 40 years. It is bound to be a deeply emotional, if not traumatic, experience. She also cites strong opposition from the community as the reason she has not returned sooner. 'It makes it very difficult for me that I am a public person; even a rumour that I was going back led to allegations that I had now become a communist', she says. 'If I go back it will not be a political move, although some are bound to see it like that. It will be because I am hungry to meet my family.' She hopes to be offered a part in a film being made in Vietnam, which would make it easier for her to return.

Kieu Chinh was one of the stars in the movie of Amy Tan's novel, *The Joy Luck Club*,[1] which addresses the issue of reunion between *émigré* Chinese in the USA and close family members still in China. Kieu Chinh plays one of the mothers, Suyuan, who was forced to abandon two young daughters in China whilst fleeing from the advancing Japanese. In exile in San Francisco, Suyuan, who by day enjoys the jolly lifestyle of the city's Chinatown, dreams of being reunited with her abandoned offspring. She dies without doing so or even knowing whether they survived, more afraid of the trauma of reunion than she realizes. Unknowingly she has transferred the yearning to her American-born daughter, June, who eventually makes the journey to meet her half-sisters – and is the one who conveys the news of their mother's death. The

[1] The story, about first and second generation Chinese migrants to San Francisco set against flashbacks of their lives in China, illustrates changes and family tensions which afflict the Vietnamese community too. For example, the phenomenon of children answering their parents back in American rather than Asian style comes across well in *The Joy Luck Club*.

immensely powerful and emotional tale is made the more poignant by the knowledge that Kieu Chinh faces similar trauma in contemplating a journey to meet the brother she can barely remember and with whom she probably has very little in common.

After California, the largest number of Vietnamese Americans have settled in Texas. Texas has had little difficulty absorbing these new immigrants who have integrated more completely into US society than those in California. Most employed Vietnamese in Texas work for US companies. As in California, the Vietnamese have favoured the cities. The largest community – up to 150,000 people – is in the oil town of Houston; smaller communities are centred on Austin, Dallas and San Antonio. They were initially attracted to Texas by jobs in the oil industry, but as the US recession hit the state they used their ingenuity to find other work. In the 1990s, the greater availability of work and cheaper housing led some Vietnamese to migrate to Texas from California and other recession-hit states. Vietnamese restaurants have proliferated in downtown Houston, which was once the preserve of Chinese restaurateurs. Houston city workers, conscious of the importance of a healthy diet, find Vietnamese cuisine with its high protein and low fat content and plentiful fresh vegetables, healthy, appetising and inexpensive: $3.99 buys a selection of 20 different dishes including soup and rice. Workers too busy to take a lunch break can have Vietnamese snack foods delivered to their premises. As in California, the Chinese Vietnamese in Texas have been the channel through which Chinese in East Asia have invested in the state.

The Houston Vietnamese community's main strength is its independence – it is more outward-looking and has a better record of competing commercially with Americans than does the California-based community. Houston has a high proportion of Vietnamese Catholics, Catholic priests amongst them. American Catholics have helped make them welcome. They are responsible for a community housing project in the Park Place district under which derelict apartment housing blocks threatened with demolition were bought by the church and sold to Vietnamese settlers at remarkably low prices – $6,000 for a one-bedroomed apartment with bathroom, kitchen and living-cum-dining room. (Being Texas, even small apartments are not that small.) The new owners, whose only extra outgoings are for utilities, have restored the apartments with great care to make comfortable homes. One street in the area has its condominium housing named after South Vietnamese cities: Saigon Condo, Hué Condo and so on.

Texas's Gulf of Mexico coastline is the scene of one of the more interesting success stories of Vietnamese America. Families of Vietnamese fishermen, *émigrés* from the southern port of Vung Tau (who came originally from northern Vietnam), have combined their native fishing skills with US business and marketing techniques to dominate the shrimp fishing industry. At the town of Seabrook half way between Houston and Galveston, for example, Vietnamese at first worked on US fish and shrimp boats. Gradually the Vietnamese, who work as families and live on the premises (on land or on the fishing vessels) thus having very low overheads, have taken over. A handful of families now runs a multi-million dollar industry that builds fishing boats, catches the fish and shrimps, runs a refrigeration plant, manages sales into the local market and also 'trucks' frozen seafoods to inland states like Kansas and Alabama and as far afield as New York. It is curious that this group of Vietnamese Americans is prospering on the very same industry which is the fastest growing export earner in Vietnam itself.

They did not reach this position of strength without a struggle. In the early 1980s, the racist Ku Klux Klan (KKK) tried to chase the immigrants out. At first they used intimidation and harassment against the Vietnamese, later they took their campaign to court. In a classic US episode of vested interest versus free enterprise, the latter prevailed, freeing the Vietnamese to expand their business. Consumers supported the Vietnamese because they were able to deliver seafood to the market at lower prices. They bought the quays and started building their own fishing vessels. As they expanded, the Vietnamese started employing Hispanics and other Americans. The KKK, who were ordered to leave the Vietnamese alone, accepted their defeat at the hands of America's newest immigrant community and the people of Texas and neighbouring states were assured of a supply of low priced seafood.

In 1924, Ho Chi Minh wrote an article about the Ku Klux Klan.[2] He recalled the organization's origins in 1866 after the American Civil War had emancipated black Americans, noting how it took its name from the Greek *kuklos*, meaning club, and told how the emancipation of blacks had ruined white landlords by depriving

[2] Reproduced in English in Bernard Fall, *Ho Chi Minh On Revolution*, Pall Mall Press, London, 1967, pp 48-51.

them of their labour force. According to Ho, the KKK, whose only policy he said was 'anti-Negro', proclaimed the supremacy of the white race and used intimidation and murder to advance their cause. 'Later', wrote Ho, 'the organization became anti-Catholic, anti-Semite, anti-worker and anti-Negro.' He noted how the Klan flourished in southern states like Texas and predicted that it was 'doomed to disappear'. Just as Ho may have been surprised that the KKK remained active well into the second half of the century, today's Vietnamese shrimp fisherfolk would be surprised to know how proud Ho Chi Minh would have been of the way his countrymen took on the KKK in their own backyard of Texas in this famous victory for what Ho would have called 'workerism' but which Americans would regard as free enterprise. The victory by the Vietnamese fisherfolk marked a significant moment in the Klan's declining power in America's south.

The story of the Vietnamese American fisherfolk is the more curious because of how they spend their wealth. As an elder of Houston's Vietnamese community explains it, the Vietnamese fisherfolk of the Gulf of Mexico are 'probably the least integrated of all Vietnamese in America'. The older generation speak little English and 'simply do not fit in to American society, with whom they have almost nothing in common'. They have little in common either with most other Vietnamese – so during the closed season for shrimp fishing they 'go home' to Vietnam and enjoy a lifestyle and climate more to their liking for at least part of the year. Though figures are not available because money tends to be carried by hand, they are likely to be contributing a significant inflow of funds and may well be supporting local Vietnamese enterprise – perhaps even helping Vietnamese fisherfolk to diversify into refrigeration and marketing. Their children, meanwhile, remain at school in the USA and, like all second generation Vietnamese Americans, are becoming more 'American' in behaviour and lifestyle.

However, the fisherfolk are also indirectly investing in the USA. Vietnamese migrants tend not to have good credit, so if a Vietnamese in Houston needs money to open or expand a business he will not go to the bank. He will approach a Vietnamese intermediary in the Catholic church who, on little more than the ethnic connection, can probably raise at least $50,000 virtually overnight. The fisherfolk are happier investing their profits in this way since it accords with their natural suspicion of banks, a characteristic of a country where banking even now is in its infancy as a source of credit or a place of secure deposit. The fishing community also finances a large Catholic church in Houston where one of the Sunday services is celebrated in Vietnamese.

Vietnamese Americans do not like the label *Viet kieu* which they think suggests they are under the control of the Hanoi government. The older ones still think of themselves as 'South Vietnamese', citizens of a nation that has ceased to exist, and they harbour bitterness against the present Vietnamese government which they blame for its demise. Young Vietnamese are less conscious of their Vietnamese identity and feel more American, although this varies from state to state. For example, the recession in California with its 'lay-offs' caused many young Vietnamese to realize that they were not after all 'full-blown Americans'. According to a community elder, they found alternative livelihoods by retreating into the Vietnamese community and providing a service wanted by that community. 'It was a sharp reminder of their Vietnamese identity and the fact that blood ties are more important than schooling', he says. Workers made redundant in Texas simply sought employment elsewhere in US firms.

Whether self-contained as in California, or well-integrated as elsewhere, Vietnamese Americans believe they are there to stay. Some of the older ones perhaps dream of returning to their motherland, but most contemplate nothing more than visits there. They talk of visiting their motherland and then returning 'home'. However poor they may be, they recognize that they have a relatively good life in the USA. Besides, given the circumstances of their departure, most Vietnamese Americans intensely dislike 'the communists'. They find it difficult to believe that *doi moi* has brought capitalism back to Vietnam and are inclined to dismiss it as a temporary aberration, pointing out that 'the communists' still control the police and the army. One intellectual has likened *doi moi* to Lenin's New Economic Policy of the early 1920s which helped revive the Soviet Union's economy, but which was reversed by Stalin after Lenin's death. He cited this as the reason Vietnamese Americans were disinclined to invest in Vietnam, preferring instead to reinvest any profits within the USA. One wealthy Vietnamese American explained why he was not putting his money into Vietnam's rebuilding programme: 'You cannot trust them, they have no law; they violate every agreement.' The attitude of another was equally straightforward: 'Once a communist, always a communist.

They haven't really changed.' A strong and at times patronizing attitude sympathizes with the lot of those 'stuck' back in Vietnam.

Yet attitudes are changing. Community leaders believe that a majority of Vietnamese Americans supported the normalization of relations between the USA and Vietnam, a significant shift in opinion since the 1980s and early 1990s. They may see it as the best chance of reunifying their families, by facilitating visits in both directions – as distinct from the single direction that has been possible since *doi moi*. Some are actively trying to build bridges by carrying on small-scale trade with Vietnam, importing handicrafts and foodstuffs for sale in the USA.

There remain a hard core who talk of reversing the Vietnamese revolution, overthrowing the communists and restoring South Vietnam as an independent nation, but few see this as anything more than empty rhetoric, a futile and meaningless display of bravado. Hanoi need not take seriously such threats. Any danger of 'counter-revolutionary' activity organized or financed from abroad has long passed. However, former political prisoners, a group still growing with new arrivals from Vietnam, are ready to call demonstrations at any public advocacy of closer US–Vietnam ties as they did when a trade delegation from Hanoi visited Washington DC, San Francisco and Houston soon after the economic embargo was lifted. They work with US veterans' groups to keep the issue of MIAs on the political agenda.

Demonstrating that the US-based community is no longer as anti-communist as before, significant numbers of Vietnamese are now returning to Vietnam – mostly at *Têt*, the New Year family festival. *Têt* is the biggest annual get-together between divided families. During *Têt* in 1995, at least 20,000 Vietnamese from Orange County and around 10,000 each from San Jose and Houston were among an estimated 80,000 Vietnamese Americans to visit their motherland. In doing so they were demonstrating that one thing they have gained by fleeing Vietnam is mobility – something denied to those left behind by reasons both of political control and cost.

It is still only a small minority of overseas Vietnamese who have made the return journey, although some have been back several times. Young Vietnamese are especially keen to find their 'roots', like the 'yuppies' of Washington DC who have established contacts with Hanoi over the Internet and are committed to using their skills and bi-lingualism for the benefit of their motherland. Young Vietnamese Americans have far fewer hang-ups about communism and the war than their parents, but often have difficulty coping with both the language and the culture on their return. They stand out in Hanoi or Ho Chi Minh City by their clothing, their accents and their wealth. Some find the experience profoundly disorientating, especially if travelling alone. Some young men go to Vietnam during their vacation to search for a wife, although others have enjoyed themselves by giving female would-be emigrants the false impression that they can offer a visa to the USA.

It is common to find Vietnamese Americans who rule out a return visit to Vietnam because they feel the communists do not like them, which is almost certainly to overestimate the ability of the government in Hanoi to keep files on those it calls the *Viet kieu*. Some, however, have penned articles critical of the Hanoi government, while others have been associated with one or other of the shadowy organizations unrealistically intent on overthrowing the communist government to 'free' Vietnam. Many others who tell you they plan to return 'next year' have no such plan, but are unwilling to reveal their very real trepidation at going back. It is difficult to underestimate the trauma of going back for those brought up in Diem's and Thieu's South Vietnam, or for those imprisoned after 1975.

Although Vietnamese Americans give an outward impression of contentment with the way fate has given them new homes in the USA, for almost all it has meant leaving close family members behind in Vietnam. Even those who 'got out' do not always consider themselves lucky. Khiem, for example, now in his seventies, managed to emigrate about five years ago, after living an austere life in Saigon. A former army officer, he had spent three years in a re-education camp. By the time he came out, most of his eight children had left the country, mainly by boat. Khiem qualified for immigration to the USA under the provision for former political prisoners. Both he and his wife had reservations about starting life again in a new land at their advanced years and with their slender understanding of English. Now in southern California, they live with one of their sons, his wife and two teenage grandchildren and have overcome most of their apprehensions. They have discovered that you do not have to speak or even understand English to enjoy life in Orange County, though they do miss friends and the social life of Saigon.

What they miss most of all is their other children. They are dispersed around the USA, Canada and Australia – and one is left in

Vietnam. So while friends probably envy them the fact that most of their immediate family 'got out', the price they had to pay for this 'freedom' is the dispersal of their family around the globe. 'We are too old to travel to see them', bemoans Khiem. 'They are too poor to come to see us, except very occasionally. I would much rather have all the family together.' Khiem recognises that he is relatively fortunate that his immediate family is intact after so many years of war, feeling that he has not had a bad life even if he did surrender quite a lot of land when they left Vietnam. He considers it to be one of life's ironies that so many of the losers in the war for Vietnam now enjoy a relatively prosperous life in the wealthiest US state, while the victors endure a life of poverty. Having suffered it himself through most of the 1980s, he speaks from bitter experience. He is not bitter about the communists and their takeover of his country, not as bitter as many of those younger than himself. Privately he admits that it would be nice to die in Vietnam, for like most Vietnamese he attaches enormous importance to the place of death and to being buried close to his ancestors. (As a second best, some Vietnamese have asked their children to return their ashes to be interred near the remains of a loved one in Vietnam, while other families have brought the ashes of a loved one out of Vietnam.) Publicly Khiem accepts that he will not return to Vietnam and his sacrifice is that he has, of economic necessity, had to follow his children into exile.

Among the refugees there is plenty of guilt towards those left behind. From Vietnam outwards, there are feeling of bitterness and anger that a sister, father or cousin is not doing more to help – either to get an individual out, or else to send money or goods back home to make life more bearable. Sometimes the anger is so intense that it leads to family splits, such as the brother in California who belatedly left Vietnam on the Orderly Departure Programme in 1985 and says he will never speak again to the sister and brother in France who failed to help him 'escape' earlier.

To hear *émigrés* speak of family members still in Vietnam is to be reminded that the vagaries of different countries' immigration laws are partly responsible for dividing Vietnam once more. The Vietnamese themselves speak of those settled in the West as being 'on a list made by God' (*danh sach cua Troi*), admitting the role fate has played in their destiny. Some were admitted for resettlement because they were loyal servants of the Americans before 1975, or because they could show 'a genuine fear of persecution' by Vietnam's communist government. Others are refused entry because they cannot, or because they are adjudged to be economic migrants seeking a better life in the West rather than genuine 'political' refugees. The USA, Canada and Australia have in fact 'creamed off' the best available talent from among the so-called 'asylum-seekers' causing an additional blow to a country which now recognizes the value of the skills it has lost – and badly needs them back.

Taken as a whole, the Vietnamese community in the USA has fared as well as any. Vietnamese Americans are both more prosperous and more integrated than those elsewhere. The story of Vietnamese settlement in the USA is a success story. Any success story has its blemishes. Most often mentioned are the gangs of young Vietnamese who prey on the houses and property of fellow Vietnamese. This may be a consequence of family alienation, although many gang members are thought to have arrived in the USA as unaccompanied youngsters who took their own chance to escape Vietnam by boat in a spirit of adventure. Drug usage among Vietnamese is not high by US standards, but is nonetheless prevalent. The 1990 US census records that 860 Vietnamese Americans were in prison at that time. Like all Americans, the recession has given rise to indebtedness: several thousand Vietnamese families in California have had their homes repossessed by banks after they failed to keep up with repayments. Unemployment among Vietnamese in the state rose from under 4% in 1989 to nearly 10% five years later. The main consequence was a steady migration away from the state to neighbouring Nevada, where Vietnamese have been attracted towards the casinos as croupiers, northwards to Washington state whose capital, Seattle, has plenty of Vietnamese restaurants, and eastwards to Texas, where cheap housing is a major attraction.

In Vietnam it is assumed that everyone who has made it to the USA is rich and therefore duty bound to share that wealth with family members left behind. Although wealthy by Vietnamese standards, quite probably owning both a house and a car for example, the Vietnamese in America think of themselves as poor by the standards of their adopted country and often have difficulty making ends meet. Yet the statistics show that while the average US per capita income exceeds $24,000 per year and the average family income of Vietnamese Americans is estimated at $22,000,[3] World Bank figures in 1995 list Vietnam as having an average per capita

---

[3] Vietnamese American estimates in this paragraph come from the Indochina Resettlement and Cultural Centre in San Jose, in a document prepared in 1994.

income of below $200 per year. The same source gives Vietnam's gross national product, shared between its 72 million people, at just under $12,000 billion, a figure similar to that estimated as the total annual income of the 1 million Vietnamese Americans. One day, say some Vietnamese Americans, the community will return en masse to Vietnam, as many Jews have returned to the homeland from which they were expelled. Quite when that happens and how many go back will depend on how quickly and how far the government in Hanoi moves away from the political and economic policies which caused them to flee their motherland in the first place. Once back they will spend their new-found wealth in Vietnam just as the gold-prospector, Le Kim, spent his after returning from California in the mid-19th century.

11

The Next Dragon?

Late in 1994 the Vietnamese government banned a book of short stories, allegedly after complaints from Buddhists priests that one of the stories denigrated Buddhism. The story in question told of a legendary Vietnamese traveller by the name of Duong Tang who was said to have introduced Buddhism to Vietnam from India around the 5th century BC. According to the story, Duong Tang later regretted wasting his time 'trying to make Buddhas out of men who were probably quite happy just being human beings'.[1] Buddhism is believed to have been introduced to Vietnam almost simultaneously by travellers from both India and China around the 2nd century AD. It first took root in the Red River delta and later, around the 10th century, became an important instrument by which Vietnamese leaders established their independence from China.

However, it was not the historical inaccuracy of the story to which the Buddhist church objected, if indeed they did object. There is some doubt as to whether the government would have banned the story in response to a protest from such quarters given the strained relations between church and state. In fact the government is believed to have realized belatedly that the allegorical story was not really about the introduction of Buddhism to Vietnam but about the coming of communism: Duong Tang represents Ho Chi Minh. The story-teller appeared to be saying that communism had never really worked in Vietnam, and that Ho Chi Minh would have been the first to acknowledge this.

Such a conclusion hardly seems revolutionary in post-*doi moi* Vietnam where both government and Party seem to have reached precisely those conclusions. The Communist Party of Vietnam is no longer communist in any sense in which Marx, Lenin or Ho Chi Minh would understand it. It has abandoned the ideology of its

[1] According to the account of the banning in the *Bangkok Post*, 22 January 1995, related by Russell Heng.

founding father without abandoning him as the symbol of the nation and its reunification. However, it is one thing to have reached those conclusions and changed the country's economic policy as a result and quite another to spell them out in literature with the implicit recognition of the error of past ways. As far as the still powerful and somewhat paranoid Party is concerned, it is too soon for such an admission to be made in public just as it is too soon to re-interpret Ho Chi Minh's contribution to the country in this way. That latter process is happening behind closed doors but is unlikely to be acknowledged in public until Ho Chi Minh's contemporaries are no longer on the scene. In this key respect, the 'second' revolution underway in Vietnam – and indeed in China – differs fundamentally from those in Russia and Eastern Europe where public figures have been more ready to admit the error of past leaders and their policies and to acknowledge openly that communism as an economic philosophy is dead.

Vietnam's leaders simply cannot afford to bury communism, as Boris Yeltsin has done in Russia for example, because it is so closely intertwined with the independence and reunification struggles. Their claim to legitimacy as rulers is founded on communism. The argument runs: 'The wise leadership of the Communist Party under chairman Ho Chi Minh enabled us to defeat the foreign enemy, regain our national independence and reunify our nation. Now the Communist Party is proudly leading the nation forward to take its rightful place in the community of nations.' In fairness it needs to be recognized that this sentiment is shared by the people to a considerable extent. Most Vietnamese (and the dissenters are mainly in the south) believe the Communist Party deserved to be entrusted with power after it evicted the French, the Japanese, the Americans and the Chinese from Vietnam and reunified the country. Most people are prepared to concede too that the Party leaders are good rulers, especially since *doi moi* for which they are given credit, which has made life easier for all.

While the Party rests its 'right' to rule Vietnam on past achievements, it exercises that rule through the Party apparatus. Power is wielded through organizations like the National Fatherland Front, which maintains control over religious and other organizations, the Women's Union, the Council of Ethnic Nationalities, the Writers' and Journalists' Associations while the army and security organizations are used to maintain order. However, having already effectively lost control of the economy to market forces, the Party in the mid-1990s is seeing its control over the people slipping away. As in China, the Party is faced with a conflict between the openness and access that is essential for capitalism to flourish and the tight control which is essential if the Party is to stay in power.

Traditionally a nominated Party member has exercised authority in every one of Vietnam's villages, but that means of control is ebbing away. As one villager in the Central Highlands explains: 'We have a village headman appointed by the Communist Party. We used to be afraid of him but not any more.' In all Vietnam's villages the loss of power of the appointed headman is symbolic of the loss of power of the Party, even if the respect accorded to national rulers remains in place. The same villager says the atmosphere in the village following *doi moi* is much more relaxed: 'We know that the Party could only reimpose its authority on our village by force, but nobody expects it to do so. Nowadays we simply ignore the Party's headman and choose our own.'

The Party may have converted almost completely to capitalism as a means of ordering the economy but it refuses to accept that, in the process, it has virtually abandoned socialism. Notwithstanding that key Western economic textbooks have been officially translated into Vietnamese, government leaders still think and speak Marxism-Leninism whilst acknowledging that market forces are now in play. 'The market system does not belong to capitalism; socialism can employ market forces too', runs a commonly expressed view, suggesting the true significance of the market system has yet to be understood. The re-education of Vietnam's communist leadership does not appear to have advanced much beyond Lesson One, which teaches that you cannot share wealth until you first have some wealth to share. The leadership's conclusion is that Vietnam first has to create that wealth (by whatever means) before socialism can be fully implemented.

Apprehension that the authorities may never get beyond Lesson One is causing foreign firms and overseas Vietnamese to hold back from making major investments in Vietnam. Already there are cases of foreign partners being ousted from small enterprises once they start to return profits. Many potential investors consider the risk of some sort of nationalization, or reneging on contractual agreements, to be too great despite a foreign investment law that appears to give the outside investor a very attractive deal. This points up another conflict facing Vietnam's leadership, that between the authority of the Party, which has traditionally been supreme, and the establishment of the rule of law as a prerequisite for encouraging investment and trade. Foreign companies are not going to do business in Vietnam unless contracts are enforced according to judicial rather than ideological or arbitrary determination. One foreigner who is especially critical of Vietnam's lack of understanding of what attracts investment says: 'Vietnam suffers from a lethal combination of arrogance and ignorance. They think they can do it themselves, but they can't. Often they have thrown out the foreign partner when the enterprise begins to make money only to see it collapse. They are unwilling to accept that the foreign partner has something – apart from money – which is necessary to make the venture work.'

Another example of the government's failure to understand how the system works was its belief that it would easily attract investment to improve the infrastructure – the roads, the ports and the electricity supply industry, for example. As the same foreign investment middleman puts it: 'The government was very disappointed to find that commercial investors want some return for their money and are not in it for charity.' Earlier the government had naively considered investment by the Americans in Vietnam's infrastructure to be part of the rehabilitation deal promised by President Nixon as part of the Paris peace process, which was never approved by Congress. Vietnam's leaders still think of their country as a victim and expect it to be compensated for being kept poor by the war and the subsequent economic embargo. Nor are they receptive to the argument of many southerners that communism was just as much to blame for keeping Vietnam poor.

The realization that those who are putting money into Vietnam now are expecting to take rather more away may eventually come from its new-found South East Asian friends, fellow members of ASEAN. These nations are themselves astute at the rules of commerce and at selling natural resources like rubber, tin and oil to fund their national development. For just as significant as the introduction of new economic policies to Vietnam is the re-orientation of foreign policy that has accompanied it. Vietnam's leaders are much clearer in their desire to rejoin the world in an economic sense and to play a full role in international trade. They regard ASEAN, and especially Singapore, as their tutors in this regard. Joining the Association has been made easier by the fact that its member governments tend to share the Vietnamese Communist Party's belief that firm government is a prerequisite for rapid economic progress. This is notwithstanding the fact that all other ASEAN governments tend to be right-wing and anti-communist.

South East Asia seems to provide proof that 'right-wing' and 'left-wing' as descriptions of political orientation have lost their relevance in the post-communist world. Measured according to traditional criteria, almost all governments around the world in the mid-1990s could be described as right-wing. Redefining socialism is a political trend far beyond South East Asia. In the UK, the Labour Party leader, Tony Blair now talks of 'collective action for common good..., rights matched by responsibilities..., and the pursuit of ethical values that endure across time'[2] but has abandoned the commitment to nationalization of public utilities and diluted the espousal of workers' rights for which his party once stood. The Labour Party has changed out of all recognition in order to retain its contemporary relevance just as Vietnam's Communist Party has. It remains communist in name alone, not in ideology where it seems at times to epitomize all that orthodox communism used to denounce. A Hanoi-based foreign banker observes: 'In Vietnam today I don't think there is anyone as capitalist as a communist, possibly because their instincts in that direction have been suppressed for so long.'

To mark the 20th anniversary of the end of the Vietnam War, the *Far Eastern Economic Review* published a cartoon demonstrating Vietnam's attitudes to the USA then and now. It contrasted Hanoi's 1975 thinking of 'Yankee go home' with the 'Yankee come back' attitude prevailing in 1995. The cartoonist could have chosen a wider time-frame encompassing 1945 – 'Yankee come to our aid' – to demonstrate how the wheel has actually turned full circle. Vietnam's leaders today want the USA to help develop the country's backward economy as desperately as Ho Chi Minh wanted them in 1945 to help liberate the country from the French. The 'middle' episode in 1975, when they rejoiced at having 'liberated' the country from the Americans, seems now like an aberration, since it is clear that the Americans were admired and respected throughout. However, to admit as much is to admit that Hanoi's wartime alliances of necessity with Beijing and Moscow gave the country little long-term benefit. Hanoi is not yet strong enough to make that admission, just as it is not yet ready to blame the country's underdevelopment on communism. Instead it chooses to hide its

[2] Writing in the (London) *Observer*, 23 April 1995.

economic and foreign policy about-turns in self-contradictory contortions about 'market socialism', or behind platitudes about being friends with all nations.

Vietnam's leaders admire their former enemy for the way its capitalist ideology has made it great and powerful. They choose not to humiliate Americans by reminding them of their military defeat at the hands of a peasant army, though privately they take much satisfaction from having cowed such a superpower. Publicly they are anxious to bury the hatchet as soon as possible for the self-interested reason that they believe only the USA has the economic might to rescue Vietnam from poverty and backwardness. This is a lesson learnt from China and indeed from all its South East Asian neighbours. Apart from its urgent desire for the levels of investment finance which only the USA seems to have and which it is busy pumping into China, Hanoi has little doubt that the USA controls international trade by raising and lifting embargoes and granting 'most favoured nation' status and other trading privileges. It has observed Washington playing its embargo card not only with regard to Vietnam but in relation to China and Japan as well as nations it has accused of sponsoring international terrorism, like Libya and Iran. Vietnam badly wants to rejoin the world trading network so that its manufactured goods as well as its oil, rice and seafoods can be traded widely around the world. Its foreign policy re-orientation is primarily economic in purpose.

However, there is a secondary purpose to mending fences with Washington. Despite its military prowess on the battlefield, Vietnam does not feel confident enough to defend itself from the hostile attention of neighbours, notably China. For one thing it lacks modern armaments: what money there is has been concentrated on development. For another, Hanoi now realizes that military might comes from economic might, even if that was not the lesson of the Vietnam war. Hanoi remains as wary of Chinese intentions as it has been since it first established independence from its powerful northern neighbour a millennium ago. That uneasiness has increased since 1988 as a result of China's assertion of its claim to the contested waters of the South China Sea.

After the Second World War, Ho Chi Minh assessed the likelihood of the victorious allies to come to Vietnam's aid concluding that the USA represented the best hope. Today, the USSR has ceased to exist and Russia is unlikely to assert itself on Vietnam's behalf. Although a shared wariness of China is a key factor uniting ASEAN nations today, none wants to go to war. In any case, several other members have their own rival claims to the parts of the South China Sea claimed by Vietnam and China. So as in 1945 Vietnam is looking to the USA to provide a measure of protection. There are no illusions in Hanoi that Washington would actually come to Vietnam's aid in a military sense, although a symbolic visit by a US warship to Cam Ranh Bay following the normalization of relations has been mooted. Even without a military role, Hanoi feels it could benefit from the kind of protective US umbrella that has allowed Taiwan and South Korea to develop their economies notwithstanding the implicit threats to their sovereignty from China and North Korea respectively.

Given the previous enmity between Hanoi and Washington there are many ironies about their relations today. The US dollar is a second currency in Vietnam and plays no small role in supporting the Vietnamese economy. The best Vietnamese music on sale in Ho Chi Minh City is imported on compact discs from California, recorded there by the Vietnamese American community, while Western pop music is imported from China on pirated discs which are at the centre of a trade dispute between China and the USA. In its eagerness to break into the Vietnamese market, American Express has pledged to restore the 11th century Temple of Literature in Hanoi dedicated to Confucius. At the beautifully restored Hotel Métropole, where American negotiators from the Office of Strategic Services stayed in 1945 as Ho Chi Minh declared Vietnam independent with the words of Thomas Jefferson, that same fondness for America and Americans is evident as the piano and violin duet play the Tennessee Waltz. Down the road, the prison that US prisoners of war dubbed 'the Hanoi Hilton' is about to become a real hotel! And as General Foods and General Electric set up outlets in the city named after their country's hated adversary, a Vietnamese 'General', Vo Nguyen Giap, the hero of Dien Bien Phu and of the 'American war', has been invited to visit the USA.

The biggest irony of all is the transformation of attitudes. Vietnam is greeting its former enemy with open arms while the USA, which 40 years ago considered Ho Chi Minh to be an agent of China, now regards unified Vietnam as an important bulwark against China. Rather late in the day, Washington has taken account of Vietnam's historical distrust of China and is turning this to its own advantage. This is an approach encouraged by all other non-communist countries in the region, including Japan, which see the normalization and strengthening of relations between Washington and Hanoi as a means of checking Chinese territorial ambitions.

The end of the American war brought Vietnam geographical unity but it is taking much longer to reunify the nation in any deeper sense. Bitterness and animosity between north and south were more evident in the early years of reunification but, even 20 years on, there remain suspicions between northerners and southerners of the older generation. The main resentment from the south is over the north's unwillingness to recognize that those Vietnamese who fought for the south were just as patriotic in their own way as those fighting for the north – and at the consequent unwillingness to honour the south's war dead. 'Vietnam will not be truly re-unified until the north recognizes the patriotism of the southern fighting force', according to one southern veteran. Some southerners believe it is time for the north to overcome its own sense of triumphalism by recognizing that its military victory was followed by just as great an economic defeat.

A minority viewpoint suggests that one way to unify Vietnam properly would be to restore its monarchy by bringing its last emperor, Bao Dai, back from exile in France – rather as the founder of the Nguyen dynasty, Gia Long, unified the country nearly two centuries ago. The suggestion is hardly intended to be taken seriously since Bao Dai remains tainted as a former 'puppet' of the French. However, he does have the advantage that he is identified neither with the north or the south and that his former imperial capital of Hué is the most 'neutral' Vietnamese city. Interestingly, the government and Party have stopped castigating Bao Dai as the 'puppet emperor' and are beginning to promote the country's imperial past for its tourist appeal.

Southern and northern intellectuals agree that the tensions that overlay superficial unity between the two halves of the country result not so much from feelings of vengeance as from insecurity on the part of the Communist Party. The northern leadership in 1975 lacked the overwhelming economic superiority that was the West German government's main advantage as it swiftly and ruthless swallowed up East Germany. In 1975 the victorious northerners tended to see the south as an economic threat – and potentially a political one too. In recent years, that perception has grown rather than diminished as the south, especially Ho Chi Minh City, has become stronger and more threatening as a result of *doi moi*. It is out of the same sense of insecurity that the leadership maintains what controls it can nationwide, including its tight controls on the press and on religious and other organizations. Veteran southerners are stoical about these limitations to their freedom, pointing out that Vietnam today is no less free than before 1975 as successive southern leaders were just as intent on maintaining control, which meant limiting freedoms.

Today another type of 'threat' is taking over as the main concern of the leadership. That is the 'dirt' brought in by the *doi moi* 'breeze', the dirt of corruption, greed, crime and prostitution and what the authorities call 'rampant individualism'. This last sums up all the above problems as well as the loss of respect for authority – typified by the motorbike racers of Hanoi – which is recognized as a key social problem today. In fact *doi moi* is helping to overcome the north-south divide, for nowadays Vietnamese are categorized less by which side they fought on in the war than by the new determining factor of wealth: 'the haves' and 'the have-nots'. The emergence of a new élite demonstrates that the economic war that has been going on throughout the country since 1975 has in its own way had just as great an impact on life-styles and society as the military war that preceded it. Young people in any case feel more in common with each other, regardless of a northern or southern upbringing, than do the older generation who are more inclined to bitterness. That fact is hardly surprising for more than half the population of Vietnam were born after the end of the war.

The way in which a younger generation is overcoming the legacy of war and division is apparent too in the contacts that are developing between young Vietnamese abroad and their compatriots and relatives back home. Young *Viet kieu* brought up in the USA are much keener to revisit their motherland than their parents. Some are even investing or returning to work there, contributing in their own way toward healing the scars of war with a spirit of patriotism that the old guard in Hanoi are having particular difficulty understanding. They ask themselves: 'How can someone who earlier fled the country now be so committed to supporting its development?'

More than the value of the war and the economic basis of socialism are being reassessed in Vietnam today. The nature of patriotism too is being re-examined in a society where a patriot used to be defined in terms of his adherence to Ho Chi Minh's thoughts. Can it be long before the young entrepreneurs of Vietnam openly question Ho Chi Minh's relevance to their lives today, just as young Indians question the teachings of Mahatma Gandhi and young Chinese challenge the thoughts of Chairman Mao? It seems inevitable that the poverty of the war years (1945-75) and the austerity of the decade of socialism that followed (1975-85) will be found wanting when contrasted with the greater affluence and prosperity of the period which followed the effective abandonment of socialism in 1986. Already many southerners openly deny that the north won the war. 'That may have been true of the American war in a strictly military sense', they say, 'but it is the capitalist ideology of the south that can clearly be seen to have won the economic war.' 'The south', they argue, 'has won the more significant war. It only remains for the north to recognize that fact.'

Vietnam's ASEAN neighbours grew rich on the Vietnam war. Thailand, Malaysia, Singapore, the Philippines and Indonesia were all threatened by communist insurgencies. All feel that the US decision to confront communism in Vietnam was fortuitous for them, buying time for them to develop while keeping their own communist insurgencies in check. All except the Philippines have now overcome these threats, more through their enhanced economic strength than military might. These countries benefited from the Vietnam war in other ways too. The Philippines and Thailand accommodated thousands of US troops in large army, naval and air bases providing a major boost to the local economies, rather as South Vietnamese cities grew wealthy on the spending of the US forces. Singapore served as an 'R and R' centre for US troops and a service centre for US military aircraft. US spending on the war was a major factor in the rapid development of South East Asia while the US defeat helped make the countries of the region more self-reliant. 'It told us in ways that were clear that never again would the Americans send young men to defend us', according to Noordin Sopiee, director-general of Malaysia's Institute of Strategic and International Studies.[3]

Together with the more advanced nations of East Asia – Japan, South Korea, Taiwan and Hong Kong – the advanced ASEAN nations of Thailand, Malaysia, Singapore and Indonesia have been dubbed the 'high-performing Asian economies' by the World Bank. These eight, more usually known as the Asian 'dragons' or 'tigers', are responsible for what the World Bank has called the 'East Asian miracle' by combining consistently high rates of growth with a

---

[3] Quoted in the *Far Eastern Economic Review*, 11 May 1995, p 30.

decline in inequality. Their economies have expanded significantly faster than most so-called 'developed' nations. Life expectancy, agricultural productivity, the private ownership of vehicles and home appliances and export performance have all risen dramatically while poverty, population growth rates and inequality have declined in an equally impressive manner.

A painstaking attempt by the World Bank to analyse why these countries have done so much better than other developing nations reached no firm conclusions.[4] A less scientific appraisal might find contributory causes in the Vietnam war, a reluctance to incur large debts and what is sometimes called 'the Confucian work ethic', with which many if not all of the peoples of the region are said to be imbued.[5] Confucius, the Chinese philosopher born in 551 BC, is perhaps given disproportionate credit for the rapid and impressive development of East Asian nation states in the late 20th century. In a further corruption of the teachings of Confucius, the East Asian miracle has even been attributed to something called 'Confucian capitalism'.

Vietnam's reform-minded leaders are preoccupied with the notion of Vietnam 'catching up' with its wealthy neighbours, even arguing that it is 'our turn'. More than 70% of Vietnam's trade is with these eight 'dragons'. Given the country's consistently high growth rates in the early 1990s, it should have every chance of itself becoming a 'dragon' eventually and of demonstrating how each successive industrial revolution in Asia takes place more rapidly than the previous one. But Vietnam has a long way to go. The same month that the World Bank published its report on the 'dragon' economies of East Asia another report from the same stable focused on Vietnam. It outlined what Vietnam had to do to catch up, pointing out that it was one of the poorest countries in the world

---

[4] *The East Asian Miracle*, OUP, Washington, September 1993. The report concludes: 'There is no single East Asian model. Rather, the eight high-performing Asian economies have used different and changing sets of policies to achieve rapid growth with equity' (p 347).
[5] This is the explanation given for the habit of East Asians to work hard. There is no evidence that Confucius actually preached hard work as an ethic, though this conclusion may have been drawn from other values which he did espouse. For example, Confucius advocated universal education for the purpose of transforming and improving society, self-discipline and deference to authority, the last derived from the notion of respect for one's parents, or filial piety (*hsiao*). The expression probably owes a lot too to the way in which a so-called 'Protestant work ethic' has been credited for rapid economic growth in both the UK and the USA at different times.

(with a gross national product per head of less than $200) and that its economic infrastructure was in a bad way 'after decades of war and mismanagement'. (The Bank would doubtless endorse the epitaph that 'communism is the longest road to capitalism.') An official of the Hanoi Chamber of Commerce said the report gave the country's leaders 'a better idea of what they need to do in the future, even though not all of the authors' advice – even if it is good – will be easy to implement in Vietnam'.[6]

As we have seen, much of the World Bank's advice is being followed as Vietnam tries to combine 'modern' Confucian values with Western economic wisdom to qualify as a 'dragon'. Its leaders may dream of overtaking China to become the auspicious 'ninth dragon', using the leap-frog principle to produce its own 'great leap forward'. However, China is comfortably in the lead even though the decline in inequality is not as pronounced there as in the existing 'dragon' economies. As China benefits from the so-called 'Chinese money' coming from Taiwan, Vietnam is hoping to turn to its own economic advantage the large Vietnamese diaspora in the USA and elsewhere, whose skills and savings could provide the means for it to achieve the coveted 'dragon' status. (Once political differences are resolved, North Korea may similarly expect to benefit from the largesse – or greed – of South Korean investors.)

'This economic dragon, travelling by *cyclo*, is likely to get a puncture before it arrives because of the bad state of the roads', according to one sceptical Western observer. His point is that for Vietnam to claim its sought-after place at the dragons' table it needs to invest heavily in its infrastructure. He believes the Vietnamese are in too much of a hurry and inclined to get their priorities wrong. For example, he questions the value of installing automatic cash dispensers before they have a proper banking system in place. Other foreign business people are more impressed, pointing out how rapidly Vietnam has moved ahead in its first ten years of *doi moi*. A telecommunications consultant says the use of modern exchanges and fibre optic lines has put Vietnam in the forefront of the telecommunications revolution – in some respects ahead even of the USA – although it remains desperately short of connections. No more than one in ten villages is linked to the telephone system, yet it is possible to direct dial or fax anywhere in the world from even a small and fairly remote Vietnamese town within seconds. Now

[6] *Vietnam: Transition to the Market: An Economic Report*, World Bank, 15 September 1993. The quoted reaction is from the *Far Eastern Economic Review*, 30 December 1993/6 January 1994 p 71.

Vietnam is planning to launch its own communications satellite. The latest computers are more widely in use in Vietnam than in other similarly 'backward' countries, while a foreign journalist was impressed to be able to rent advanced television editing equipment from Vietnam Television that was 'more advanced and cheaper than I could have found in Bangkok'.

The Vietnamese people say the mythical 'dragon' originates from Vietnam and that they are themselves the descendants of a marriage between the legendary dragon king, Lac Long Quan, and the beautiful princess Au Co, who bore him 100 sons. They say the Chinese subsequently adopted the symbol as their own though the Chinese would doubtless disagree. At any rate, in both China and Vietnam the dragon is associated with imperial power and honour. Because the oriental dragon is always benevolent (unlike its occidental counterpart) it is appropriate that it has come to symbolize prosperity and rapid but mainly equitable growth. The Vietnamese dragon is waking up as the world's 13th most populous nation tries to take its place among its prosperous 'dragon' neighbours.

Vietnam's own 'nine dragons', the mighty Song Cuu Long or Mekong River, could be the vehicle for the country's economic take-off as the Pearl River has been for China. Since pre-colonial times the 2,600-mile long Mekong, which rises in Tibet and flows through Burma, Laos, Thailand, Cambodia and Vietnam, has served as an international frontier. It marked the limits of French-ruled Indochina and, after 1975, divided communist South East Asia from its non-communist neighbours. With the abandonment of communism as an economic system in all three states of Indochina that great divide has ceased to have much significance, rather as the abandonment of communism in Eastern Europe rendered the iron curtain frontier unnecessary. The economic changes in South East Asia are as significant for that region as were those a few years earlier in Europe. With Vietnam as a member, ASEAN has become a larger grouping in population terms than the European Union, linking more than 400 million people. The desire of Laos and Cambodia to follow Vietnam into ASEAN can be compared with the enthusiasm of Europe's former communist countries to join the European Union.

The Mekong will not disappear as the Berlin wall and Europe's barbed wire barriers have, but its symbolism as part of the so-called 'bamboo curtain' separating off Asia's communist states has gone. This has in turn encouraged trading across previously tightly restricted borders. This is very much in the spirit of the World Trade Organization with its aim to boost the level of international trade and is sure to have a beneficial effect on the economies of this previously rather backward corner of Asia. Leaders of the Mekong riparian nations now sup at the same table where they plan the most mutually beneficial use of the Mekong and its waters. They include China, so development of the Mekong's resources is a shared interest between China and its southern neighbours which could help to put the minds of the latter at rest about the former's regional ambitions.

The Mekong could become as significant a means of winning the war against backwardness and underdevelopment as the Ho Chi Minh trail was in winning the military struggle. Its upper reaches are an important 'backdoor' into China's land-locked Yunnan province, facilitating a lively trade in cars smuggled from Thailand through Laos into China. The provincial government of Yunnan wants to open up this backdoor further to both trade and travellers to give the province an alternative route to the sea, thus helping it catch up with China's prosperous and fast growing south-eastern provinces. The province authorities would like to dynamite rapids on the Mekong between Laos and Burma to create a commercially viable waterway between China and Thailand. Thai businesses are investing heavily in Yunnan. A further set of rapids in southern Laos limits the extent to which the upper Mekong is reachable from the sea. However there is considerable scope for the expansion of local river traffic lower down, between Vietnam and Cambodia, as well as for developing the river's hydro-electric potential to drive the region's industrial revolution. Electricity produced along Mekong tributaries is already a major export of Laos, the most mountainous of the riparian states. Thailand, China and Vietnam, which are all concerned about meeting their future energy needs, have strong interests in developing the river's hydro-electric potential.

One significant demonstration of how the breaking down of political barriers has fuelled economic and trade links was the bridging of the Mekong in 1993 between Nong Khai in Thailand and Vientiane, the capital of Laos, the first time the Mekong has been bridged below Yunnan. This scheme was first proposed nearly 50 years ago but was delayed by the years of war. It was financed by Australia which is now looking at the feasibility of bridging parts of the Mekong's great delta in Vietnam. Meanwhile, the Asian Development Bank is looking at the feasibility of building roads from Thailand to Vietnam – one through Cambodia to Ho Chi Minh City, and another across Laos to Vinh or Danang in central Vietnam – and of connecting the riparian states by railway. The only international rail links at present are between Vietnam and China, but they are not fully utilized. The Bank looks ahead to the time, not too distant it hopes, when it will be possible to travel by road or railway from Singapore to Beijing via Hanoi or Kunming, the capital of Yunnan. Within Vietnam there are plans to dredge some of the Mekong ports, like Can Tho, to enable them to take ocean-going vessels. Then rice from the Mekong delta could be shipped directly abroad instead of being transshipped through Saigon port. Nothing would do more to develop the delta as an international rice bowl as well as to encourage the growth there of agricultural and aquatic industries. Whatever its other potential economic purposes, the Mekong's single most important role will continue to be that of nourishing the rice growing lands of South East Asia.

Vietnam in the mid-1990s lends itself to comparison with other Asian nations at earlier stages in their development. Foreign visitors are struck by similarities. The one most frequently cited is with Indonesia in the late 1960s and early 1970s after President Suharto had taken power from the leftward leaning President Sukarno. Suharto set out to reverse socialist policies and encourage foreign investment. Indonesia then was a country growing rich on oil and with enormous developmental ambitions but still lacking infrastructure. Rather as Vietnam's authorities do now, the government kept a tight rein on the people arguing: 'We cannot afford to allow free political activity until we have put right the economy.' A less savoury comparison with Indonesia suggests Vietnam has already followed its large southern neighbour into that stage in laisser faire development at which money is worshipped as gods were before. The challenge for the Vietnamese leadership is to avoid the widening of a poverty-wealth gap which has been a feature of Indonesian development, which neighbouring Malaysia has managed to avoid.

Comparisons with Indonesia are especially marked physically in the small villages that constitute the suburbs of both Hanoi and Ho Chi Minh City which have a definite feel of 1970s Jakarta, according to one veteran of both countries. 'They are banning the *cyclos* from the city centres just as they did in Jakarta at that time', he points out. Those with longer memories experience a feel of Malaysia at an earlier stage. They say that like Malaysia in the 1960s, Vietnam is a country trying to exploit its substantial natural resources in order to develop. What Vietnam shares with both Indonesia and Malaysia, as well as more recent developer China, is the good fortune to be sitting on large reserves of hydrocarbons which it recognizes as the key to affording the rapid development to which it aspires.

Veteran travellers draw comparisons between Vietnam's lack of tourist facilities and Nepal in the 1960s – a back-packer's paradise but not well equipped to attract the more affluent class of visitor. Vietnam is still considered a pioneering destination by intrepid travellers who do not insist on luxury buses and hotels. The pioneers relish the chance to explore this 'new frontier' nation but their spending power falls far short of the government's expectations and hopes. Yet wealthier tourists expect more extensive facilities and are not prepared to eat in cheap cafés or do their sight-seeing from *cyclos*. Vietnam is keen to attract investment to improve its tourist industry so that it can earn the foreign exchange that comes from foreign visitors. It is conscious of the way the economy of Thailand has taken off by encouraging tourism, though anxious at the same time to avoid the more seedy side of tourism in the Thai capital, Bangkok. The 'pleasure' industries associated with tourism are coming fast: nightclubs and discotheques are opening in both Hanoi and Ho Chi Minh City and the ubiquitous singers from the Philippines who play the clubs throughout South East Asia can now be heard in Vietnam.

From the business community, both occidental and oriental, there are plenty of comparisons with China which are generally favourable to Vietnam. Says a Taiwanese businessman who has invested in both countries: 'Compared with China, Vietnam is not so steeped in socialism as not to understand how capitalism works. The Vietnamese are more determined to get things done than the Chinese. Once they have learnt how to do something they are very dedicated workers.' Vietnamese leaders are proud to hear such comments because, whilst denying that *doi moi* is following a Chinese example, they talk often about 'avoiding the mistakes made by China'. A pertinent question is: 'Are they any better placed than their counterparts in Beijing to recognize and avoid those mistakes?' If Vietnam is to avoid the public rifts between government and foreign investors which have afflicted business in China during the mid-1990s it needs to live down a reputation for arbitrariness. This is especially true if it is to attract back its own human resource, the *Viet kieu*, with their investment dollars.

Another potential similarity with China comes from what might be seen as the cultural consequences of opening up. For example, the freeing of controls on printing and publishing in China has led to the publication of a stream of pornography. Many millions of 'dirty' books have been seized as the authorities attempt to crackdown on what they see as an unsavoury consequence of economic reform. While publishing remains the exclusive preserve of the state, state enterprises are now required to pay their way so they publish what people want to buy rather than what their leaders think they should read. The publication and distribution of pornography earns large profits for the 'mafia' who run it. State enterprises in Vietnam are under similar pressure to pay their way. It is likely that Vietnam too will feel a need to reimpose controls in a belated attempt to 'batten down the hatch' and prevent cultural degradation, as China has tried to do.

Other negative effects of development experienced by China are already being felt. They include the drift to the cities of peasants in search of job opportunities and 'spontaneous decentralization' as foreign investment in the regions weakens the authority of the centre, no longer the prime source of provincial finance. There is also trepidation in Hanoi that the soliciting of bribes should ever reach the levels reported from China, where prestige cars and an overseas education for one's children are not infrequently demanded as the price for an official to give approval to a deal. But no Chinese 'disease' is feared more than inflation which it has been said led to the Tiananmen Square democracy movement. Vietnamese leaders are acutely conscious that rising prices can easily lead to social discontent.

Vietnam has its own comparisons, or models of development, that it would like to emulate. Undoubtedly its favourite model is Singapore whose efficient, clean and prosperous nation is everything Vietnam's leaders could want. Singapore's leaders believe their decision to trade with Vietnam throughout the embargo period helped to win Vietnam over to the cause of free trade. Another model for Vietnam is South Korea. Seemingly making a point about their own political path, Vietnam's leaders point out that South Korea would not be the economic miracle it is today without 17 years of authoritarian rule. A similar sentiment is expressed about Taiwan, another model whose prosperity is now helping Vietnam to develop through investment.

It is no coincidence that Vietnam's role models, like the USA itself, are capitalism's success stories. Vietnam also admires Japan as the first Asian nation to join the Western world – in an economic sense – and seems hell-bent on following the Japanese example. Vietnamese leaders took comfort from the wife of the former Japanese prime minister, Morihiro Hosokawa, who drew a comparison with her own upbringing in post-war Japan when visiting rural north Vietnam with her husband in 1992: 'These people have even more commitment and dedication than we did, and their spirit is so strong. I'm sure they will grow prosperous very soon.'

A T-shirt popular in Moscow in the early 1990s declared 'The Party is over' against a hammer and sickle motif. Anyone trying to sell such a T-shirt in Vietnam would face imprisonment, the surest sign that the Communist Party there is not 'over' and remains in power. However, it has been considerably weakened by its surrender of control over the economy to a combination of market forces and foreign capital. The collapse of international communism and the ending of the aid and ideological support that formerly hailed from Moscow was a body blow, although the introduction of *doi moi* and the end of centralized planning have been similarly catastrophic for the Party's hold on power. One authority says the Party 'has moved from being the orthodox implementer of the plan to being the dominant political force in a market economy'.[7] The key question now is: 'How long can it retain this dominant position?' The same authority suggests that if the Communist Party is to survive in Vietnam it may need to model itself on the *Kuomintang* of Taiwan, the People's Action Party of Singapore or *Golkar* in Indonesia – all of which have remained in power by ushering in greater prosperity for their people. The lesson of these successes in holding on to the reins of power have not been lost on Vietnam's leadership.

---

[7] Michael C. Williams, *Vietnam at the Crossroads, op cit*, p 88.

Bibliography

The following books were consulted, or are helpful aids to an understanding of the Vietnam war and modern Vietnam. The editions cited are those in paperback most readily available, or are those used by the author, and are not necessarily the only editions. The Bibliography is not intended to be comprehensive.

Pre-colonial Vietnam
Tate, D. J. M., *The Making of Modern South East Asia: Vol. 1 The European Conquest*, Oxford University Press, Kuala Lumpur, 1971.
Tate, D. J. M., *The Making of Modern South East Asia: Vol. 2 Economic and Social Change*, Oxford University Press, Kuala Lumpur, 1979.

The origins of the war
Charlton, Michael and Moncrieff, Anthony, *Many Reasons Why: The American Involvement in Vietnam,* Scolar Press, London, 1978.
Fitzgerald, Frances, *Fire in the Lake: The Vietnamese and the Americans in Vietnam*, Little Brown and Co, Boston, 1972.
Horowitz, David, *From Yalta to Vietnam*, Pelican, London, 1967.
Patti, Archimedes, *Why Vietnam? Prelude to America's Albatross*, University of California Press, Berkeley, 1980.

War memoirs
Karnow, Stanley, *Vietnam: A History,* Viking, London, 1983.
Ky, Nguyen Cao, *Twenty Years and Twenty Days*, Stein and Day, New York, 1976.
McNamara, Robert, *In Retrospect: The Tragedy and Lessons of Vietnam*, Times Books, New York, 1995.
Pentagon Papers, The, Routledge and Kegan Paul, London, 1971.
Shawcross, William, *Sideshow: Kissinger, Nixon and the Destruction of Cambodia,* Fontana, London, 1980.
Sheehan, Neil, *A Bright Shining Lie*, Picador, London, 1989.
Snepp, Frank, *Decent Interval: The American Debacle in Vietnam and the Fall of Saigon*, Allen Lane, London, 1980.

Terzani, Tiziano, *Giai Phong: The Fall and Liberation of Saigon*, Angus and Robertson, London, 1976.
Young, Gavin, *Worlds Apart*, Penguin, London, 1987.

Ho Chi Minh and the perspective from Hanoi
Burchett, Wilfred, *Grasshoppers and Elephants: Why Vietnam Fell*, Urizen, New York, 1977.
Dung, General Van Tien, *Our Great Spring Victory*, Monthly Review Press, New York, 1977.
Fell, Bernard B., *Ho Chi Minh on Revolution*, Pall Mall Press, London, 1967.
Giap, Vo Nguyen, *The Military Art of People's War: Selected Writings*, Monthly Review Press, New York, 1970.
Lacouture, Jean, *Ho Chi Minh* (a biography), Pelican, London, 1969.
Macdonald, Peter, *Giap* (a biography), Fourth Estate, London, 1993.

After the war was over
Hiebert, Murray, *Vietnam Notebook*, Far Eastern Economic Review, Hong Kong, 1993.
Sheehan, Neil, *Two Cities: Hanoi and Saigon*, Jonathan Cape, London, 1993.
Williams, Michael C., *Vietnam at the Crossroads*, Royal Institute of International Affairs/Pinter, London, 1992.
World Bank, *The East Asian Miracle,* Oxford University Press, New York, 1993.
World Bank, *Vietnam: Transition to the Market: An Economic Report,* World Bank, 15 September 1993.

Novels of the war years and after
Butler, Robert Olen, *A Good Scent from a Strange Mountain*, Minerva, London, 1993.
Duras, Marguerite, *The Lover*, Flamingo, London, 1986.
Greene, Graham, *The Quiet American*, Penguin, London, 1956.
Grey, Anthony, *Saigon,* Weidenfeld and Nicolson, London, 1982.
Kaiko, Takeshi, *Into the Black Sun,* Kodansha International, Tokyo, 1980.
le Carré, John, *The Honourable Schoolboy,* Hodder and Stoughton, London 1972.
Mullin, Chris, *The Last Man out of Saigon,* Corgi, London, 1986.
West, Morris, *The Ambassador,* New English Library, London, 1965.

Literature from contemporary Vietnam (editions in English)
Bao Ninh, *The Sorrow of War,* Secker and Warburg, London, 1993.
Duong Thu Huong, *Paradise of the Blind,* Morrow/Penguin, New York, 1993.
Terada, Alice, *Under the Starfruit Tree: Folktales from Vietnam,* University of Hawaii, Honolulu, 1989.
Thiep, Huy Thiep, *The General Retires and Other Stories,* Oxford University Press, Singapore, 1992.
Vien, Nguyen Khac and Huu Ngoc (ed), *Vietnamese Literature* (an anthology), Foreign Languages Publishing House, Hanoi.

Travelogues and guides

Brownmiller, Susan, *Seeing Vietnam: Encounters of the Road and Heart,* Harper Perennial, New York, 1994.

Downie, Sue, *Down Highway One,* Allen and Unwin, Sydney, 1993.

Lewis, Norman, *A Dragon Apparent: Travels in Indochina,* Jonathan Cape, London, 1951.

Lonely Planet Guide, *Vietnam,* Hawthorn, Australia, 1993.

Trade and Travel Publications, *Vietnam, Laos and Cambodia Handbook 1995,* Bath, UK 1994/Passport Books, Chicago, 1994.

Wintle, Justin, *Romancing Vietnam: Inside the Boat Country,* Viking/Penguin, London, 1991.

Index